**Psychology
in
Progress**

General editor: Peter Herriot

Philosophical
Problems
in Psychology

Psychology in Progress

Philosophical Problems in Psychology

edited by
NEIL BOLTON

METHUEN

First published in 1979 *by*
Methuen & Co Ltd
11 *New Fetter Lane London* EC4P 4EE
Published in the USA by
Methuen, Inc
733 Third Avenue, New York, NY 10017

Typeset by Northumberland Press Ltd
Gateshead Tyne and Wear
and printed in Great Britain at the
University Press, Cambridge

ISBN 0 416 70980 X (*hardbound*)
ISBN 0 416 70990 7 (*paperback*)

Contents

Notes on the contributors

Margaret A. Boden is Reader in Philosophy and Psychology at the University of Sussex. She is the author of *Purposive Explanation in Psychology* (Harvard University Press, 1972), *Artificial Intelligence and Natural Man* (Harvester Press, 1977) and several papers in philosophical and psychological journals.

Neil Bolton is Professor of Education at the University of Sheffield, having previously lectured in psychology at the Universities of Newcastle and Durham. He has written *The Psychology of Thinking* (Methuen, 1972), *Concept Formation* (Pergamon Press, 1977) and papers in psychological journals.

John M. Heaton has held various posts in the National Health Service, been research assistant at the Institute of Ophthalmology and has practised privately in psychotherapy since 1961. He is the author of *The Eye: Phenomenology and Psychology of Function and Disorder* (Tavistock, 1968) and papers in medical and philosophical journals.

Wolfe Mays is Reader in Philosophy at the University of Manchester as well as visiting professor at Northwestern University and the University of Wisconsin-Milwaukee. His books include *Whitehead's Philosophy of Science and Metaphysics* (M. Nijhoff), *Arthur Koestler* (Lutterworth Press) and *The Philosophy of Whitehead* (Allen and Unwin). He is also the editor of *The Journal of the British Society for Phenomenology*.

Colin McGinn lectures in philosophy at University College, London. He has published papers in *Mind, Journal of Philosophy, Analysis, Journal of Philosophical Logic* and *Philosophical Studies* on philosophical logic, epistemology and philosophy of language.

Michael Morgan is Professor of Psychology at the University of Durham and was formerly a lecturer in experimental psychology at the University of Cambridge. He is the authour of *Molyneux's Question* (Cambridge University Press, 1977) and papers in *Perception, Animal Behaviour, Quarterly Journal of Experimental Psychology* and *Psychology and Behaviour*.

Philip Pettit is Professor of Philosophy and chairman of the School of Interdisciplinary Human Studies at the University of Bradford. He has written *On the Idea of Phenomenology* (Scepter, 1969) and *The Concept of Structuralism* (Gill and MacMillan/University of California Press, 1975, 1977). He is co-editor with Christopher Hookway of *Action and Interpretation* (Cambridge University Press, 1978).

Arthur Still lectures in psychology at the University of Durham. He has published papers in the *Quarterly Journal of Experimental Psychology, Journal of Experimental Psychology* and *Animal Behaviour*, as well as other journals.

Norman Wetherick is Senior Lecturer in Psychology at Aberdeen University. He has published various papers in psychological and philosophical journals.

Editor's introduction

Whilst philosophers writing on the philosophy of mind do not by and large make use of the results of psychological investigations, although papers by Nagel (1971) and Davidson (1976) provide notable exceptions to this rule, psychologists for their part tend not to make any detailed reference to philosophical analysis. The present volume was written as part of an attempt to bring these two disciplines into closer relationship. Although the contributors have dealt with a variety of topics, it is true to say, I believe, that each chapter reflects the interrelation of philosophy and psychology rather than focussing upon one to the exclusion of the other. And what has emerged from this preoccupation is an emphasis on the importance of the concept of action. If there is one concern which unites all the authors contributing to this book, it is the question of the form a science of human action can take. It is this question which provides the major theme of the book and which has dictated the sequence of the contributions. One consequence of this singlemindedness is that other important questions within the philosophy of mind are treated as subsidiary to the main theme. Thus, for example, the mind–body problem is referred to in the papers by McGinn and Boden, but, although important in their reasoning, it is not the focus of their chapters. Similarly, it may be argued that Heaton's paper is relevant to the traditional philosophical problem of personal identity, although the paper itself has as its central concern the nature of theory in psychotherapy.

It has been widely claimed that human behaviour cannot be understood simply from within the causal framework of natural science, since it must be characterized essentially as consisting of meaningful actions, not of mere patterns of responses (for example Taylor, 1964). Action, it is argued, is accounted for by reference to the reasons of the agent, and reasons cannot be identified with causes: behaviour is not an effect produced by an antecedent condition but the consequence of an interpretation. It has been concluded, therefore, that psychology needs to shift to a new paradigm, in which investigators interpret their subjects' behaviour in the way that one interprets a text (Harré and Secord, 1972; Gauld and Shotter, 1977). However, recognizing the centrality of rationality for an explanation of behaviour does not necessarily commit one to postulating a sharp dichotomy between causes and reasons or to believing that our present positivist psychology must give way to a new hermeneutic psychology. For, if reasons are to determine behaviour they must in some sense function as causes and can then be treated as intervening variables within a causal sequence (Macklin, 1972; Macintyre, 1971). On the other hand, it may well be that the rationality of human action both determines most significantly the direction of our inquiries into behaviour and sets limits to the possibilities of precise and exhaustive prediction. It is such a view which is elaborated in the first section of this book.

Both Pettit and McGinn argue that explanation within psychology must be an elaboration of the commonsense way of explaining behaviour through searching for the reasons behind actions and that the relationship between mental events (beliefs, desires, etc.) and behaviour is a causal one. In explaining behaviour there is no more fundamental assumption than 'that the action produced by any state of belief and concern is that action, or at least a member of that set of actions, which is rational in the light of the state in question' (Pettit, p. 9). However, the more successful we are in specifying the causes of a particular action, the less generally applicable are the conditions we discover, for they will be peculiar to the agent at the time of his acting. Rationalization, McGinn points out, is idiographic, not nomothetic. That is to say, the language of rationality will not produce exact laws describing the relationships between reasons and actions; but, since reasons and actions must fall under some rubric of lawful relations, the only kind this could be is a physical one. Reasons and actions must in principle be physically describable, but this means only that each particular mental event which causes an action is identical with some particular physical event which causes a bodily movement; it does not mean that rationalizing explanation is reducible to physical explanation, since mental events may be identical with diverse kinds of physical events in the brain.

The beliefs that man is essentially characterized as a rational agent and that mental events correspond to physical events occurring in the brain are, I believe, shared by two of the most influential, contemporary perspectives in psychology, Piagetian theory and information processing. Both, however, go far beyond 'commonsense' and hold out the hope of discovering general structures beneath the apparent complexity of behaviour. For Piaget, the universals of behaviour are located within the general structures of action, and Mays shows that a proper understanding of the basic Piagetian concepts requires a grasp of the philosophical problems with which Piaget was concerned. He points to affinities between Piagetian theory and the phenomenology of Husserl. Morgan, in discussing the nature of phenomenal space, quotes Piaget's dictum that geometrical intuition has its origin in internalized action and concludes, after reviewing developments in geometrical theory since Kant, that the geometry of phenomenal space is the geometry of our actions, its rules reflecting their necessary organization. Consequently, the objects of phenomenal geometry do not occur within a private, interior realm but are programmes for action that can be communicated to others (and hence are amenable to experimental manipulation). Wetherick proposes that the structure with which psychology is concerned is one that has the capacity to model other structures and, building upon this through, for example, work with computer programs, psychology can establish itself as a science. Boden, too, argues that the use of the computational metaphor in psychology is entirely consistent with a humanistic perspective and with the language of reasons and intentions. She is not concerned with the question of the possible limits of artificial intelligence, but with demonstrating the usefulness of this work for making more precise our understanding of cognitive processes. The computer analogy is valid, Boden maintains, because seeing the human brain's function as modelling or representing the world allows us to understand how subjective processes such as intentions and beliefs can be grounded in objective causal mechanisms.

Whilst these four chapters are informed by a common concern for founding what might be called an empirical psychology of human action, what unites the last three chapters of the book is an awareness of the possible limits of such a framework. Still considers the objections that have been voiced against artificial intelligence and concludes that the computer analogy, which is at the centre of cognitive psychology, cannot be conclusively refuted, largely since one can never rule out the possibility of a propositional representation of processes alleged to be outside the capacities of present computer programs. Far from this fact guaranteeing the validity of the computer metaphor, however, it may be that its very irrefutability reflects a totally spurious convergence of reasoning (like Ptolemaic astronomy), to escape from which we need to consider a point of view that is diametrically opposed to the assumption that the mind works by constructing a representation of the world. Still sees Gibson's (1966) ecological optics as such a perspective and points to the similarity between Gibson's views and the phenomenological notion of 'being-in-the-world'. My own chapter seeks to vindicate the notion of pre-reflective awareness, principally through an examination of Husserl's phenomenology, and it is suggested that phenomenological analysis leads us to reject the dualism of the model of intentional acts informing sensory content. Our acts must be seen within a context that both precedes and transcends them, and any psychological model which seeks objectivity by ignoring this context will seriously mislead us. Heaton shows in the final chapter that this is precisely what various theories of therapy have done. They masquerade as general theories of human nature, whereas they ought to confront us with an understanding of the way in which language represents, so that we can recognize what can and what cannot be said.

Whilst the contributions to this volume are organized in such a way as to bring out the interplay between the philosophical analysis of action and its scientific investigation, each chapter may be read independently, and psychology students who are unfamiliar with philosophical analysis might prefer to begin with the more directly psychological chapters. It is my belief that the philosophy of psychology should occupy a more central position than it does at present in the psychology curriculum and I hope that this book of original contributions may help to convince the reader, if he needs convincing, that joining together philosophical and psychological concerns can only be of benefit to both.

NEIL BOLTON

References

Davidson, D. (1976) Philosophy as psychology. In S. C. Brown (ed.) *Philosophy and Psychology*. London: Macmillan.

Gibson, J. J. (1966) *The Senses Considered as Perceptual Systems*. London: Allen and Unwin.

Gauld, A. and Shotter, J. (1977) *Human Action and its Psychological Investigation*. London: Routledge and Kegan Paul.

Harré, R. and Secord, P. F. (1972) *The Explanation of Social Behaviour*. Oxford: Blackwell.

Macintyre, A. (1971) The antecedents of action. In A. Macintyre, *Against the Self-images of the Age*. London: Duckworth.

Macklin, R. (1972) Reasons vs. causes in explanation of action. *Philos. Phenom. Res. 33*: 78–89.

Nagel, T. (1971) Brain bisection and the unity of consciousness. *Synthese 22*: 396–413.

Taylor, C. (1964) *The Explanation of Behaviour*. London: Routledge and Kegan Paul.

Part I
Reason and action

1 Rationalization and the art of explaining action

Philip Pettit

Introduction

It is our ordinary scheme of action explanation which identifies for us those events that we regard as actions. Among the events to which a human being gives rise without the intervention of other agencies, we confer the title of 'actions' on those which we explain as the appropriate issue of a certain state of mind. The agent views his situation as offering certain options, let us say, considers that the matters which most concern him are such and such and, by way of doing what he takes to satisfy those concerns, performs one of the options. Here we would have little hesitation in describing the event constituted by that performance as an action. But even in cases where the agent cannot be imagined to go through explicit phases of reasoning, we are prepared to take a similar line. A person who raises his hand to his forehead and brushes off a fly, however casually he does so, would normally be said also to have performed an action. Here too we take it that the event in question occurs as the appropriate outcome of the state of mind. The agent notices something on his forehead and, concerned to get rid of the irritation, is led to sweep his hand across his brow.

An event which constitutes an action must be the appropriate outcome, I said, of an agent's state of mind. The qualification that it must be appropriate is designed for the negative purpose of ruling out of the court of actions any events which are, so to speak, caused in the wrong way. What it prescribes positively, i.e. how exactly an action must be occasioned by a state of mind to be its appropriate outcome, is a point which we must leave in obscurity. But, to give an example of an event ruled out as an action, consider the following possibility. Someone interrupts me at work and I reflect as I make my response that, if I present myself as somewhat flustered by his arrival, I shall probably get him to leave fairly quickly. However these considerations, simply insofar as they distract and disorientate me, have the result that I do present myself as flustered. In such a case, though we may be unclear about the reasons, we would not regard the event as an action; it is not something that the agent strictly does.

The prescription that an action must be the appropriate issue of the agent's state of mind does not, it should be noticed, eliminate the set of what we might call accidental actions. Suppose that I am led to offer help by the consideration of someone's plight but the effect of my doing so is that I offend the person in question. My giving offence is, equally with my offering help, the appropriate outcome of my state of mind. It must be so since, at least on the most plausible account of the individuation of actions, it is one and the same action as my offering help (see Davidson, 1971a; cf. Goldman, 1970). I may not have sought to give offence as such but I did seek a course of behaviour which turned out to have an offensive effect.

When we find it unfitting to apply the ordinary scheme of action explanation to events which a person brings about without intermediary cause, we judge that those events are not properly actions. Thus we usually cast beyond the pale of action such various things as digesting and breathing, coughing and burping, blushing and laughing, seeing and believing, wanting and hoping. These responses we choose to make sense of in some way other than by representing them as actions. They are allocated to other categories within our general theory of human beings.

The point in rehearsing these platitudes about the identification of actions is to emphasize that if we seek within the human studies for a discipline of action explanation, we must take our starting point in the common scheme of explanation. Since it is that scheme which sets apart among human responses those events that we describe as actions, we cannot be sure that we shall not have changed the subject matter if we take our departure from elsewhere. We may judge, as the behaviourists did, that we should begin afresh in studying human responses scientifically, and that we should try to construct our own categorizations among those responses. If we do so, however, we should not presume that we may describe our enterprise, without being misleading, as an attempt to explain human action.

This essay is concerned with the prospects, so far as they are subject to philosophical scrutiny, for a science of human action or behaviour. I take it, on the basis of the foregoing considerations, that if such a science is possible, it must come of a refinement and elaboration of the ordinary scheme of action explanation. In the first section I give a brisk exposition of that scheme and try to locate the points at which one might think of sharpening it. In the second section I set out a problem which, I believe, renders any attempt to sharpen the scheme, and produce a science of human behaviour, futile. And in the third section I consider what room remains for the development of specialized skill in the explanation of action. I argue that even if one cannot improve on the ordinary scheme of explanation, one may hope to do better than average in applying it to the behaviour of individuals and groups. There is reason to expect specialists to surpass people of commonsense in explaining particular actions or action patterns, a point which I illustrate briefly at the end of the section.

The paper, it should be said, is closely related to Pettit (1976 and 1978) and is heavily indebted to the work of the American philosopher Donald Davidson, some of whose papers are mentioned in the bibliography. A number of important topics have had to be ignored, most notably: the agent's own knowledge of the beliefs and concerns underlying his action and the knowledge available to an audience from his verbal reports on the matter. I assume that an agent does not have any special kind of knowledge of his beliefs and concerns, though he may know more than others. And on the question of verbal reports I take the point often made by Davidson that the interpretation of such reports raises just the problems raised by the explanation of actions.

The common scheme of action explanation

The sorts of accounts which are given of action in everyday life are legion but for the sake of perspective we may divide them into four rough categories. Some accounts refer us to the *character traits* of agents, some to their *motivating states*, i.e. the emotions or impulses with which they are visited from time to time, others invoke the agents' *concerns* or desires or priorities and others again the *intentions* with which they act on different occasions. The items mentioned in the four categories of explanation each bear on the goals of the agent but they do so in different ways (see Pettit, 1976).

To know an agent's intention in acting, as I use the term, is to know the description or aspect under which the agent represents the action to himself as the thing he is attempting, or is about to attempt, to do. Knowledge of the intention, that is to say, gives us the primary characterization of the action. It follows that knowledge of the intention is of no use in explaining why the action was performed except to the extent that we have not yet even identified properly the action to be explained: we know it perhaps just as a bodily movement and, assuming that it is an action, we ask why it occurred. The explanation of actions described by reference to the intentions they embody is provided in terms of concerns, states and traits.

Among these three types of explanation, that which deals in concerns is the basic one. To know a person's concerns in acting is to know the descriptions or aspects under which the action appealed to the agent as the thing to be done. It is to see that he desired the intended action on the grounds that it promised enjoyment, monetary reward and some benefit to his friends, for example. (As intended, an action may also be appealing, in which case knowledge of the intention gives knowledge of one concern satisfied by the action; but usually an action is intended under a very specific description which, just as such, we would not expect to engage a person's concerns.) We look to general descriptions or aspects in order to understand why a project should have been found attractive. The introduction of such descriptions is explanatory because it refers us to dispositions which we are ready to ascribe to any human being. We hold to a background model of human desire in which it is entirely unsurprising, for example, that someone should be moved by the prospect of enjoyment, monetary reward or benefit to his friends.

One reason for saying that the explanation by concerns is more basic than explanation by states or traits is that while we always take such explanation to be available we often assume that an action may involve no particular impulse or emotion, or no particular personality trait. But, even more important than this, when we have recourse to states or traits in explaining an action, we do so on the supposition that the agent is moved by a particular concern or set of concerns. The recourse serves, in supplementation of the more basic level of explanation, to indicate why the concerns invoked should have been operative just then, or in just that combination. It is when a supposed pattern of concerns is found surprising for some reason that mention of a visitation of feeling or a habit of personality serves an explanatory purpose. In rendering the pattern less surprising it reinforces the action explanation in which the concerns are invoked.

The line of thought which we have been following indicates that the principal form of action explanation allowed for within the ordinary scheme is explanation by agent concerns. At this point we must mention that in the full explanation of an action we make reference not just to such concerns but also to the agent's beliefs. It is in view of his beliefs, where this is a catch-all category for his perceptions, judgements, inferences and standing commitments, that an agent sees that he has such and such options, with such and such possible outcomes, and that he views those outcomes as each being relatively more or less attractive, on the basis of his concerns, than the others. Within the form of explanation in question what is taken to occasion the action is a state of mind involving, apart from concerns, a complex of such beliefs.

Focussing then on the explanation by concerns let us try to see what it involves. A first question to settle is whether it should be viewed as a species of causal explanation. When this is decided, we may formulate some more specific questions about how it is implemented in practice.

The question of the causal or other status of action explanation has been, at least until recently, a major point of debate in analytical philosophy. The present orthodoxy appears to be that it is causal and, since I agree with this view, I will not spend much time trying to establish it (see Davidson, 1963). Those who oppose the causal construal maintain that there is a logical connection between the event mentioned in the explanans and that mentioned in the explanandum: that is, so far as we are concerned, between the event of the agent coming to be of a certain pattern of beliefs and concerns and the event constituted by his action. What this logical connection is said to mean is that it is logically inevitable that if the first of these events occurs, the second will do so, or *vice versa*. Sometimes the connection is said to run in both directions, sometimes in only one. But in any case it is taken to preclude the possibility of the mental event, as we may call it, being the cause of the behavioural one. It is supposed to put the mental event–action event pair on a par with event pairs, such as the following, which clearly do not involve a causal connection:

1 John is born in 1960. John reaches age 10 in 1970.
2 I say 'Shucks'. I say 'Sh'.
3 My sister has a child. I become an uncle.

The logical connection argument, as it is called, is both ill expressed and unconvincing. It is ill expressed because the question of whether two events bear a logical connection depends on how they are described. Indeed any two events f and g can be described so that it is logically inevitable that if one occurs the other occurs: for example, f can be described as 'the event such that it is identical with f and there is an event g', so that if an event fitting that description occurs it is logically inevitable that an event g occurs. It may be that my intending to do X and my doing it, described as such, are logically connected but they are not so connected when the first event in the pair is redescribed as 'the intending which I went through at time t', or 'the intending that was uncharacteristic of me'.

But let us be charitable and, ignoring the question of formulation, take the logical connection argument to say that the mental event invoked in action explanation bears to the action explained a connection of the kind exemplified by 1–3, and that such a connection is incompatible with a causal one. So expressed, the argument turns out to be quite unconvincing. For whereas it would be indeed out of place to say that the first event in any of the examples 1–3 was the cause of the second, we are required to say this of the events mentioned in an action explanation if the first is really held to explain the second. An explanation of an agent doing such and such would be given by: 'He came to see an action of doing such and such as the only alternative to one of doing so and so and doing such and such appeared more desirable to him at the time.' The explanation would be reduced to nothing however if we were then told: 'Of course his seeing things in that way was not the cause of his doing what he did.' This establishes that we think of the mental event involved in explanation of an action, unlike the first event in any of our examples 1–3, as being causally related to the event with which it is matched.

The question of status appears then to be settled. The explanation of actions by reference to states of belief and concern represents those actions as the determined causal issue of the mental states. In charting our ordinary scheme of action explanation, and in particular explanation by reference to beliefs and concerns, we must turn now to the question of application. How is it, in the explanatory practice of everyday life, that we manage to apply the scheme to individual pieces of behaviour, isolating in each case a causally efficacious state of mind responsible for the action? How do we determine which beliefs and desires to invoke in accounting for the behaviour?

The query may be distinguished into two questions. The first is: how do we know which action a given array of beliefs and concerns will produce? How do we project from the mental state to the behaviour? And the second is: how do we know which beliefs and concerns to ascribe to someone, independently of seeing the action they produce? How do we find effect-independent indices of the mental state? Granted the operation of causally productive states of belief and concern, the first problem has to do with the tracing of effects, and the second with the identification of indices. We may expect our ordinary scheme of action explanation to give us ways of handling both problems. But if we are interested in sharpening up the ordinary scheme, we may also expect that there will be room for improving on the ways in which the problems are handled. The point will be made again.

The problem of tracing the effects of beliefs and concerns is solved in the application of our ordinary scheme by what we may call the assumption of rationality. We assume as we attempt to make sense of one another's behaviour, and indeed also of our own, that the action produced by any state of belief and concern is that action, or at least a member of that set of actions, which is rational in the light of the state in question. And what is it for our action to be rational in the light of a state of belief and concern? Roughly, we can say that the action must be represented by the agent in the mental state as a way of realizing something which, granted the state he is in, he finds more attractive than anything which he thinks can be realized by the available alternatives. In order to work out which of a set of options has this property for an agent, we need to know the concerns which determine what he finds attractive, the relative weights which he attaches to these concerns and the decision principles which guide him in his attitude to actions that may give any of a number of outcomes.

This outline statement of the assumption of rationality is sufficient for our purposes but it may be mentioned that decision theory is an attempt to spell it out in detail and also to sharpen it up (see Jeffrey, 1965). Decision theory takes from utility theory the assumption that concerns allow us to construct a single numerical index representing the aggregate attraction to an agent of each of the outcomes which may be secured by this action. This solves the weighting problem dramatically. In a situation of certainty with regard to the outcome of each action it is naturally taken that the rational strategy is to choose the option with the highest associated index: to maximize utility. The problem which then remains, and that to which decision theory is mainly devoted, is to isolate the intuitively rational strategy or strategies in a situation where the outcome of one or more options can only be probabilistically determined, or is downright uncertain. For someone who considers refining and elaborating the ordinary scheme of action explanation, decision theory will appear as just the sort of enterprise to press ahead with. It promises to open up the possibility of a rigorous science where before there was only a rough explanatory scheme.

And what now of our second problem? How are effect-independent indices of belief and concern identified in the application of our ordinary scheme of action explanation? I will say, in nice parallel to our response to the first problem: by the assumption of humanity. To assume humanity in dealing with another person is to take it that in forming and maintaining beliefs and desires he is as the common run of men and women. His perceptions display the same rough patterns of figure on ground, his generalizations are made on similar inductive canons, his deductions follow approximately the same rules of logic. He is a person subject to the ordinary inclinations of our species, but also he is susceptible in the general way to the effects of whatever training and education he has received. Over time he exhibits a certain stability in his beliefs and concerns. If any such disposition changes, there is certain to be some cause of the change: the dispositions do not form a randomly mutating set (see Grundy, 1973 and Lewis, 1974).

The assumption of humanity is idealized and explicated, though only so far as beliefs are concerned, in the rules of inductive and deductive logic. I shall take it as obvious that in rough practical form we apply the assumption daily in our efforts at divining one another's states of mind. The point which I wish to highlight is that in drawing in this way on the assumption of humanity we solve the second problem associated with our ordinary scheme of action explanation. By supposing humanity in the agents whose behaviour we wish to explain we give ourselves a fair means of establishing their beliefs and concerns in any situation independently of seeing what actions they perform. That is, we provide ourselves with effect-independent indices of the mental states which we take to produce their actions.

In this section we have seen that within our ordinary scheme of action explanation the explanation by concerns has a special place, that this explanation is of the regular causal sort and that in pursuing it we make use of the twin assumptions of rationality and humanity. It is time now to consider how we might sharpen up the ordinary scheme in seeking to develop a science of human behaviour, and whether the attempt to develop such a discipline has any chance of success. Our ordinary scheme falls far short of science in the sense that it gives us little predictive control of behaviour. Given an action and granted humanity and rationality then we may be able to make a shrewd guess at the agent's state of belief and concern. What we are not able to do however, except very rarely, is to pick out that state in advance and predict the action that ensues.

The impossibility of a science of action

The way to sharpen up the ordinary scheme of action explanation is, it would appear, to seek more exact indices of beliefs and concerns than those which are supplied by the assumption of humanity. We might envisage refinement of the scheme along the following lines. We tighten up the assumption of humanity in a given case, taking certain indices to betoken unequivocally a particular state of mind. If an action follows which is not the action we would expect on the assumption of rationality then we modify that assumption in order to see whether the link between our sharp indices and that action is generally realized. We make this move in every case in the search for correlations between states of mind that have sharp indices and actions. At the cost of modifying or even replacing the assumption of rationality, we work towards laws which have the advantage that we can tell for certain that they apply, at least in principle, independently of seeing whether the behavioural effects that they predict are realized. With such laws we would be rid of the vagueness of the ordinary scheme of action explanation. We would be in possession of a theory that we might expect, by the usual process of falsification and amendment, to develop into an ever more powerful tool for predicting human behaviour.

The envisaged sharpening of our ordinary scheme cannot, unfortunately, be taken as a serious prospect. The problem is that the assumption of rationality is so deeply embedded in our habits of thought about action that so long as we treat someone as a person in his full senses we must take his behaviour to be rational in the light of his beliefs and concerns, whatever the indices say that those beliefs and concerns were. If our indices tell us that an agent's frame of mind was such as rationally to make him perform a particular action and it turns out that he performs another action which is rationally incompatible with that frame, we naturally conclude that the indices were misleading or that the agent changed his mind between our reading the signs and his doing the action. On no account do we tolerate the idea that we have found reason to amend or in any way alter the original principle that human agents act in the way rationalized by their beliefs and desires (see Davidson, 1974; Pettit, 1978).

Our scheme of action explanation might be spelled out as a set of sentences which we hold true. Among those sentences the assumption of rationality has the special status, I suggest, of being contextually *a priori* (see Quine, 1953 and Putnam, 1977). What this means is that there is no evidence we can envisage which would lead us to revise it, as a sentence held true of human beings in general; in any imaginable instance we would rather revise some other sentence or sentences. The assumption may not be absolutely *a priori* because there is nothing to close the possibility that someone might develop a presently unimagined theory involving its denial, or at least the denial of its nearest translational equivalent, a theory which would naturally command our allegiance once developed. All that is claimed is that in the context of our present theory the assumption presents itself to us as one which no imaginable circumstance would lead us to amend. The claim, rather than being seen as a blunt assertion, may be taken as a challenge. The reader is invited to imagine a case where on the basis of the indices of someone's state of mind, and the consequent apparently irrational behaviour, he would seriously consider amending the proposition that human agents act in the way rationalized by their beliefs and desires. The suggestion is that in any such case the reader would deny the evidence of the indices and preserve the rational face of the behaviour or, at the very limit, that he would conclude that the agent was not properly a human agent at all, being in some respect out of his senses.

Even if the reader admits the force of this challenge, and accepts the claim that the assumption of rationality has contextual *a priori* status within our view of persons, it may be wondered why this should be so. The least venturesome, and a perfectly plausible answer is that our epistemological priorities, which incline us towards simplicity, generality, economy and so on, would be offended by our giving up on the assumption of rationality in the face of any imaginable circumstance of behaviour: or more precisely, that they would be offended by our giving up on the assumption in the absence of a comprehensive alternative to our present theory of persons (see Quine and Ullian, 1970). Epistemologically, the cost of rejecting the principle of agent rationality would be greater, in the absence of a comprehensive alternative theory, than the cost of rejecting one of the other sentences which are engaged by any troublesome example. Thus, in such a case, minimizing the mutilation of our beliefs, we would hold on to the assumption and look for some other sentence to reject: and this, even to the point of denying that the agent in question was properly human.

It is not surprising that we should find a contextually *a priori* assumption written into the theory of persons which underlies the ordinary scheme of action explanation. Within any theory, even the most explicitly scientific, it is possible to locate sentences which no imaginable circumstance would lead adherents to revise, sentences which none the less may come to be revised with the acceptance of some presently unenvisaged theory. Thus consider the status within our theory of measurement for middle-sized objects near at hand of the sentence 'If object A is longer than object B, and object B is longer than object C, then object A is longer than object C'. This sentence, which we might dub the principle of the transitivity of length, is embedded within our beliefs at a depth which makes it contextually *a priori*. No piece of evidence we can imagine would lead us, while in full possession of our epistemological senses, to question it. Any difficult case that we can envisage would suggest revision of some other belief which it would be less costly for us to let go. Thus, given an apparent counter-example to the principle, we would naturally conclude that one or more of the objects, or perhaps the measuring instrument itself, was changing in length over the time required for measurement. And yet the fact that this is so does not rule out the possibility that some radical alternative to our present theory may be elaborated in which the translational equivalent of the principle is denied, an alternative which would command our preference on the usual epistemological grounds of being more simple, more general, more economic, or whatever. What is claimed is that the principle of the transitivity of length is contextually *a priori*, not that it is absolutely so.

But enough has been said of the status of the assumption of rationality, we must now explain why that status is a source of difficulty. Very simply, the reason is that the assumption is in potential conflict with any law involving exact indices that might be developed in the course of sharpening the ordinary scheme of action explanation. As things are in our existing practice, if the indices suggest a particular state of belief and concern in an agent and then the agent acts in a manner rationally incompatible with that state, the indices are sufficiently inexact to allow us to assume that we were misled by them. We may suppose that contrary to appearances the agent was in a state of such a kind as rationally to produce the action, thereby preserving the assumption of rationality. However, if we were to postulate certain exact indices and then seek to formulate laws which might be tied to them, we would be bound to come into conflict with the assumption sooner or later: this we indicated already in sketching the enterprise of sharpening our ordinary scheme of action explanation. The reason is simple: if the assumption of rationality were compatible with the fixing of exact indices for states of belief and concern, then it is hard to see why these indices should not already have been located during the long history of application of the ordinary scheme.

What appears from our reflections then is that while the ordinary scheme of action explanation looks ripe for sharpening into an exact predictive science of behaviour, the status accorded within the scheme to the assumption of rationality makes such sharpening impossible. We are deeply committed to viewing one another as rational agents and this commitment renders futile the attempt to develop an exact science out of our ordinary scheme. The empty possibility is there, as indicated in our discussion of the contextual aspect of *a priori* sentences, that a theory may be developed which would revoke the assumption of rationality and yet command our allegiance. But this is of no practical consolation to the professional psychologist or sociologist who seeks a science of behaviour. The possibility is empty in that we have absolutely no idea of what might constitute its realization.

The promised art of action explanation

In the introduction to this paper we saw that a science of human behaviour must take its starting point in the common scheme of action explanation, since it is by reference to the scheme that we define action in the first place. The first section analysed the ordinary scheme and indicated where it might be sharpened into a science but the second section showed that the prospect for sharpening was nil: the assumption of rationality within the ordinary scheme leaves no room for the development of scientific laws. The question which we now face is whether there is hope, if not of a predictive science of behaviour, at least of a discipline of behavioural explanation. Is there any place at all for professional skill in the business of explaining action?

I believe that there is place for such skill, for the reason that while commonsense may be enough for an understanding of our scheme of action explanation, it need not be thought to offer the most enlightened guidelines on our application of it. The application of a regular predictive theory is not something problematic since all we have to do in explaining an event is to find among the laws which might explain it that law, and normally there will be only one, whose indices are fulfilled. However, the application of our explanatory scheme for actions is problematic, precisely for the reason that the indices of states of belief and concern are inexact. Among those mental states from which a given action might have rationally proceeded, the indices will leave it more or less unclear which was actually the agent's state. Thus the person applying the theory in explanation of the action will have discretion to exercise in his choice of best explanation. The fact of the discretion means that there is room, at least in principle, for improvement on the commonsense habits of applying the ordinary scheme of action explanation. There is a point at which professional skill may enter into the enterprise of explaining behaviour.

Abstractly considered, the task of applying the scheme of action explanation to a given piece of behaviour is one of optimization. The problem is to select the mental state which optimally satisfies a number of competing constraints that derive from the twin assumptions of humanity and rationality. The beliefs and concerns which make up the state must rationalize what the agent does, they must square with his background and past behaviour, and they must be such as could have been formed and maintained by a 'normal' person. There need be no perfect solution to such an optimization problem, though some solutions will clearly be preferable to others, putting less strain for example on the humanity of the agent under discussion. Thus there may often be room for improvement, through the efforts of professional dedication, on the solutions favoured by commonsense for any range of actions. (I owe the optimization parallel to Nick Jardine.)

This possibility becomes more live when one considers the pressures to which commonsense is subject in suggesting lines of action explanation. Here I will mention two main sources of pressure in order to indicate the room which exists, if not for a science of human behaviour, at least for an art of behavioural explanation.

Explanations of action are often, as it has been put, negotiated between the agent and his audience. The agent may suggest or insinuate an explanation for what he has done which, if it is accepted, he will vindicate in his future behaviour, continuing to act on the beliefs and concerns which his original action has been taken to evince. Alternatively the audience may make an offer, perhaps a counter-offer, of an explanation, the joint acceptance of which will set the stage for further behaviour and response. For an example of the process we may think of the boy and girl situation, where the more or less ambiguous overtures of one or the other party have a definite outcome only when they receive a common interpretation. But examples abound through the spectrum of human relationships, friendly and hostile. When the explanation of an action is agreed, however tacitly, between an agent and his audience, the explanation will be chosen by way of initiating or renewing a shared sense of future exchanges. It will be selected by the parties with a view to inaugurating or reinforcing a certain sort of relationship between them.

The first pressure on commonsense explanation of action stems from this link between explanation and relationship. If in explaining some-one's doings I am constrained by my sense of our relationship, then I may well be led towards a less than optimal account of what he does. I may be too kind for example, making unrealistic excuses on his behalf, or I may not be kind enough, readily finding evidence of a less than fully human sensibility. More than likely it will be the case that an uninvolved concern for optimizing over the demands of humanity and rationality would avoid both extremes.

But commonsense is not limited just by the pressure of relationships. A second limitation springs from a pressure, scarcely avoidable in commonsense patterns of explanation, against imputing reflexive con-cerns in any widespread way to human beings. A reflexive concern is not a desire to get something straightforward like money, power or fellowship but a desire to appear, in one's own eyes perhaps as well as in the eyes of others, to have just such a straightforward desire. We may readily avow, drawing on nothing other than the assumption of humanity, that people are often moved by reflexive concerns. But the problem with commonsense explanation is that this avowal cannot be systematically applied in accounting for behaviour (see Pettit, 1978).

Commonsense applications of our scheme of action explanation introduce concerns which any agent, just by being possessed of commonsense, may expect to be ascribed to him on the basis of what he does. It is because of this that we may allow that any such agent is liable to be moved by the reflexive concern to have the concern in question ascribed to him. But if it became a matter of common-sense practice to ascribe the reflexive concern in such a case then this pattern would be displaced. We would have to allow that the agent might expect to have the reflexive concern ascribed to him in this case. And then we would be pushed a level further to admit that the agent was liable to be moved by the higher order reflexive concern to have the first order reflexive concern ascribed to him. Nothing would be gained by such a shifting of levels and so, almost as if by general conspiracy, commonsense explanations tend to rest with the imputation of ground-floor non-reflexive concerns.

What we may well look for then, beyond the commonsense way of explaining action, is a style of explanation which would resist the non-reflexive pressure, and the pressure of existing relationships, in construing people's behaviour. This explanatory art would take the ordinary scheme of action explanation and would seek in every case to optimize over the demands of humanity and rationality. It would constitute, in a phrase which may be mischievous for its overtones, an effort at impartial rationalization.

But in order that I may not be accused of inventing a new idol for the shrines of psychological and social inquiry, let me just mention in conclusion that the art of rationalization seems already to be a flourishing discipline. Within psychotherapy for example, whether of a Freudian or Laingian persuasion, it has become a commonplace that the therapist should seek out a positive style of explanation for behaviour which within the patient's circle of relationships was taken, perhaps even by himself, as immoral, morbid or mad. The therapist is not a detached theorist because part of his job is to form a relationship with the patient on the basis of this new style of explanation. He seeks to liberate the person by revealing the possibility of a new self-image and a new pattern of social exchange.

Another area where rationalization is of the essence is the social psychology or microsociology of behaviour. Consider the typical approach of the social psychologist, for example, to the behaviour of hooligans. He has no truck with the hostile and distancing explanations suggested by middle-aged commonsense which would put down the hooligans as delinquents who have not learned to control their passions. He rejects the pressure of such a corrective relationship and, usually through plumbing the possibility of reflexive concerns, seeks to put a more rational, if not a more flattering, face on the behaviour. Thus he may conjecture that the hooligan activities among the group in question are taken to evince bravery and that they are performed, at least partly, out of a reflexive concern to be judged as brave by peers.

For a final example of rationalization at work among professional students of human behaviour I can quote from Stanley Milgram's attempt to explain the behaviour of the subjects in his notorious experiment. What he has to explain is how so many ordinary people could have been willing in his mock-up of a learning experiment to administer to the learner what they took to be painful and dangerous electric shocks. In his explanation he avoids straining our assumption of humanity by positing undreamt of sadistic inclinations in his subjects. Instead, following Goffman, he conjectures that they conform to the experimenter's instructions out of a reflexive concern to be seen as having the attitudes appropriate to their relatively inferior position.

> The experimental situation is so constructed that there is no way the subject can stop shocking the learner without violating the experimenter's self-definition. The subject cannot break off and at the same time protect the authority's definitions of his own competence. Thus, the subject fears that if he breaks off, he will appear arrogant, untoward, and rude. (Milgram, 1974, p. 150)

If the comments of the last few paragraphs are fair then we have discovered at the end of our journey a not unhappy state of affairs. It appears that the philosophical worries about the project for a science of human behaviour which I tried to formulate in the earlier parts of this paper have been anticipated in the practice of psychological and sociological inquiry. I do not think that all students of human behaviour will be happy to be told that their task is one of rationalization but it is encouraging that many have proceeded as if they were open to that accolade.

References

Davidson, D. (1963) Actions, reasons and causes. *Journal of Philosophy 60*.
Davidson, D. (1967) The logical form of action sentences. In N. Rescher (ed.) *The Logic of Decision and Action*. Pittsburgh: University of Pittsburgh Press.
Davidson, D. (1970) Action and reaction. *Inquiry 13*.
Davidson, D. (1971a) Agency. In R. Binkley, R. Bronaugh and A. Marris (eds) *Agent, Action and Reason*. Toronto: University of Toronto Press.
Davidson, D. (1971b) Mental events. In L. Foster and J. Swanson (eds) *Experience and Theory*. Boston: Belknap.
Davidson, D. (1973) Freedom to act. In T. Honderich (ed.) *Essays on Freedom of Action*. London: Routledge and Kegan Paul.

Davidson, D. (1974) Philosophy as psychology. In S. C. Brown (ed.) *Philosophy and Psychology*. London: Macmillan.

Goldman, A. I. (1970) *A Theory of Human Action*. Princeton: Princeton University Press.

Grandy, R. (1973) Reference, meaning and belief. *Journal of Philosophy 70*.

Jeffrey, R. (1965) *The Logic of Decision*. New York: McGraw-Hill.

Lewis, D. (1974) Radical interpretation. *Synthese 27*.

Mackie, J. L. (1974) *The Cement of the Universe*. Oxford: Oxford University Press.

Milgram, S. (1974) *Obedience and Authority*. London: Tavistock.

Pettit, P. (1976) Making actions intelligible. In Rom Harré (ed.) *Life Sentences*. London: John Wiley and Son.

Pettit, P. (1978) Rational Man Theory. In Christopher Hookway and P. Pettit (eds) *Action and Interpretation*. Cambridge: Cambridge University Press.

Putnam, H. (1977) 'Two dogmas' revisited. In Gilbert Ryle (ed.) *Contemporary Aspects of Philosophy*. Oriel Press.

Quine, W. V. O. (1953) Two dogmas of empiricism. In *From a Logical Point of View*. Cambridge, Mass.: Harvard University Press.

Quine, W. V. O. and Ullian, J. (1970) *The Web of Belief*. New York: Random House.

2 Action and its explanation

Colin McGinn

Psychologists have accustomed themselves to operating with an un-differentiated concept of 'behaviour'. This custom encourages neglect of, and insensitivity to, a significant distinction among the events of bodily movement which (in part) comprise a person's biography: I mean the distinction between those episodes of movement which befall us, in which we are patient; and those, on the other hand, which we initiate, of which we are agent. The partition of behavioural events this distinction imposes is central to our commonsense theory of persons; it lies behind our attributions of responsibility and is pre-supposed to the idea of rationality. But what is the mark that dis-tinguishes between active and passive, between what we do and what merely happens to us? What is the principle of the distinction gestured towards by these locutions? This is precisely the question of what qualifies a bodily movement as an *action*. In what follows I shall return an answer to that question, and set forth some distinctive features of our ordinary scheme for explaining such events. The hope is that a measure of clarity on what is involved here will show this scheme to be legitimate, ineliminable and a paradigm of psychological explanation.[1]

I

It seems clear at once that the concept of *intention* is integral to the notion of agency. For surely, if a piece of behaviour is intentional, it is something the agent does – it is an action. Spilling the ink is an action if the agent spills it intentionally. However, it may seem that, though sufficient for agency, intentionality is not necessary; for we may also perform actions *un*intentionally. Spilling the ink may qualify as something done, though the agent did not intend to do it. Are mistakes not precisely unintentional actions? This is, of course, an entirely correct observation: but it does not follow that intention is not the crux of the action/non-action distinction. For the possibility is left open that, wherever an action is performed unintentionally, there is always an intentional action in the immediate offing. The way this may come about is made plain by the following example: I may unintentionally pour a glass of vodka into the sink, supposing it mere water; but I did intentionally empty the contents of the glass. And in the general case my unintentionally doing one thing is invariably accompanied by my intentionally doing another.

But what is the exact relation between these things done, between pouring away the vodka and emptying the glass? The answer I shall endorse is that it is the relation of strict numerical identity: 'pouring away the vodka' and 'emptying the glass' are descriptions of the very same action, much as 'the start of World War II' and 'the invasion of Poland' may refer to the same event, and 'the evening star' and 'the morning star' refer to the same physical object. That it is the same event that is brought under different descriptions in the action case is best appreciated by focussing on the bodily movement: my hand tips the glass; I believe this to satisfy the description 'pouring away water', but in fact it satisfies a description I disbelieve of it, 'pouring away vodka'. Described as 'emptying the glass' we rate the movement as intentional, but described as 'pouring away the vodka' we call it unintentional. Now the thesis is to be that every action can be described under an aspect that makes it true to say it was intentional. Since, in the general case, an action will satisfy many descriptions the agent does not believe of it, we must always take it that a statement of intentionality is relative to some description. This suggests that we revise our intentional criterion of agency to read thus: a behavioural event qualifies as an action if and only if it satisfies (or is believed by the agent to satisfy) *some* description relative to which it was intentional. By this standard pouring away the vodka will count as an action, because it is identical with intentionally emptying the glass.

A convenient way to state this feature of the concept of intention is to say that actions are intentional or otherwise only *under a given description*.[2] This in turn is best understood in terms of the notion of semantic intensionality or opacity. In the sentence 'It was intentional of A that *e* occurred', where *e* is an action, we cannot guarantee that substituting descriptions of the same action for '*e*' will preserve the truth or falsity of the sentence. Thus, in respect of the aforementioned example, substituting 'emptying the glass' will yield a truth, but replacing that description by 'pouring away the vodka' will lead from truth to falsity, even though these descriptions designate the same action. Put in these terms, our criterion is to the effect that an event *e* is an action if and only if there exists at least one description such that when substituted into an intensional sentence of the above sort a truth results. Notice that, though the criterion is itself intensional, it characterizes a concept that is extensional: for sentences of the form '*e* is an action' do not exhibit opacity – if an event qualifies as an action under one description it qualifies under all. (It is because of the existential form of the criterion that it delivers the extensional concept of agency from the intensional concept of intention.) If a movement satisfies no intentional description, then it fails to count as an action: reflex knee-jerks and getting knocked over are thus (correctly) excluded from the class of actions. It seems, then, that, though further refinement may be required, our criterion draws the line in intuitively the right place.

A natural protest at this point is that the criterion for action in terms of intention is an attempt to illuminate the already obscure by the more obscure, and so does not advance the discussion. This is not in itself a good objection if the criterion successfully articulates a significant conceptual connection; but it is a fair question to ask what is involved in a bodily movement's being intentional. Can we connect intention with some other concept in an illuminating way? It seems that we can: acting intentionally seems intimately related to acting for a *reason*. When I empty the glass intentionally I do it for a reason, perhaps so that I can refill it with vodka; but if my knee jerks reflexively no reason can be ascribed to me. When I do something intentionally I do it for a reason, even when my reason was just that I wanted to do it (as in 'I did it for no reason'). The notion of reason, like the notion of intention, is intensional: an agent has a reason to perform an action only under certain of its descriptions. I had a reason to empty my glass, though not to pour away the vodka. The sentence 'A did *e* for a reason' therefore produces an opaque context. Given this connection between acting for a reason and acting intentionally, nothing stops us saying that an event qualifies as an action just in case it is done for a reason, by the equivalence of 'done for a reason' and 'done intentionally'. We shall have to enquire more closely into the precise relation between reasons and intentions later, and into what it is to be done *for* a reason; the more immediate question concerns what a reason is. When we know what is involved in having a reason for acting we shall understand better what intentionality is, and hence what makes a movement an action.

A reason is best conceived as a desire and belief in a certain sort of combination. If my reason for boiling the kettle is to make tea, then I desire to make tea and I believe that boiling the kettle will contribute towards the satisfaction of that desire. From the specification of the action and the statement of my reason – 'to make tea' – you can reconstruct the desire from which I acted and the belief which guided me. To know the desire is to know the end or purpose of the action, and to know the belief is to know the means (or believed means) to its attainment. Given any two members of this triad – desire, belief, action – it is possible to infer the other, but each singly leaves the remaining two undetermined. We come to know an agent's reason in acting when we see from which desires and beliefs his action (under a certain description) may be inferred; we see which desires and beliefs the action was performed 'in the light of'. Given those desires and beliefs we appreciate why the action was, for that agent then, a reasonable thing to do: if we had his desires and beliefs, we too should be disposed to act as he did, and reasonably. The components of an agent's reason can be construed as premises in a piece of practical reasoning. Practical reasoning is reasoning about what to *do*, and it involves taking account of one's desires and one's beliefs about certain courses of action. It is to be contrasted with so-called theoretical reasoning, in which the question is what to *believe*. The premises implicated in theoretical reasoning are the objects solely of belief, which is why the question of what the theoretical reasoner *desires* is irrelevant to the assessment of the correctness of his reasoning. But in practical reasoning, where desires or judgements of value feature as premises, it is relevant, in assessing the person's reasoning, to take his desires into account. We might represent a little piece of practical reasoning as follows:

1. *A* desires to have tea
2. Boiling the kettle is a (the best) means *A* has for getting tea

   3 Boiling the kettle is therefore a good or desirable thing for *A* to do.

We may imagine the agent running through this 'practical syllogism' to its conclusion and, upon the basis of this reasoning, boiling the kettle. The conclusion (3) corresponds to a desire of the agent's to act in a certain way, where this desire leads to the appropriate action unmediated by further practical reasoning. Observe that the desire expressed in (1) need not itself be specified in terms of any particular action type as its object; it may just concern a certain state of affairs the agent desires to obtain, for example that tea be imbibed by him. Prospective actions enter the picture with the second premise (2), which serves to link the desire with a type of action that will (the agent believes) contribute towards the obtaining of the state of affairs in question. By thus connecting the initiating desire with a type of action a proportionate desirability comes to attach to the type of action itself: means become desirable in proportion as they lead to the satisfaction of ends. Once the desire is transferred to a type of action believed by the agent to be a means within his power of satisfying the desire, the agent is prepared to act: he does what the syllogism, in accordance with which he has reasoned, recommends that he do. Whenever an agent acts for a reason we can assume some such reasoning to have occurred. We can thus say that an action is a bodily movement issuing from such practical reasoning as is codified in the practical syllogism. This makes it clear that a reason is a rationally structured combination of desires and beliefs.

   The above account of practical reasoning is obviously much simplified; it does not provide for the presence of other desires and beliefs of the agent which may bear upon his decision whether to boil the kettle; in particular it does not reckon with conflict of desire. Very often, adopting one course of action at the behest of a certain desire may (predictably) result in the frustration of another; and a particular performed action is bound to have descriptions not intended by the agent, with respect to which he may be indifferent or concerned, as in the vodka case. The isolated practical syllogism deals only in actions under a single description; it is therefore blind to inevitable accompaniments of an intended type of action and to the myriad of descriptions the performed action *de facto* instantiates. And because the syllogism deals in single act descriptions, a particular action may be recommended by one such syllogism and proscribed by another. The difficulty of much practical reasoning, not mirrored in theoretical reasoning, is that of ensuring that what is actually done conforms optimally with one's desires taken as a whole. The coefficient of adversity being what it is, what we gain on the roundabout we frequently lose on the swings.

II

We have dwelt so far upon the *analysis* of the concept of action, i.e. upon the *a priori* conceptual connections between this concept and certain others. The question to be taken up now is whether, and if so how, the concepts called upon in the analysis of the concept of action can be employed in the (empirical) *explanation* of action. Now it is a fact that we do answer questions of the form 'Why did *A* φ?' (where 'φ' is schematic for verbs of action) by citing a reason – either in our own case or on behalf of another. That is, we do often purport to explain why an action took place by ascribing desires and beliefs that constitute the agent's reason for acting that way. Depending upon what is evident from context, we may cite either a belief or a desire; but we must assume that a desire-belief *pair* is implicated in the explanation, though one or the other will not need explicit mention. Desire without belief is blind, and belief without desire is purposeless. When we come to know an agent's reason for acting we learn what it was about the action, given his beliefs and desires, that made it appeal to him; and we learn that he acted *because* it thus appealed to him. This type of explanation may be called *rationalization*. The intentional criterion of agency connects with rationalization in this way: a bodily movement counts (analytically) as an action if and only if it admits of that style of explanation. Indeed, it is doubtful that we should recognize the action/non-action distinction *unless* we operated the scheme of rationalizing explanation.

Rationalization introduces an element of justification: knowing the agent's reason we appreciate why, from his point of view, what he did was a rational thing to do; we see of which practical syllogism his action was the 'conclusion'. This justificatory feature of rationalization is dependent upon the fact that the mental states and events we cite by way of action explanation are, or involve, propositional attitudes; i.e. they are states defined and constituted by possession of a specific propositional (or sentential) content, a content canonically expressed by a 'that'-clause. An action is presented as reasonable by dint of its relation, as described, to desires and beliefs possessed of specific propositional contents. In this respect, theoretical and practical reasoning compare: when we are told why a man *believes* a certain proposition we learn how that belief is rationally related to other beliefs he possesses, by virtue of their propositional contents. This distinctive feature of propositional attitudes, as contrasted with the non-mental states and events we call upon to explain non-intentional events, confers upon desires and beliefs, in their capacity as explanatory concepts, a certain duality of role. On the one hand, they enjoy logical relations, as represented in the practical syllogism; but they are also, what propositions themselves are not, states whose presence and operation serves to explain the occurrence of certain concrete events.

We have said what it is about desires and beliefs that justifies actions, but does this exhaust their explanatory role? It seems that it does not; some further relation between reasons and actions is needed. An agent may have desires and beliefs that make reasonable a certain type of action, yet not perform that action; or he may perform the action thus made reasonable, but not *because* of that reason. For a reason to explain why an action occurred it is not enough that the reason be present and the action occur; the action must be done *for* the reason. It is in virtue of what the 'because' imports that reasons explain why actions occur as well as represent them as rational. When one event occurs because of another the natural and obvious account of the relation involved is that it is *causation*. And the case of reasons and actions seems to invite just such an account: reasons cause actions, and rationalization is a species of causal explanation. Here then is the second role of rationalizing propositional attitudes: they cause, and causally explain, actions. Reasons are rational causes. The practical syllogism is therefore not merely a means of reconstructing practical reasoning; it is also a sketch for a certain special sort of causal explanation. The conception of explanation by reasons this duality of role suggests is certainly attractive, but before we can accept it we must satisfy ourselves upon a number of vexed and delicate points. Can rationalization consistently incorporate rational and causal elements?

The question may (and should) be broken into two parts: one about causation, the other about causal explanation. It was suggested that reasons could not serve to explain actions unless they caused actions; but it does not follow that if reasons cause actions they explain them. Nor can we assume that, if a reason causes an action *and* justifies it, then citing the reason causally explains the action; there is even the possibility that reasons explain actions by justifying them and reasons cause actions but that reasons do not *causally* explain actions. This is because the concept of causation is extensional while that of explanation is intensional; or as we might put it, causation is a relation between events howsoever described, but causal explanation relates sentences and so the descriptions under which the events are brought are relevant to the truth-value of an explanation statement. Thus, if '*a* caused *b*' is true, then it remains true no matter which descriptions of *a* and *b* are substituted into the original sentence. But not all descriptions of *a* which thus yield a truth will be such as to afford an explanation of why *b* occurred. It might be that the event you told me of in the kitchen caused the event you told me of in the bathroom, but it is no explanation of why the latter event occurred that it was caused by the event spoken of in the kitchen. But if these events are in fact a fire and a short-circuit respectively, then being informed of *these* descriptions can be explanation enough. The truth of the corresponding explanation statement is sensitive to which properties of the events are recorded in the descriptions that pick out the causally related events. And these properties of cause and effect must be related in such a way that the instantiation of one explains the instantiation of the other. Now we can see why reasons could be causes of action but not, *so described*, explanatory of actions; propositional attitude descriptions might just not be the descriptions under which reasons are explanatory – we might, for example, have to describe them physically. We can see too that reasons might cause actions and, under their mental descriptions, justify actions, though these descriptions were party to no causal explanation of the action. We can even see that reasons be causes and explain by dint of justifying actions but not be *causally* explanatory, i.e. the instantiation of a reason-description not be causally relevant to the instantiation of an action description. The short-circuit causes the fire and its being a short-circuit causally explains, because it is causally productive of, the effect's being a fire; but it might be that a particular desire causes an action though its being that desire is not causally responsible for the action's being of the type it is – even if these properties are related in a justifying and otherwise (i.e. non-causally) explanatory way.

Now in fact I think that none of these possibilities is realized: rationalization really is a species of causal explanation. But it is important to be clear about what is involved in the claim that it is: for one thing, it would not follow from the rejection of rationalization as pseudo-explanation that reasons are not causes; for another, there are certain objections, to be considered directly, to what has been said so far whose rebuttal requires a clear distinction between the extensional notion of causation and the intensional one of explanation.

Just as our original question can be split into two, so the objection I am about to consider is really two-pronged; one prong concerning causation, the other causal explanation. The first proceeds from the generally agreed point that events can be related as cause and effect only if their being thus related is a matter of empirical fact, not susceptible of *a priori* demonstration. Or, to put the requirement another way, it must be the case that cause and effect are identifiable in logically independent ways, so that the obtaining of the causal relation between them is an *a posteriori* matter. This condition is plainly met, for example, by 'The short-circuit caused the fire'. But the statement 'He crossed the road because he intended (desired) to cross the road' seems to fail this necessary condition; the putative cause seems inferable *a priori* from its alleged effect, especially if we make it explicit that he crossed the road intentionally. And yet, on the other hand, it seems right to maintain that the action and the intention or desire (or their activation) are distinct events, causally related. We use the word 'because' here, and what relation can it be expressing save that of causation? We are thus presented with a minor antinomy: the relation seems causal, but it appears to violate the necessary condition we just acquiesced in accepting. One way out of the puzzle is the following. Consider as a parallel case 'The cause of the fire caused the fire'. This statement seems true enough, indeed analytically so; and it mentions distinct events. Yet it does not have the status of an *a posteriori* truth. In this case the solution seems obvious: the cause of the fire can be otherwise described than *as* the cause of the fire – say as 'the short-circuit' – and under *that* description there is no hint of logical connection. The proper formulation of the requirement, then, is that the events be describ*able* in such a way as to make the corresponding causal statement empirical and synthetic.

Could we try the same tactic in the case of reasons and actions? We could if we allowed ourselves to suppose that desires and beliefs and intentions (or the events involving these states that cause actions) satisfied physical descriptions, i.e. were identical with events in the brain. And similarly we could, in principle, re-describe the action as a collocation of muscle contractions and the like. Under those descriptions reasons and actions *would* be displayed as logically independent; there would be no inferring the cause from the description of the effect. Since the identity theory is already plausible – and more will be said in its support later – it seems that it gives a means of resolving this problem about causation. The point is just that actions are often described by allusion to their mental causes, and these causes themselves (so described) have some sort of *a priori* connection with their effects in action; but both events also admit of other descriptions which succeed in meeting the necessary condition we laid down. (A parallel point could be made about statements of perceptual causation – 'The presence of object *a* in the visual field of P caused P to see *a*' – again the perceptual event must be so describable as not to entail that *a* was its cause.)

The second objection may allow that the first can be thus met, but claims to discern a difficulty in the idea that reasons, so described, can be causally *explanatory*. The 'because' in the sentence 'He crossed the road because he desired to cross the road' may introduce a genuine cause, but in such a style as to make its mention non-explanatory: for the descriptions employed are not related in that way required for authentic causal explanation. The ground for this doubt is similar to the previous doubt about causation: for a sentence of the form 'A because B' to count as an explanation, it must be the case that the explanandum sentence A is suitably related to the explanans sentence B. These sentences are not thus suitably related, so the objection runs, if (i) it is possible to make an *a priori* inference from the explanandum to the explanans, and (ii) it is *a priori* that if an object satisfies the conditions stated in the explanans it satisfies those of the explanandum. In short, there must not be any analytic or definitional connection between the sentence whose truth is to be explained and the sentence whose truth is alleged to do the explaining. Both requirements would be clearly violated by the putative explanation 'The fire occurred because the cause of the fire occurred'. Now the objection is that our reason-action sentence about the road crossing is in the same case. For (i) the explanans is inferable from the explanandum just by the definition of acting intentionally, and (ii) it is 'part of the concept' of desire (or intention) that, if certain conditions obtain, an action of a certain type is apt to be performed. The general nature of the difficulty is that the predicates used to pick out cause and effect are not empirically related, and so the alleged explanation seems not to supply any new information about the event to be explained. It would be a mistake to think that the objection could be evaded after the pattern of the solution for the case of causation. For that solution exploited the extensionality of the causal relation; but the concept of explanation is intensional – it relates sentences, not events *tout court* – and so to re-describe the mentioned events, say in physical terms, would be precisely to concede that, after all, rationalization is pseudo-explanation. To defend the thesis that citing reasons can be genuinely explanatory, we need to show that they can explain when described *as reasons*. Now that we have distinguished causation and causal explanation, we see that different kinds of answer are needed to the two-pronged challenge.

It is instructive to compare the case of rationalization to that of the explanation of physical events by reference to gross physical dispositions. Suppose we say 'The sugar cube dissolved in the water because it was water-soluble'. Here too there is a strong feeling that the explanans may be inferred *a priori* from the explanandum, and that it is *a priori* that if sugar is disposed to dissolve in water and it is placed in water, then it dissolves. As in the rationalization case, we have an event characterized in such a way that (i) we can infer the disposition (solubility or the desire to cross the road) of which it (the event) is a manifestation, and (ii) this disposition is itself characterized in terms of the events that manifest it (dissolvings and crossings of roads). Yet, in spite of these *a priori* connections, we do apparently employ the schemes of rationalization and reference to gross physical dispositions to answer 'Why'-questions. How can this be? In the case of gross dispositions a plausible answer is that to cite such a disposition by way of explanation of some event is to imply therein that there exists some other explanation of the event which shows no hint of *a priori* connection, and which is related in a specially intimate way to the – admittedly feeble – explanation in terms of the gross disposition. For solubility this further explanation would consist in a detailed empirical statement of the sugar's micro-structure and a chemical theory stating how this micro-structure makes for dissolution in water. It is just because the original 'because' sentence entails the existence of such a powerful kind of explanation that we regard it as informative and to a degree itself explanatory; it is as if mention of the disposition initially specified in terms of its manifestations goes proxy for an, in principle, available scientific explanation in which the disposition is otherwise characterized. We operate the gross scheme of explanation because we believe, and it is an inductively well-founded belief, that there is such an *underlying* system of explanation.

Now one might well be tempted to take the same line in the case of reasons: we attribute explanatory force to the scheme of rationalization because we believe there to be, perhaps on general empirical grounds, some such underlying explanatory system, by reference to which actions would be fully and indisputably explained. It seems clear that the only plausible candidate for this role would be explanation in terms of events in the brain: reasons, as they feature in explanation of action, would thus go proxy for brain conditions. (This suggestion would not amount to the same redescriptive manoeuvre we rejected earlier: for on the present proposal the reason is *already* explanatory, by virtue of its relation to the underlying system.)

However, I do not believe this is the correct way of looking at the matter. It is true that, in both cases, we find ourselves obliged to shift to some other sentence or sentences in order to convert the initial feeble explanation into a full-blooded one; but I think the shifts are of different orders. Making an honest explanation of the invocation of solubility involves a vertical shift to underlying structure; and this is what makes reference to such a disposition explanatory of its manifestations. But in the case of reasons, on the other hand, we typically seek further enlightenment as to why an action was performed, not by enquiring after which brain events were responsible for the corresponding bodily movement, but rather by relating the given intention or desire to *some other intention or desire*, whose presence is not *a priori* inferable from the presence of the given one and from which alone it is not possible to infer the type of action that will manifest its presence. Thus it might be that the agent intended (desired) to cross the road because he intended (desired) to draw money from the bank. And there is no way that this *further* reason could be deduced from the explanandum sentence 'He crossed the road intentionally'. He might, as we say, have crossed the road for any number of reasons; and so it is informative and explanatory to be told which of these it actually was. Nor is it true that the desire to draw money from the bank is definitionally specified in terms of what, on this occasion, manifested that desire, namely crossing the road. So the predicates occurring in *this* explanans and explanandum are related in the required *a posteriori* and synthetic way. In a sense, then, it isn't explanatory to say that a man ϕed intentionally because he desired to ϕ; but this by no means exhausts the resources of the rationalizing scheme – there is, as it were, the possibility of horizontal mobility within it.[3] And typically when we ask why an action of a certain description was performed we wish to be informed of the agent's further reason – which desire constituted the *first* premise of his practical reasoning. What has to be stressed is that explanation relates sentences, and an explanation is informative just in so far as it supplies a sentence which gives a non-trivial reason why the sentence whose truth we already know is true. Within the scheme of rationalizing explanation there is more than one way in which this can happen.

If it were asked why we should take the entailed full-blooded explanation to involve a further reason rather than reference to brain conditions, after the model of gross physical dispositions, I should reply that part of the answer has to do with the descriptions under which we are interested in explaining actions. When we move to a microstructural basis for the case of solubility the appropriate description of the event to be explained is still 'a dissolving in water', or else this predicate is straightforwardly reducible to predicates of the small bodies involved in dissolution. But in the case of intentional descriptions of actions the move to antecedent causally operative brain states as the explanatory correlates of reasons requires a radical redescription of the event to be explained, as say muscle innervations and contractions. Since these are quite new descriptions, to which action descriptions are irreducible (*vide infra*), such a move is open to the charge of simply changing the subject. This makes for a significant asymmetry with the solubility case, and shows that there is not between propositional attitudes and brain conditions an intimacy of relation comparable to that between physical dispositions and their structural bases. Because rationalization does not derive its efficacy by pointing outside itself to an underlying system of physical explanation, it enjoys a certain autonomy and irreducibility not shared by the dispositional scheme of explanation. Despite, or perhaps because of, this autonomy, reasons may be invoked to explain the actions they cause, where this causal explanation peculiarly involves the (conditional) justification of the action in question.

III

We started by defining actions as intentional events; we then related the property of being intentional to explanation in terms of reasons. The question arises of exactly how desires and beliefs are connected with intending and with an event's being intentional. We have claimed, in effect, that appropriate desires and beliefs are *necessary* conditions for having a certain intention and for a movement's being intentional; but it is a question whether *sufficient* conditions are forthcoming. I shall assume, what is not totally uncontroversial, that every action is preceded and caused by an intention, where an intention is to be conceived as a sort of propositional attitude. My first question then is whether having a reason is sufficient for intending to perform the recommended action. This question is of some significance, since if such conditions can be provided intentions will have been reduced to other sorts of propositional attitude – desires and beliefs – and so need not be recognized as mental states *sui generis*. The second question is whether we can define intentional action in terms of reasons plus causation. These are in fact large and complex questions, and my remarks will only scratch their surface.

As to the first, reflection discloses that a man could possess desires and beliefs recommending a certain course of action and yet refrain from forming the intention to undertake it. This is obvious for reasons at large, since we have many reasons we form no intention to act upon. But it also seems true if we restrict the desires and beliefs upon which an intention may be alleged to supervene: a man could have a strong desire (perhaps, in some sense, his strongest) for a certain state of affairs, and believe the means to be at hand and within his power, yet still not intend to perform the indicated action. Thus an agent could reason to the conclusion of a practical syllogism, know that an action is desirable all things considered, and still not intend the action: intention is therefore a mental state super-added to desire and belief.

As to the second question, it is possible for a reason to cause a bodily movement of a kind made rational by that reason and yet the movement not be intentional. For example: a man may notice that swerving his car will save his own life at the expense of the lives of others; he therefore has a good reason to swerve; however, he is so appalled by this selfish thought that he physically shudders; this causes him accidentally to swerve the car: this movement was thus both caused and made reasonable by his desire and belief, but it was not intentional and so was not an action. Notice that the difficulty could not be mended by introducing a prior intention: for our man could form the intention to swerve and be so appalled by *this* that he swerves as before. So reason (or intention) plus causation do not add up to intentional action.

Now for both of these cases – intention and intentional action – one might try to excogitate refinements of the conditions which aim at sufficiency – give a fuller specification of the non-intentional mental states that are supposed sufficient for intending, place conditions on the kind of way reasons must cause movements if they are to be intentional – but it is clear that, even if possible, this is not child's play. What all this suggests is that the concept of the intentional is essentially richer than the conceptual materials provided by desire, belief and causation. To put it antiquely: the conative faculty of the mind (that having to do with intention or the 'will') is distinct from, and irreducible to, the affective (desire) and cognitive (belief) faculties. This suspicion is reinforced by the following observation: intention is conceptually linked to action in a way that desire, though admittedly itself a mover to action, is not. For, while we may desire what we cannot (or believe we cannot) achieve, we cannot, from the nature of intention, intend what we believe is impossible of attainment. Intention is thus necessarily a disposition to action in a way that desire is not. However, although the transition from reason to intention is a transition to a state of mind genuinely distinct from the former, there is a certain curiosity to be remarked: for though intention seems necessary for action and a mental state *sui generis* it does not seem that it plays any essential *explanatory* role in rationalization. Once we have a performed action it seems that we can explain its occurrence adequately in terms of the agent's desires and beliefs, along perhaps with other mental events like noticings; the agent's intention need not be mentioned. This is perhaps because intentions seem supervenient upon other mental states and events in this sense: that two agents could not be alike in all mental respects specified without using the concept of intention and yet be unlike in a mental respect which is so specified. (It is consistent with this that we cannot give sufficient conditions for the formation of an intention.) The explanatory redundancy of intention in the enterprise of rationalization seems related to its *ex post facto* character: once an action is performed we know there was a corresponding intention, and we can reconstruct the intention from a knowledge of the agent's reason. If we were in the business of predicting actions, we might have to reckon more seriously with the conditions – if there be such – under which intentions are formed.

IV

If rationalization is to be a scheme of testable empirical explanation, it must relate to the publicly observable facts of behaviour. That is, if we wish to apply it to the actions of another we must be able to appeal to information about his behaviour by way of support for our mentalistic attributions; we must be able to tell, on the basis of the agent's behaviour, what his desires, beliefs, etc., are. In considering whether, and how, this condition is met it is absolutely essential to distinguish two questions: can truths about an agent's reasons be *reduced* to truths about his behaviour? and, are attributions of reasons *evidentially supported* by truths about behaviour?

There is a simple and compelling argument to show that no behaviourist reduction of the first sort is possible, as follows. For such a reduction to be effected we would need to associate with each desire or belief some kind of behaviour such that necessarily an agent has that desire or belief if and only if he evinces, or is disposed to evince, that kind of behaviour. Thus it might be proposed that for me to want to get to the other side of the river is just for me to be disposed to cross the bridge. The main defect of this proposal, and analogous ones linking belief and behaviour, is that possession of a certain desire does not dispose the agent to a certain kind of behaviour unless he also has appropriate *beliefs*, i.e. those relating the desire to a type of action. I am disposed to cross the bridge only if I believe that this is a good way of satisfying the desire in question; and a parallel observation holds of belief *vis-à-vis* desire. The point is that desires and beliefs dispose to behaviour only in pairs, so there is no associating a kind of behaviour with one component of such a pair independently of a determination of the other (actually matters are more complex since, as noted below, desire-belief pairs themselves interact with each other in the production of behaviour). This means that a behaviourist reduction is feasible only if it appeals to mental conditions in its purported reduction biconditionals – i.e. it succeeds only if it fails; so it fails. Nor could we hope to carry out the reduction upon desire-belief pairs, since the components of such pairs may correlate with quite other behaviour kinds when combined with other beliefs and desires, and nothing in the proposed reduction reflects this property of detachment and re-combination.

However, it would be a great error to infer from this irreducibility that explanation by attribution of reasons is unconstrained by behavioural evidence. Information about the truth-value of sentences in a certain class may afford evidence for assigning truth-values to sentences of another class, though there is no possibility of *translating* the sentences of the latter class into sentences of the former. Of course, it is a subtle and intricate matter how exactly we use facts about behaviour to verify a propositional attitude psychology in respect of a given agent; but it is patent that we do regard episodes of behaviour, including crucially speech behaviour, as evidence – in the end the only evidence – for or against a particular mental attribution or set of such. Broadly speaking, it is a question of arriving at that total assignment of propositional attitudes to the agent which makes maximum *sense* of his observed behaviour. Each attribution of desire or belief should pull its weight in our best overall account of why he behaves as he does. In fact, rationalizing explanation may fairly be compared with other sorts of theory subject to test according to the hypothetico-deductive method. Rationalization is warrantable in the light of behavioural facts without being reducible thereto.

V

Nothing in the conception of a reason as so far expounded requires that reasons be *conscious*: room has been left for rationalization by appeal to *un*conscious reasons. And indeed many of Freud's case studies invite metapsychological interpretation as precisely rationalization by unconscious beliefs and desires.[4] What an agent (or patient) avers to be his reason for acting in a certain way may not be his real reason, i.e. the reason that in fact rationalizes and causes the action in question. What 'rationalizes' in the Freudian sense of that term may not rationalize in our sense. The really operative reason, as contrasted with the agent's ostensible reason, may be unavailable to his consciousness and difficult to discover; it may have to be conjectured from a wide range of actions without benefit of explicit avowal, perhaps on the basis of a psychoanalytic theory of the formation of certain desires and beliefs during the person's psychological development. Nevertheless, it appears that where an action is explained by such unconscious desires and beliefs the rationalizing scheme is conformed to: an unconscious desire is attributed and a belief, commonly of a phantastic kind, links this desire with a kind of action whose performance in some way leads to the satisfaction of the motivating desire: according to Freudian theory, dreams, the parapraxes and neurotic actions generally would fall under this characterization. The unconscious reason both causes and makes rational (from the agent's – possibly phantastic – point of view) the problematic action; and in discovering this we become able to re-describe an apparently senseless action as done for a reason which makes it intelligible to us – we come to see its point. Indeed the recognition of unconscious desires and beliefs seems forced upon us, as it was upon Freud, precisely by the pressure to find sense in a pattern of behaviour not explicable by the agent's acknowledged reasons.

This account of (one aspect of) psychoanalytic explanation raises the interesting problem of what makes a propositional attitude un-conscious, of what differentiates conscious from unconscious reasons. Here is a tentative answer to this question. An uncontroversial start on the problem is provided by the observation that for a desire (say) to be unconscious is for its possessor not to know or believe that he has that desire. The belief one has when one knows one has a certain desire I shall call a *second-order* belief; it has the form 'A believes that he desires that p'. This second-order belief is plainly a mental state distinct from the desire which is its object and (I shall claim) is caused by it. Normally, it is automatic that a first-order desire should cause a second-order belief consisting in the knowledge that one has that first-order desire. But suppose that normal mechanism were somehow interrupted, so that the usual corresponding second-order belief is not produced. Then clearly the person in question would have no (direct) knowledge of the desire in question, i.e. it would be unconscious. This suggests that a conscious reason is simply a reason we know we have because it (perhaps in concert with other states and mechanisms) causes us to have a second-order belief concerning it; while an un-conscious reason is one that does not, for some psychologically explicable reason, give rise causally to any such second-order belief. The difference between conscious and unconscious mental states, on this view, is not that conscious states enjoy some special quality of mental luminescence, nor that there exist in the mind two topo-graphically distinct compartments, one designated 'conscious' and the other 'unconscious', and we are to think of desires as periodically migrating from one compartment to the other – as a result of repres-sion or therapy, as the case may be. Rather, just as a desire may cause or fail to cause an action, depending upon what else is true of the agent, so it may cause or fail to cause a belief about itself, depending upon the person's psychological condition. On occasion actions may be caused and rationalized by a reason which fails to cause a second-order belief of which it is object. In such circumstances, the reason is unconscious.

Given this general picture, repression operates by interrupting the normal causation of higher-order beliefs. Now repression, I should claim, is itself a kind of intentional action, albeit a purely mental one; it is a project whose purpose is to keep certain desires from con-sciousness. But, if so, we seem faced with something of a paradox: if repression is a kind of action directed upon propositional attitudes, does it not involve the formation of second-order beliefs about those desires? The project to repress comprises a wish or inclination to shield from consciousness desires (or beliefs) with a certain disturbing quality and beliefs locating the attitudes possessed of that quality. But then it appears that repression requires beliefs of the form 'I believe that I desire that p', i.e. it brings with it consciousness of what is to be repressed and is thus self-defeating. This is certainly a *prima facie* difficulty with my account, but it is also a difficulty for other accounts I know of.[5] I suggest that we avoid the threatened paradox by invoking the concept of repression under a description. It is natural to assume that desires are identified as subjects for repression under descriptions which, so to speak, disclose the identity of the desire in question, for example as 'the desire to do away with my father'. But if the project to repress identified the disturbing desires under descriptions which did not reveal *which* desire it was – e.g. 'any disturbing thought or desire engendered in infancy' – then the appropriate desires could be located and the interruption initiated without the repressing agent becoming aware of these desires as such. So understood it seems that repression could be undertaken without the necessity to know which are the forbidden desires. Though no doubt crude and over-simplified this account of unconscious reasons seems to offer an intelligible, and demythologized, picture of their station in the mind.

VI

Told that reasons causally explain actions one naturally asks whether such explanation conforms to the so-called deductive-nomological model: i.e. does rationalization explain by subsuming the particular case under some general law?[6] In the present case the required covering law would be a lawlike generalization linking reasons and actions, to the effect that whenever an agent had certain desires and beliefs he would perform an action of a certain sort. It would be mere dogmatism to insist that rationalization *must* conform to this model if it is to be explanatory at all, but it is of interest to enquire whether it in fact does. The question is not an easy one to settle; I confine myself to a couple of relevant observations. What is instantly apparent in this regard is that the rough and ready generalizations we incautiously assert concerning what people are apt to do given certain desires and beliefs would need a lot of refinement and qualification if they were to be pressed into the deductive-nomological schema. This can be appreciated by considering what may go into a course of deliberative practical reasoning: desires must be assessed for relevance and weighed one against another, beliefs must be surveyed and subjective probabilities recorded and compared, and these beliefs must then be reckoned in the light of the pattern of desires. That is, in concrete practical reasoning large tracts of the agent's store of propositional attitudes are somehow brought to bear and evaluated in scarcely articulable ways prior to the performance of the action. This is clearest when the reasoning is explicit and deliberate, but the same holds when it is not. We can call this feature – that desires and beliefs eventuate in behaviour only as conditioned by further desires and beliefs – the *holistic* nature of practical reasoning. Suppose now that, in pursuit of a law of action, we tried to supplement the practical syllogism that *ex post facto* abstracts from this holism by inserting into the antecedent of the putative law conditions adequate to capture all that went into the performance of an action of a certain type. That is, suppose that, *per impossibile*, we specified causally sufficient mental conditions for the action in question. Would the result qualify as a general law of action? It seems not, for the closer we asymptote to sufficiency, by taking account of the holism, the further we depart from generality: we record the mental antecedents of a particular agent's action, but the detail and complexity induced by the holistic operation of his propositional attitudes will make the 'law' peculiar to him, indeed to him at the time of acting. Now when we rationalize a particular action what we learn is why *that* agent did it, we come to know something about him; but this tells us little about why others act as they do, even when they act in the same way. Rationalization is, as psychologists say, idiographic, not nomothetic.

So two ideas converge to cast doubt upon the thesis that rationalization is deductive-nomological: that reasons operate holistically, and that rationalization is idiographic. In fact, we might even say that it is *because* of the holistic character of the mental in its relation to action that explanation by reasons is idiographic. The doubt springs from the fact that a particular piece of rationalization, when filled out, fails to be *generalizable*: what was sufficient to make me cross the road on a certain occasion will almost certainly never be repeated. Accordingly, we cannot hope to state general causal laws relating reasons and actions, and so explanation by reasons does not take the form of deduction from known laws of action in conjunction with singular premises about reasons.

But if there are no laws relating reasons and actions, are we not caught in an inconsistency, since causality implies lawfulness? That is, given the generally accepted principle that causally related events must instantiate laws, how can it fail to be true that there are reason-action laws to back singular causal statements about reasons and actions? In fact there is no inconsistency here, for a reason by now familiar to us: just as events are explained by other events only under some of their descriptions, so they instantiate laws only as described in certain ways – as can be seen from our earlier examples. What is notable here is that reasons explain actions under descriptions which do not bring them under laws. Nevertheless, they must fall under laws as described in some vocabulary or other, by the generally accepted principle. By elimination it seems that the only kind of law this could be would be a physical law: but if reasons and actions instantiate physical laws, they must be physically describable, i.e. they must be physical events.[7] Indeed these might just be the descriptions to whose existence we appealed in demonstrating the 'logical in-dependence' of a reason and the action it causes.

It appears, then, that our earlier claims together imply a version of the psycho-physical identity thesis. This was, perhaps, already plain in respect of actions: they are each severally identical with particular movements of the body, describable in purely physical terms. But it is something of a surprise to find it entailed that the mental events which cause actions are also physical events, occurring in the brain. This conclusion can also be reached by a somewhat different route, on the basis of certain plausible principles about action causation. Individual actions, we said, are identical with particular bodily move-ments. Bodily movements are evidently caused by events in the nervous system. But from these facts two things follow by the extensionality of the causal relation: reasons cause bodily movements, and brain events cause actions. So the same events are caused both by reasons and by brain events. But surely these causes cannot be distinct events, since that would imply that their effects were caused twice over, i.e. their occurrence would be causally over-determined. Since distinctness implies that unacceptable consequence, it seems we must conclude that the mental antecedents of action are identical with the physical events which cause the bodily movements with which actions themselves are identical. The events alluded to in rationaliza-tion turn out to be physical events, i.e. these mentally described events also satisfy physical descriptions.

This conclusion may prompt the hope, or fear, that, after all, rationalization is reducible to, and therefore in principle replaceable by, purely physical explanation. That does not follow, however. For the physicalist thesis just advocated was only to the effect that each *particular* mental event which causes an action is identical with some particular physical event which causes a bodily movement; it did not claim that the mental properties which qualify a mental event as falling under a mental description are identical with the physical properties each such event instantiates. And for a reduction to be possible mental and physical properties must be identical, or at least necessarily one–one correlated. Just as each action of a certain intentionally identified kind is identical with some bodily movement though the movements may be of physically diverse kinds, so mental events in general may be severally identical with physical events in the brain though these latter fail to match up with respect to kind. Indeed strong arguments can be given to show that any such reduction is impossible.[8] Since an identity thesis and the impossibility of reduction are compatible, and also individually plausible, we can acknowledge both the autonomy of psychological explanation and the identification of mental events with physical. The descriptions under which reasons explain actions are not reducible to the descriptions under which (if we knew them) brain events explain bodily movements: but these descriptions may yet describe the same things.

When we choose to view the behavioural events that comprise a person's biography as subject to the distinction between intentional and non-intentional, as here advocated, we cannot help but see him in his capacity as Rational Animal: we see him as acting for reasons – reasons which explain and justify what he does. It seems to me that psychologists have tended, through failure to appreciate the character and efficacy of rationalizing explanation, either to neglect it and to seek instead (usually unsuccessfully) for some other type of explanation, often couched in factitious vocabulary, or to treat such everyday explanations as somehow epiphenomenal, as idle by-products of other sorts of mental or quasi-mental phenomena – in short, to regard rationalization as mere pseudo-explanation. If, to the contrary, the legitimacy of such explanation were fully recognized – as it seems evident that it should – we might come to see the springs of action as issuing, very often, from nothing other than the dictates of rationality, than which there is nothing deeper.

Notes

1 Much (though by no means all) of what follows consists of a selective digest of the works of Donald Davidson on the philosophy of action and mind. For further detail, and to chart my departures and supplementations, the following articles should be consulted: (1963) Actions, reasons, and causes. *Journal of Philosophy* 60: 685–700; (1967) Causal relations. *Journal of*

Philosophy 64: 691–703; (1971) Agency. In R. Binkley (ed.) *Agent, Action and Reason.* Toronto: University of Toronto Press, pp. 3–25; (1971) Mental events. In L. Foster and J. Swanson (eds) *Experience and Theory.* Boston: Belknap, pp. 79–101; (1973) Freedom to act. In T. Honderich (ed.) *Essays on Freedom of Action.* London: Routledge and Kegan Paul, pp. 139–56; (1974) Thought and talk. In Guttenplan (ed.) *Mind and Language.* Oxford; (1976) Psychology as philosophy. In Glover (ed.) *Philosophy of Mind.* Oxford; (1973) The material mind. In Suppes (ed.) *Logic, Methodology and Philosophy of Science IV.* North-Holland; (1977) Hempel on explaining action. *Erkenntnis.* I am also indebted to Christopher Peacocke and Anita Avramides for stimulation.

2 For an early statement of this viewpoint see G. E. M. Anscombe (1957) *Intention* (Oxford: Blackwell), p. 46f. Davidson developed the point.

3 This position commits me to the view that the most proximate mental cause of an action – that represented by the last line of a practical syllogism – is not what typically explains the action. What explains the action is a desire (etc.) – that represented in general by the first line of such a syllogism – which causes the action by causing the interpolated proximate desire.

4 A good example is the case of the Rat Man, well expounded in R. Wollheim (1971) *Sigmund Freud.* London: Fontana.

5 Cf. Sartre's discussion of the censor and the unconscious in (1957) *Being and Nothingness.* London: Methuen, pp. 50–4

6 For an exposition of this account of explanation in application to action see C. G. Hempel (1965) *Aspects of Scientific Explanation.* London, pp. 463–86.

7 This argument was first stated by Davidson (1971) in Mental events.

8 This is more fully discussed in my (1978) Mental states, natural kinds and psychophysical laws. *Proceedings of the Aristotelian Society, Supp. Vol.*

Part II
The psychology of action

3 Genetic epistemology and theories of adaptive behaviour

Wolfe Mays

Introduction

Piaget's studies in the field of intellectual development have brought about the same kind of revolution in our way of looking at the child's mind as Freud's has done in the field of emotional development. He has opened up to experimental investigation the whole subject of concept formation which up to the appearance of his early publications in the 1920s had been largely the preserve of philosophers in their epistemological treatises. John Locke, for example, poured scorn on the theory of innate ideas by arguing that children have no inkling of such abstract logical principles as that of identity or non-contradiction. As he puts it:

> But alas, amongst *children*, *idiots*, *savages*, and the grossly *illiterate*, what general maxims are to be found? What universal principles of knowledge? ... Such kind of general propositions are seldom mentioned in the huts of *Indians*, much less are they to be found in the thoughts of *children* or any impressions of them on the minds of *naturals*. They are the language and business of the schools and academies of learned nations, accustomed to that sort of conversation or learning. (Locke, 1974, p. 24)

Although this might seem to be a robust reaction on Locke's part to the Cartesian theory of innate ideas, his approach with its consequent *tabula rasa* theory of the mind was in some ways just as much *a priori* as that of the Cartesian view. It was not based on either controlled observation or experimental procedures, and might be said to be largely impressionistic in character.

Piaget's interest in the way our knowledge develops has led him to be criticized by philosophers for being too psychological and empirical, and by psychologists for being too philosophical and logical. There is little doubt that that part of his work which has occasioned the most interest, at least among psychologists, has been his experiments carried out by himself and his collaborators. These are largely concerned, among other things, with the development of the child's ideas of logic, number, space, time, speed, quantity, etc. They are fascinating to observe and usually easy to repeat, especially as they do not require much apparatus or thinking about the theoretical issues involved. Most discussions of Piaget's work tend to concentrate on his experiments and the various stages he claims to find in the child's intellectual development. Psychologists when they come to evaluate these experiments either try to show their limitations or their applicability to children in different social environments and in other parts of the world.

Piaget's own theoretical contributions have therefore in the main tended to be ignored by the working psychologist on the ground of their excessive obscurity, or regarded as an irrelevant accretion to his experimental studies. I am not myself of this opinion, as his experiments obtain their significance from the theoretical framework in terms of which they have been formulated. When divorced from this framework the experiments become merely problem-solving tasks or even intelligence test items.

The problem of adaptive behaviour

What I shall be primarily concerned with in this paper is an aspect of Piaget's thought which is fundamental for his genetic epistemology, namely, his theory of adaptive behaviour, which runs like a thread through his earlier and later work. I shall compare it with other similar theories which regard the adaptive process as a kind of balance or equilibrium achieved between the needs of the subject and the demands made on him by his environment. I shall also examine in some detail one important critique of Piaget's theory.

A fundamental feature of Piaget's theory of adaptive behaviour, as we shall see, is his use of the concepts of assimilation and accommodation together with that of equilibrium to describe the way the individual adapts himself to his environment. These concepts are usually taken as being purely of biological origin. If one accepts this interpretation, then Piaget's position would seem to have an element of incoherence about it. How, it may be asked, can equilibrium systems, even of the feedback variety, which are inherently causal, be used to describe our desires, aims and expectations, an account of which needs to be given in terms of motives and not in terms of causes? Further, how can logico-mathematical and moral norms which are manifestly non-empirical be dependent on what are plainly empirical operations?

A number of psychologists and philosophers have consequently been highly critical of Piaget's approach to the problem of adaptive behaviour. Bruner has claimed that Piaget has neglected motivational questions like 'the nature of the unfolding and development of his [the child's] drives', (Bruner, 1959, p. 369) and he considers the notion of equilibrium as used by Piaget as a kind of 'surplus baggage' which perhaps gives him a comforting sense of continuity with his earlier biological apprenticeship (Bruner, 1959, p. 369). Mischel has argued that analogies drawn between intellectual and biological adaptation obscure crucial differences between them. 'Biological equilibria', he argues, 'are maintained by the causal interaction of specifiable physical forces, but psychological equilibration cannot be understood in terms of such homeostatic models' (Mischel, 1971, p. 323).

However, the difficulties which critics have found in Piaget's theory of adaptive behaviour are partly due to their failing to take adequate account of the fact that Piaget's theory is also concerned with the question of needs: with the subject's direct consciousness of his needs in the form of feelings, aims and expectations, by means of which he directs his actions towards certain ends. For Piaget too, on a conceptual level, our understanding of norms, logico-mathematical and moral, has to be distinguished from the activities by which they have been acquired.

Further, Piaget's use of the notion of equilibrium is closely connected with his holistic approach to the problem of learning. In contrast to the more atomistic conception of stimulus-response theory which asserts that learning arises from chance associations of independent elements, learning for Piaget arises from the subject's inborn and acquired action schemes (practical and cognitive) becoming modified and hence restructured in terms of his situation. It is true, however, as some critics have not failed to note, that the notion of equilibrium as used by Piaget has a wide application. Not only does it apply to organic systems, but also to habit, symbolic behaviour, as well as to the higher reaches of reasoning and formal thought. For example, Piaget regards cognitive operations as being concerned with the combining of elements into more inclusive systems or wholes, and he looks upon the product of this synthesis as a form of equilibrium. As thus used the notion of equilibrium bears a marked resemblance to the final stage of the Hegelian dialectic triad (thesis, antithesis, synthesis) where a balance is achieved between contrary terms.

At the higher cognitive levels, the notion of equilibrium then refers to the resultant of such processes of cognitive synthesis which combine elements into more comprehensive systems. A simple arithmetical operation such as $2 + 2 = 4$ would come under this head, since Piaget considers its epistemic or intuitive aspect (as opposed to its logico-formal aspect) as a synthetic rather than an analytic operation. But what needs emphasizing is that the concept of a system as an organized unity is a perfectly general one, although its particular manner of exemplification may differ from instance to instance. Such systems, Piaget contends, occur at a large number of different levels: biological, perceptual and intellectual. Each system may be regarded as a particular instance of this more general concept, which therefore does not seem to have primarily a biological character, although, of course, it might have an ontological or metaphysical one.

Assimilation, accommodation and equilibrium

I shall now look a little more closely at Piaget's use of the notion of equilibrium in his analysis of learning behaviour. In accepting this kind of approach, Piaget seems to have been guided by the work of Edouard Claparède, his predecessor in his chair at Geneva (and founder of the Institut J. J. Rousseau). Claparède, in his account of adaptive behaviour, described it in terms of the homeostatic model of equilibrium. He believed this model to be more applicable than a mechanical one to an essentially need-motivated organism, whose behaviour is directed towards certain ends.

On a behavioural level Claparède identified 'need' with the rupture of the equilibrium of an organism. All behaviour, Claparède argued, has for its function the maintenance or restoration of this equilibrium: mental activity, like life itself, is to be conceived as the perpetual readjustment of an equilibrium perpetually broken. Although

Claparède might seem to be giving a purely biological explanation of human motivation, he also takes account of our consciousness of needs. As Piaget (1954, pp. 3–4) tells us, Claparède has shown that a behavioural disequilibrium is translated in the subject by an affective impression *sui generis* which is consciousness of the need – the behaviour ends when the need is satisfied. This scheme, Piaget remarks, 'is very general: no nutrition without alimentary needs; no work without needs; no act of intelligence without a question, that is without a felt lacuna, therefore without disequilibrium, therefore without need' (Piaget, 1954).[2] The notions of equilibrium and disequilibrium are then used by both Claparède and Piaget to describe our success or failure in satisfying some particular need.

On Piaget's view a need is not a permanent mental state or disposition, but is always defined in terms of the subject's specific situation, and this may vary from moment to moment. Thus in adapting ourselves to this situation, our action schemes (innate and acquired) are at the same time modified by it. The process of adaptation therefore has, he says, two facets: assimilation and accommodation.

(a) *Assimilation*, the way in which certain features of the environment become integrated within a particular action scheme, so that the character of the scheme is thereby changed: in other words we learn from experience. Thus, to take a simple example, a child may learn to suck his thumb in place of the maternal breast or feeding bottle.

(b) *Accommodation*, which is concerned with the way the environmental situation modifies our action schemes. Thus, the young child's primitive sucking behaviour becomes adapted to different kinds of object to those which originally elicited it.

Piaget then defines adaptation somewhat formally as an equilibrium between the two processes of assimilation and accommodation (Piaget, 1952, p. 6). Or to put it in more homely language, it is the way in which the child learns to adapt his behaviour to the changes in his immediate environment.

Piaget believes that the new-born child begins life with certain inborn action schemes or tendencies towards such activities as sucking or grasping. But, as he points out, an element of learning enters even the simplest of such schemes. For example, the sucking reaction needs to be stimulated a number of times before it can be established. When an action scheme fails to attain its objective, trial and error movements ensue. If any such movement proves successful in achieving a particular end, it will henceforth become assimilated (or integrated) within the original scheme which is thereby modified – for example the baby will learn to suck its thumb. Like Claparède, Piaget recognized that needs and an awareness of an end direct the most elementary gropings of the child. It is therefore doubtful whether on their view trial and error behaviour can be regarded as being purely fortuitous. As Piaget points out (1952, p. 148), the behaviour of the child is always intentionally directed towards an end sought after and desired, and he even finds it in the eight-months-old child who sets aside obstacles in order to attain an objective.

Lewin, Sartre and Piaget on human motivation

Piaget shows a certain sympathy for the work of Kurt Lewin, the Gestalt psychologist, in the field of human motivation (see Lewin, 1935), partly because the latter, unlike the classical Gestalt psychologists, takes account of the influence of the past history of the subject in affecting his present behaviour. Lewin was particularly critical of attempts to explain motivation in terms of instincts and dispositions. These he likened to the essences postulated by Aristotelian physics to explain physical phenomena. He compared his own position with that of Galileo, who rejected the Aristotelian view that bodies fall because of some occult quality or gravitational essence. The acceleration of a falling body is rather to be regarded as a function of the general configuration of forces acting upon it. In the same way, Lewin argues, the anger manifested by a person is a resultant not only of some inherent psychological disposition, but is a function of the total field of which the subject forms part.

According to Lewin what makes an object desirable or undesirable for a particular subject is not the object as such, but the total configuration of the field. Piaget illustrates this point as follows. If you are walking along a pavement and notice children playing football in the road, and they kick the ball a fair distance away from them, you will not usually have the least desire to go after the ball. But if it were to land at your feet, you may then experience a sudden urge or need to kick it. The ball has acquired a new character as a function of this field, namely, as a result of its landing in front of you.

To describe the field of action, Lewin introduced the notion of 'hodological space' (from the Greek *hodos*, path). And by this he had in mind the physical and social environment, which he believed we experience as made up of attracting and repelling forces directed towards or away from objects. These forces he assumed will fluctuate in accordance with the variation in the child's needs. Thus a lollipop will to a normal child have a considerable appeal or attractive power, but for the satiated child it will have a strong negative or repulsive character. When a child is, for example, faced with a specific task to perform, he may have to overcome certain obstacles before he can complete it. In order for this to happen, Lewin argued (and he constructed experiments to show this), there has to be a restructuring of the field: old forms need to be broken up and restructured into new ones. This process of the restructuring of forms may be illustrated by a simple perceptual example – the familiar puzzle picture in which one has to discover a face hidden in the branches of a tree. By changing our way of looking at the picture, stressing certain elements and neglecting others, the hidden face will suddenly appear. Similarly, Köhler's ape had to reconstitute its field of action in order to use the nearby stick to draw the banana towards itself.

Lewin's hodological space, expressed in terms of a mixture of topology and dynamics then polarizes itself according to certain forces which attract or repel. A further example of this phenomenon is the case of an animal presented with food, to which it is attracted when hungry and indifferent when satiated. Piaget, commenting on Lewin's use of hodological space as a descriptive tool, believes that in a number of cases it throws light on the problem of motivation, but in others it seems to be merely a translation into more complex language of our everyday observations of the dynamics of motivated behaviour.

It may seem strange in this context to refer to Sartre's theory of the emotions, especially as Piaget has himself described it as a form of irrationalism, presumably because Sartre sometimes refers to the transformations effected by the subject on his environment when under emotional stress as 'magical' (Piaget, 1971, 132–3). However, in his account of emotional behaviour, Sartre (1971) took over and adapted to his own purpose Lewin's concept of hodological space, which has built into it the Gestalt conception of the 'breaking and reconstituting of forms'. He then went on to identify hodological space with the real space of the human world, which is primarily an action space rather than a perceptual one. Lewin, it is true, expresses this action space in the abstract language of topology and dynamics. Nevertheless, Lewin's conception comes closer to the primitive's and child's picture of the world as made up of objects which act upon us as if endowed with vital functions, a world which also directly exhibits such properties as being 'welcome' or 'hostile'.

As Sartre puts it, 'in this way we can draw up a "hodological" chart of our *Umwelt*, a chart that will vary in function with our actions and our needs'. From this point of view, he goes on, the world around us is therefore the *Umwelt*, 'the world of our desires, our needs and of our activities' (Sartre, 1971, p. 62). This world is not the physical world, but the human world in which our actions take place – the behavioural environment. To illustrate the difference between these two sorts of environment, Koffka (1935, pp. 27–8) relates the German legend of a horseman riding in winter over frozen Lake Constance fully believing that he was galloping across a snow-covered plain. On arriving at the other side of the lake and on learning that he had just ridden across Lake Constance, he fell dead from his horse. As Koffka points out, the rider's behavioural environment, the world in which he was living, his *Umwelt* had been a snow-covered plain, but his physical environment unbeknown to him had been Lake Constance.

It is this life-world which for Sartre is transformed by our emotions. When all ways are barred, he says, and we have to act, an unbearable tension is set up in us. We therefore try to change the world: reconstitute or transform it (Sartre, 1971, pp. 63–6). We may faint and thus successfully blot out the stressful situation, or, as in Sartre's own example of the grapes beyond our reach, say that they are too green and walk away. It is unfortunate that Sartre uses the word 'magical' to describe such emotional transformations, as most of them are merely examples of a Gestalt change. The Gestalt psychologists have given numerous examples of such transformations of the affective field, as well as in that of perception and cognition, where we break up an old configuration and reconstitute it as a new one. The picture puzzle example is a case in point.

On Sartre's view an emotion, for example anger, is an abrupt solution to a conflict (Sartre, 1971, p. 45), where there is a switch from what might be termed a higher level of human activity to a more primitive form in terms of which the whole situation becomes reorganized. Although Sartre uses Lewin's 'breaking and reconstituting of forms' model, he does not think that Lewin stresses sufficiently the part played by the conscious subject. As Fell puts it:

Mere specification of the situation provoking the emotional reaction (e.g., an experimental problem designed to frustrate all possible attempts at solution) is not in itself sufficient to account for the nature of the emotional reaction: it may be anger, it may be fear of the experimenter, it may be laughter at the absurdity of one's situation (Fell, 1965, p. 121).

To explain a particular emotional response we need to take account of the subject's feelings, purposes and the ends he has in view. What Sartre seems to be doing is grafting the concept of intentionality, i.e. that consciousness is always directed towards an object, on to Lewin's hodological space. By carrying out this operation, Sartre broadens the concept of intentionality to include purpose. The conscious emotional act is then a pragmatic one: it is an attempt to transform our world (Fell, 1965, p. 131).

Fell (1965, pp. 120–1, 131) also makes the interesting point that Sartre's theory not only introduced intentionality, but also took over Janet's thesis that emotion is an inferior, less well-adapted or 'set-back' behaviour which is then combined with Lewin's 'breaking and reconstituting of forms' model. On Janet's view, emotion is a behaviour of disadaptation or defeat, as when someone confronted with an apparently insurmountable problem bursts into tears. Sartre believes, however, that Janet's view that in emotion we move on to a lower, more primitive level of action, has to be supplemented to take account of the total situation in which the subject finds himself.

Claparède in his theory of needs generalized Janet's position, since Janet's 'set-back' behaviour can be considered as the achievement of a form of equilibrium, albeit at a lower level. Piaget states Claparède's position as follows:

> As Claparède has shown, a need is always a manifestation of disequilibrium: there is need when something, either outside ourselves or within us (physically or mentally) is changed and behavior has to be adjusted as a function of this change. For example, hunger or fatigue will provoke a search for nourishment or rest: encountering an external object will lead to a need to play ... or it leads to a question or a theoretical problem ... Conversely, action terminates when a need is satisfied, that is to say, when equilibrium is re-established between the new factor which has provoked the need and the mental organization that existed prior to the introduction of this factor. (Piaget, 1968a, pp. 6–7)

If an emotion is classified as a manifestation of a thwarted need which now achieves its satisfaction and hence equilibrium at a lower level of behaviour, then Janet's theory of emotions could be subsumed under Claparède's more general theory of needs. Although Piaget largely accepts Claparède's account, he does not think that the latter sufficiently appreciated that goal-directed behaviour depends, as Lewin has shown, on the total field and not only on a relation between the subject and the particular objective. And Sartre, as we have seen, has made a somewhat similar objection to Janet's theory.

Piaget's theory of needs not only has a psychological application, but also a sociological one. In this respect it resembles Sartre's account of needs in his *Critique* (1960). Sartre here identifies need with a conscious awareness of a 'lack' which arises from scarcity in our physical environment: this leads to alienation and hence social conflict. Piaget describes the same sort of sociological phenomenon in terms of his disequilibrium/equilibrium model. He makes the point that Marx's sociological theory involves a theory of equilibrium and that through the existence of social conflict and continual opposition, history comes to be conceived as a succession of more or less powerful disequilibria (i.e., class struggles), which precede the final equilibrium – the advent of socialism (Piaget, 1965, pp. 39, 48, 76–7). Thus Piaget's equilibrium theory when applied to the sociological field plays the same role as the dialectic does in Marx's social thought.

Piaget believes that there are two modes of approach to any human activity: (a) diachronic (genetic or historical) – the way this psychological, social or economic activity has developed through time; and (b) synchronic (normative) – the end-result of the historical process, the structure or system whose elements can be studied normatively in terms of rules, values and meaningful signs. Piaget (1965, p. 48) notes that this dual approach is also to be found in Marx: Marx studies historically the material factors of production which determine social groupings, but he assumes that from the start elementary social values are attached to human work, for example its efficacy, so that such work is evaluated normatively.

Implication and assimilation

An interesting feature of Piaget's genetic epistemology is his view that implication is the basic relationship holding between conscious experiences, which he clearly differentiates from the causal relationships holding between physiological processes. Piaget (1968b, pp. 186–9) argues that it is meaningless to apply the notion of causality, physical or physiological, to our experience of concepts and values between which only such implicatory relations hold. From this point of view Piaget's position resembles Husserl's and Brentano's, who distinguished between the intensional relations involved in our mental acts and the causal ones applicable to natural phenomena.

Piaget regards the relation of implication as being common to the system of meanings, to our recognitions, to acts of understanding – to all that differentiates a psychic from a physical process. The relation of implication is then taken by him in this wide sense to cover all conscious affective, perceptual and cognitive relationships, including the most primitive pre-logical ones. On the other hand, Piaget considers implication in the strict sense in which it is used in logic to be a particular use of this more general relation.

In using the notion of implication in this extended sense, Piaget once more reflects Claparède's position. He quotes Claparède's view that the feeling of necessary connection between mental events is not the result of learning from past experience, but is of a more primitive character. Claparède maintained, Piaget goes on, that if a child is burnt a single time in touching a stove he will act afterwards as if he thought the stove will necessarily burn him if he touches it. Implication for Claparède, interpreted in this wide sense, seems to come to much the same thing as intentionality. Without it, he says, we could not learn from experience: anything might be connected with anything else, as Hume claimed (Piaget, 1952, p. 404). Our expectations about the future, our projects, therefore always have such an implicatory or intensional character.

Claparède re-interpreted the Pavlovian concept of the conditioned reflex in terms of this wider conception of implication. He used it to refer to the connection between perceived data having a similarity of meaning – between a sign and a thing signified. Thus, he says, 'B is implied in A when, A being given, the subject behaves toward it as he would behave toward B' (Piaget, 1952, p. 404). In the case of Pavlov's dog, when the coloured pink A is presented with the food B, the dog reacts to A as if B were contained, were implied by A. Claparède believes that if this connection were a case of simple association rather than implication, the pink colour would simply evoke in the dog's memory the recollection of the food, without being followed by any reaction signifying that the colour pink is taken for the food, and functions like it (Piaget, 1952, p. 404).

This kind of approach to the problem of conditioning might appear to be a form of anthropomorphism to the behaviouristically minded psychologist, especially as it seems to give animals at least some primitive understanding of meaning as well as something akin to conscious remembering. However, I think that both Claparède and Piaget would be willing to attribute to such animals as dogs, dolphins and apes the ability to recognize, remember and coordinate things in a simple way, as well as the capacity for taking a perceived object as signifying another, as yet unseen.

Piaget (1952, p. 406) amplifies Claparède's remarks when he states that in the case of Pavlov's dog, the pink colour elicits the salivary and gastric reflexes because it has acquired significance by being assimilated to an action scheme, namely, that of feeding. The process of learning is then, for Piaget, not basically a juxtaposition (or association), as behaviourists contend, but rather one of organized systems adapting themselves to changed conditions. It is, he argues, only in terms of such an assimilatory (action) scheme that stimulus A implies response B.

The view that in conditioning we deal with elements which have a systematic meaningful character is also held by Merleau-Ponty, who under the influence of Gestalt psychology and Husserlian phenomenology argued that sensation and reaction are linked together by their common participation in a unitary structure. 'In fact the reflexes themselves are never blind processes: they adjust themselves to a "direction" of the situation, and express our orientation towards a "behavioural setting" ... It is this global presence of the situation which gives meaning to the partial stimuli and causes them to acquire importance, value or existence for the organism' (Merleau-Ponty, 1962, p. 79). Merleau-Ponty therefore stresses that the response to a specific stimulus is determined by the total pattern of the situation and by the organic and psychological factors in the structured organism.

Piaget believes that in order for any particular experience to become meaningful it has to be related (or assimilated) to some practical or cognitive scheme. In other words, its present meaning is always dependent on what we have experienced in the past. Thus when a man perceives an object, he identifies it by means of a spatial scheme, as a shape standing out against a background. When a baby pulls his blanket towards himself to obtain some object placed on it and beyond his reach, he is assimilating it to a certain action scheme. Or on a more intellectual plane, when a biologist classifies the specimens he has collected, his perceptions are assimilated into an already existing scheme of concepts (or logical categories).

Although the notion of assimilation also has a biological significance for Piaget, it would seem that some of the conceptual aspects of the notion have been his guide rather than the biological ones. This at least seems to have been the case with Claparède who compared the method of testing hypotheses with his account of trial and error learning (Piaget, 1952, p. 396). He identifies 'need' with the question or problem for which one tries to find a solution in hypothetical reasoning, and the specific scheme of action (the trial) which satisfies the need, with the testing of the successful hypothesis. Piaget's assimilatory schemes with their implicatory structures as used in perception and thought would seem to have the characteristics of such hypotheses: they are anticipatory in character and generate action and thought.

Zaner (1964, pp. 230–3)[3] has pointed out that Piaget's account of assimilation as a process of identifying a thing as belonging to a certain class or scheme resembles Husserl's account of 'associative pairing' or the seeing of similarities between pairs of things. We may see a red circle and a red square as similar in respect to colour and at the same time different as far as their shape is concerned. Thus a child who has previously handled a red rattle will henceforth attempt to grasp other red objects which he sees (or put them in a class of grasped noise-producing objects). However, he speedily learns to distinguish those red objects which are to be avoided, such as a fire, from those like rattles which are comparatively innocuous. Assimilation and 'associative pairing' cover the processes by which we learn to group objects under certain categories rather than others. It will be seen that the process of assimilation involves the relating of elements similar to each other, so that instead of two independent classes we obtain only one.

Hamlyn on assimilation and accommodation

Perhaps the most important critic of Piaget's account of assimilation and accommodation has been David Hamlyn. Hamlyn would seem to see more value in Piaget's formal approach to knowledge than what he takes to be his biological approach. He tells us that Piaget in his account of assimilation is largely concerned with the way an instance is put under a universal principle. As Hamlyn puts it, 'we have the concept in question only when we are both able to see a range of things as falling under the concept and also in the position to know what it is for them so to fall, what it is that makes them instances' (Hamlyn, 1967, pp. 37–8). He goes on to say that for this reason there is inevitably 'in the process of acquiring concepts a delicate balance between a kind of abstract understanding of what it is to be an X and a knowledge of what things conform to this criterion' (1967, p. 38).

These points, he continues, are essentially Kantian, but are also found in a certain sense in Piaget, although in this case 'A strictly philosophical point is tricked out under the guise of a rather vague and certainly misleading psychological or biological theory' (p. 38). And here he is specifically referring to Piaget's processes of accommodation and assimilation and the balance achieved between them. What Piaget's position then really comes to for Hamlyn is that 'our knowledge of objects is partly determined by what these objects are in themselves, partly by how we regard them' (p. 39). This, Hamlyn believes, reduces itself to the above point concerning the relationship between concepts and instances.

Further, Hamlyn goes on, the view that perception and the acquisition of knowledge involve accommodation and assimilation amounts to the idea that there is a mutual modification of subject and object. This sort of view depends, he says, on analogies which are supposed to exist between perception and other situations in which there is a reciprocal causal relationship, as is the case, for example, in biological structures where the attainment of a balance is the function of an organism. But for Hamlyn 'the relationship which comes to exist between concept and object in perception is not a causal relationship at all'. And he brings this point out further by saying 'to have a concept of X is to know what it is for something to be an X' (p. 39).

The biological model is further misleading, we are told, since 'It suggests that the balance to be attained is one between something about the individual which is essentially subjective, i.e. the concept, and something about the world around us which is clearly objective, i.e. the object' (p. 39). But, Hamlyn argues, in fitting something to a concept we are not imposing on it a subjective point of view, 'The objectivity of a concept is bound up with the idea that it must be inter-subjective, inter-personal, just as knowledge is' (p. 39). The growth of knowledge cannot therefore be looked upon as some kind of transaction between individual and environment, as if social, inter-personal factors have no part to play. Hence Hamlyn concludes there is a serious under-estimation of the social: Piaget's biological model rules out the social factor and thereby undermines the objectivity of knowledge. It is most important, Hamlyn says, 'to note the extent to which notions like that of knowledge and concepts are social ideas' (p. 40).

Piaget would, however, agree that these notions have an inter-subjective character and to some extent are socially determined. From his earliest work onwards he has noted the influence of social factors in the development of reason and objective knowledge, although he is careful to avoid any form of sociologism. Piaget emphasizes that in its development the child's mind and its basic structures adapt themselves to the social as well as physical environment. Although he asserts that both logical and moral (value) theory are bound up with the fact that we live in a society, he would not, like, for example, Durkheim, wish to reduce norms to social facts.

Thus, subject to the condition that mental factors also have their part to play in the development of rationality, Piaget does recognize that social life is a necessary condition for the development of logic and rational argument, involving an appeal to truth criteria. It is this, he tells us, which transforms the individual in his very nature, making him pass from a state of ego-centrism to one of cooperation with others. It would therefore seem that as far as the objectivity of knowledge is concerned, there is little difference between Piaget's and Hamlyn's positions.

It is true that in his later writings Piaget tended to emphasize intellectual or formal features rather than social ones in his account of concept formation. But the importance of the social factor is implicit in such works as *The Language and Thought of the Child*, *Judgment and Reasoning in the Child* and *The Moral Judgment of the Child* as well as his more sociological writings. The view that Piaget's biological model rules out the social factor seems to arise from the belief that for Piaget the notions of assimilation and accommodation are to be interpreted largely in biological terms, and not also in social, practical and conceptual ones. In any case it is possible to use the equilibrium model to deal with problems in social psychology: Lewin constructed his hodological space for this purpose; and in economics and social theory equilibrium models are common. And as we have seen Piaget applied this model to explain social change.

It ought also not to be overlooked that the use of the notion of assimilation in French is precisely connected with the way an object is placed under a general principle. One of its meanings is *to like*, *compare*, in addition to the more obvious biological use of assimilation on the model of the body 'ingesting food and drink'. It is worth noting that biological models were also used by Plato, who explicated knowledge as 'conception' or 'child-bearing'.[4] One might therefore also criticize the use of the term 'concept' because of its metaphorical connection with child-birth. The truth of the matter is that in philosophy, as well as in other disciplines, words are taken from common usage or other fields of enquiry and applied to the new field in the hope that they may help in its elucidation. They may in the process of translation take on a radically different meaning, although overtones of their earlier meaning may still remain.

Piaget is then in more general agreement with Hamlyn than may appear at first sight. Indeed Piaget may have taken over the concept of assimilation from such French philosophers as Brunschvicg, Lalande and Meyerson as well as from Claparède. Its use, however, goes back to Aristotle. And Wundt used it to refer to the organization of sensations into meaningful perceptions. Max Scheler used it in a sense similar to that of Piaget and Claparède, and distinguished between 'association by contiguity' (Hume's notion) and 'association by similarity' or assimilation. He went on to argue that since spatial instantaneousness and temporal succession are based on association by similarity, so for that matter is association by contiguity (Scheler, 1973, pp. 421, 442, 443n, 464).

Sartre, when commenting on the use of the concept of assimilation by these French philosophers, caustically remarked that after reading their work

> ... we have all believed that the spidery mind trapped things in its web, covered them with a white spit and slowly swallowed them, reducing them to its own substance. What is a table, a rock, a house? A certain assemblage of 'contents of consciousness', a class of such contents. O digestive philosophy! Yet nothing seemed more obvious ... Nutrition, assimilation! Assimilation, Lalande said, of things to ideas, of ideas by ideas, of minds by minds ... The simplest and plainest among us vainly looked for something solid, something not just mental (Sartre, 1970, p. 4).

Sartre is here poking fun at French idealist philosophy by giving the formal meaning of assimilation a more evident biological (rather than metaphorical) interpretation. And this seems to be what Hamlyn has done certainly with more justification in his criticism of Piaget. Sartre might, however, have put Piaget's and Hamlyn's positions under a similar head, since both in their accounts of conceptual knowledge are concerned with the relating of elements into more general systems, and this is what putting an object (instance) under a general principle comes to.

On the plane of concrete behaviour Piaget's action schemes come closer to Sartre's more pragmatic approach to knowledge. Commenting on Piaget's position Hamlyn thinks it no surprise that what Piaget calls the stage of concrete operations must in general precede that of abstract operations. 'As Aristotle said', he goes on, 'while in knowledge the general is prior in itself, the particular is prior relative to us. This is what Piaget's point comes down to' (Hamlyn, 1967, p. 40). Hamlyn in this last remark does appear to identify Piaget's concrete and abstract operations with the distinction between reflective knowledge of a general concept and our perceptual recognition of an instance of it. But this identification is not quite precise, since (1) concrete and abstract operations are not passively perceived or contemplated in thought: they comprise activities, in one case sensori-motor and in the other cognitive (conceptual); and (2) concrete operations are not particular instances of abstract operations, since they refer rather to our skilful activities of whose rationale we may be largely unconscious, whereas abstract (i.e. cognitive) operations refer rather to our reflective thought processes.

Hamlyn's comment on Piaget's view that the concrete stage must temporally precede in the child's development the abstract one, is that 'it is clearly futile to expect a child to move from one extreme to the other, and the concrete and the particular is clearly more obvious than the abstract and the general' (1967, p. 40). However, the problem Piaget would appear to be concerned with here is not simply the question of the concrete and particular being more obvious than the abstract and general, namely, that one comes to recognize particulars before one comes to grasp the universals they exemplify. When Piaget, for example, talks of concrete operations he is rather concerned with the carrying out of some concrete task so as to achieve a particular aim, and not with, say, consciously recognizing the universal red in some object, as is the case when we see the red carpet in front of us.

Although Hamlyn undoubtedly emphasizes the social nature of knowledge, his above account does seem to be a contemplative one (of the 'knowing that' type), where we intuit universals and their instances. And this seems to be implied in his remark that 'to have a concept of X is to know what it is for something to be an X' (1967, p. 39). Having a concept here then means something like understanding an idea rather than manifesting a particular intellectual skill or activity. Piaget maintains that, at the more elementary level of child thought, concepts only exhibit themselves through such practical activities as classifying, ordering, etc., as forms of 'knowing how' rather than 'knowing that'. We are unable to apply clear-cut distinctions relating to universals and particulars at this level of child thought to which pragmatic rather than conceptual criteria apply. Hamlyn (1967, p. 25) clearly recognizes that in a skill such as riding a bicycle, 'knowing how' comes to play a role and that technique and under-standing cannot be divorced from each other. However, he does not seem to stress, as Piaget does, that logico-mathematical concepts first obtain their exemplification through the child's practical skills.

When Piaget talks of concrete operations he tends to identify them with what he has termed 'unconscious cognitive activities' (Piaget, 1972, 36–47), where we carry out a task without having clearly before our minds the exact procedures and methods used. Thus a child may crawl on all fours without being aware of the precise order in which he moves his hands and feet, or he may be able to establish the equality of two rows of counters without being able to justify verbally his reasons for doing this. The difference between concrete and abstract operations then might be said to be that between the habitual applica-tion of a rule and its conscious application.

When Piaget then uses the notion of assimilation on a sensori-motor level, he is concerned with action schemes and their relation to certain perceived objects in the child's environment. On the other hand, on the level of reflective consciousness he is concerned with our under-standing of concepts and the relation between them, as well as their application to particular instances (i.e., putting an instance under a general principle). Although broad resemblances do exist in the way the notion of assimilation functions at both levels, Piaget, nevertheless, believes that there are important differences. In the former, motiva-tion plays its role, i.e. there is some awareness of the ends to be achieved, but no clear awareness of the methods used to achieve them. It may be that Piaget is remiss for using the term 'assimilation' in both these senses. However, on the conceptual level at least it is consistent with a certain French usage. One must remember that Piaget's work was directed to a French-speaking audience in the first place and not to an Anglo-Saxon one, who might regard his use of this concept as a kind of 'surplus baggage'.

Finally let us look at Hamlyn's statement that because Piaget talks of assimilation on the conceptual level he is introducing causality in the realm of consciousness, and that the relation between a concept and an object cannot be a causal one. Once again there is a greater affinity between Hamlyn's and Piaget's views than might seem to be the case. As we have already seen, Piaget would hold that the relations between conscious data are of an implicatory nature. Thus the rela-tion between a concept, say red, and a perceived object exemplifying it would be a conceptual and not a causal one, i.e. one of similarity.

On a conceptual level Piaget's account of the part played by meaningful cognitive structures in our experience has much in common with that of Husserl. Husserl was not only concerned with the nature of meaning, but also, especially in his later work, with showing how the spatio-temporal and logical structures of commonsense and science were based on more primitive experiential structures. Piaget does perhaps stress the genetic dimension more than Husserl does. Nevertheless, the latter did put forward a genetic phenomenology, and was in his account of the life-world influenced, as he acknowledged, by the work of Lévy-Bruhl on primitive mentality.

Husserl, as E. Marbach notes, was in the 30s concerned with problems of the factual genesis of conceptual knowledge and was interested in studies of early childhood. 'I would like to think,' he writes, 'that just as Husserl was stimulated by Lévy-Bruhl's ethnological work on primitive mentality, he may well have read and been stimulated by Piaget's early writings, which were published during his life-time' (Marbach, 1977, p. 103).

Conclusion

My prime concern throughout this paper has been to show that Piaget gives a developmental account of logico-mathematical knowledge. For example, he has demonstrated that classificatory and serial structures initially exhibit themselves in the child's simple manipulation of objects, and only a later date take on a propositional form. Piaget's essential point is that there is a continuity between the different levels of logico-mathematical structures, occurring at the varied phases of intellectual development. He refuses to believe that there is an *a priori* realm of logico-mathematical entities, the private preserve, as it were, of logicians and mathematicians. And it is precisely the function of genetic epistemology, as Piaget conceives it, to show that there is a continuity between logico-mathematical knowledge and our other more practical kinds of behaviour.

One conclusion of this paper is that in order to understand Piaget's theory of adaptive behaviour, one needs to take into account his more theoretical views, i.e., his genetic epistemology. One must remember that Piaget refuses to accept a philosophical empiricism, a view endemic to most Anglo-Saxon psychological thinking. Such a view takes the socio-physical world of the child as being identical with that of the adult, the only difference being that the adult has learned more about it. Piaget, on the contrary, believes that the child's socio-physical world has a much less structured character than the adult's, and that his logic is also of a fairly rudimentary kind.

We have seen that some of the criticisms which have been raised against Piaget's concepts of assimilation and accommodation, namely that he imports biological concepts into the psychological field, are unjustified, as these concepts have a more general character. It is Piaget's claim that it is precisely in terms of these processes that the child comes to construct not only his logico-mathematical concepts, but also his conception of the socio-physical world. One cannot therefore detach, as is sometimes done, the numerous experimental studies Piaget has carried out in the field of concept formation from his discussions in genetic epistemology.

This is a perennial source of much of the confusion which empiricist philosophers and psychologists claim to find in Piaget's work. They thus overlook that his experimental studies are primarily meant to show how the abstract concepts of logic, mathematics and physics, can be given an experiential grounding. It is true to say that the use of Piaget's work in the educational field, for example, in the teaching of mathematics and physics, is only a spin-off from his genetic epistemology, and that such application has never been the prime motor behind his enquiries. As Piaget once remarked 'l'application c'est le diable'.

Notes

1 See, for example, Piaget's very early view that the whole and part relation is common to both life and mind in his (1976) Autobiography, *Piaget Sampler* (ed. Sarah F. Campbell). New York: John Wiley and Sons, p. 120.
2 Translated by Theodore Mischel (1971), 'Piaget: cognitive conflict and motivation', p. 327.
3 See also Wolfe Mays (1977), Genetic analysis and experience: Husserl and Piaget. *Journal of the British Society for Phenomenology*, January, pp. 54-5.
4 On this point see James M. Edie (1975), Identity and metaphor: a phenomenological theory of polysemy. *Journal of the British Society for Phenomenology*, January, p. 39.

References

Bruner, J. S. (1959) Inhelder's and Piaget's 'Growth of Logical Thinking'. *British Journal of Psychology 50*: 369.
Fell, J. P. (1965) *Emotion in the Thought of Sartre*. New York and London: Columbia University Press.
Hamlyn, D. W. (1967) The logical and psychological aspects of learning. In

R. S. Peters (ed.) *The Concept of Education*. London: Routledge and Kegan Paul.

Koffka, K. (1935) *Principles of Gestalt Psychology*. New York: Harcourt Brace.

Lewin, K. (1935) *A Dynamic Theory of Personality*. New York and London: McGraw-Hill.

Locke, J. (1974) *An Essay Concerning Human Understanding* (ed. John Yolton), Vol. I. London: Dent, Everyman Library.

Marbach, E. (1977) Husserls reine phänomenologie und Piagets genetische psychologie. *Tijdschrift voor Filosofie*.

Merleau-Ponty, M. (1962) *Phenomenology of Perception* (trans. Colin Smith). London: Routledge and Kegan Paul.

Mischel, T. (1971) Piaget: cognitive conflict and motivation. In Theodore Mischel (ed.) *Cognitive Development and Epistemology*. New York and London: Academic Press.

Piaget, J. (1952) *The Origins of Intelligence in Children* (trans. Margaret Cook). New York: International Universities Press.

Piaget, J. (1954) *Les relations entre l'affectivité et l'intelligence dans le developpement mental de l'enfant*. Paris: Centre de documentation univ.

Piaget, J. (1965) *Etudes Sociologiques*. Geneva: Droz.

Piaget, J. (1968a) *Six Psychological Studies* (trans. Anita Tenzer, ed. David Elkind). London: University of London Press.

Piaget, J. (1968b) Explanation in psychology and psychophysiological parallelism. In Paul Fraisse and Jean Piaget (eds) *Experimental Psychology: its scope and method*, Vol. I (trans. Judith Chambers). London: Routledge and Kegan Paul.

Piaget, J. (1971) *Insights and Illusions of Philosophy* (trans. Wolfe Mays). Cleveland: World Publishing Co.

Piaget, J. (1972) Inconscient affectif et inconscient cognitif. *Problèmes de psychologie génétique*. Paris: Denöel/Gonthier.

Sartre, J.-P. (1960) *Critique de la raison dialectique*. Paris: Gallimard.

Sartre, J.-P. (1970) Intentionality: a fundamental idea of Husserl's Phenomenology (trans. Joseph P. Fell). *Journal of the British Society for Phenomenology*, May.

Sartre, J.-P. (1971) *Sketch for a Theory of the Emotions* (trans. Philip Mairet). London: Methuen.

Scheler, M. (1973) *Formalism in Ethics and Non-formal Ethics of Values* (trans. Manfred S. Frings and Roger L. Funk). Evanston: Northwestern University Press.

Zaner, R. M. (1964) *The Problem of Embodiment*. The Hague: Martinus Nijhoff.

4 The two spaces

Michael Morgan

...it is beyond doubt that primary spatial intuition depends
upon imagery, like all preoperational and intuitive thought:
but it is no less clear that these images mean nothing in
themselves, except in so far as they refer to possible actions,
to which the objects are assimilated and receive their spatial
determinations... Geometrical intuition is thus in its origin
a set of internalized actions, of which the image is only a
symbol....

J. Piaget
Genetic Epistemology, p. 207

In this essay I shall be concerned with the idea, which has been
expressed in various ways by philosophers, mathematicians, physicists
and psychologists, that there are two spaces: one the space of ordinary
physical objects, and the other a *mental, subjective* or *phenomenal* space.[1]
In particular, I shall consider the idea that phenomenal space has its
own intrinsic metric, a metric which makes it possible to ask whether
it is an Euclidean or a non-Euclidean space. It has seemed to me useful
to begin with a rather lengthy historical introduction to the problem
of phenomenal geometry before proceeding to a critical analysis.
Readers who are familiar with Kant's theory of geometry may,
however, overlook approximately the first half of the chapter and
begin at the second section.

Historical

It is strange, but true, that the philosopher who did more than any other to encourage the idea that there are two spaces was resolutely opposed to spatial dualism. Kant argued that space is entirely a representation and that what it represents should not be thought of as space-like. He regarded the practising scientist's tendency to identify the spatial and temporal aspects of his experience with the real properties of objects as inelegant: or, as he put it in his own way, 'merely empirical'. In other words, the fact that the scientist distinguishes only a sub-set of perceptual attributes as belonging to things as they really are is itself just a fact of psychology, or of appearance. We do not think that there are two 'colour worlds', one the realm of physical colours and the other of phenomenal colours. Why should we think that there are two spaces?

To carry the representational programme (see Still, this volume) to its logical conclusion, Kant proposed, we should therefore admit that all aspects of our perceptual experience, including space and time, are phenomena; and that we know nothing about the nature of the objects giving rise to these appearances other than that which is revealed in the phenomena themselves. 'What objects may be in themselves, and apart from all this receptivity of our sensibility, remains completely unknown to us. We know nothing but our mode of perceiving them – a mode which is peculiar to us, and not necessarily shared in by every being, though, certainly, by every human being.' (A 42)[2]

The psychological implications of the last remark should not escape notice, and have indeed been the subject of much critical comment by philosophers such as Strawson, who regarded Kant's psychology as a needless excrescence upon the otherwise admirably austere architecture of his system. What Kant seems to be suggesting is that we just happen to be innately fashioned so that we perceive things in space and time, just as some of us (but not all) are fashioned to see things as 'coloured'. True, there is no spatial or temporal equivalent of colour blindness in people, but Kant seems to suggest that if we consider other organisms, there might be. It would thus appear to be the business of psychologists to investigate the causes of our spatial and temporal intuitions, treating them as phenomena in the same way as we are used to regarding smells and colours. As Strawson put it:

> It is true that Kant thought of himself as investigating the general structure of ideas and principals which is presupposed in all our empirical knowledge; but he thought of this investigation as possible

only because he conceived of it also, and primarily, as an investigation into the structure and workings of the cognitive capacities of beings such as ourselves. The idiom of the work is throughout a psychological idiom. Whatever necessities Kant found in our conception of experience he ascribes to the nature of our faculties. (*The Bounds of Sense*, p. 19)

This aspect of Kant's reasoning may be contrasted with what Strawson calls the 'austere' aspect, in which the aim is to seek the minimum properties that experience must have to qualify as experience. From this latter point of view, space and time become necessary aspects of our experience, not merely contingent aspects like colours and smells. As Kant explains:

Tastes and colours are not necessary conditions under which alone objects can be for us objects of the senses . . . Further, no one can have *a priori* a representation of a colour or of any taste; whereas since space concerns only the pure form of intuition, and therefore involves no sensation whatsoever, and nothing empirical, all kinds of determinations of space can and must be represented *a priori*, if concepts of figures and of their relations are to arise. Through space alone is it possible that things should be outer objects to us. (*Critique of Pure Reason*, A 29)

Kant's argument that a spatial order of objects is a necessary feature of experience is a complex one, and not always convincing. A simple set of phenomena that merely *were* would not, according to Kant, define a thinking subject and would not constitute 'experience'. A distinction is required between the subject who has the experience and the object of that experience. (On this view certain dreams or ecstatic happenings would not qualify as experiences.) For this to be so the objects of experience must be supposed to have some existence independently of the subject and to have an independent order and arrangement. Kant claims that this independent order and arrangement is the spatial order, and that without this spatial order, therefore, experience would be impossible.

This argument is even run in reverse gear, to dispose of the doubts about the reality of space which the merely constitutional-psychological approach had appeared to raise. Here the argument is more convincing. It is a condition of posing the question about the reality of space that we distinguish phenomena from the independently existing objects which cause them, as, for example, when we distinguish a colour from a wavelength. But a concept of space is necessary to make the distinction between things that happen *in* us, and those that happen *outside* us, intelligible at all. Therefore the question is unintelligible, and outside its range of meaningful application, if applied to space itself. The argument is developed in the 'Fourth Paralogism of Pure Reason' to counter idealism of the Berkelean variety.

All this is very salutary, and perhaps the best antidote against the other aspect of the *Critique* with its idealist talk about space being a 'representation only', as being 'peculiar to us, and not necessarily shared in by every being', and with its repeated claim that we can know nothing about objects apart from the 'receptivity of our sensibility'. But it was the speculative metaphysical influence of Kant, rather than the critical, that had the greater impact upon psychology. Kant was generally understood as saying that spatial intuition is an innate psychological faculty, and this led in the nineteenth century to a sometimes bitter dispute between those who, like Hering, thought that they were supporting Kant, and those on the other hand, such as Helmholtz, who argued that we obtain our spatial intuition from 'experience'. Here is how Helmholtz himself described the influence of Kant:

> In the recent form of this [nativist] view, especially as developed by E. Hering, there is an ideated subjective visual space wherein the sensations of the separate nerve fibres are supposed to be registered according to certain innate laws. Thus, in this theory, not only is Kant's suggestion adopted, that the general perception of space is an original form of our ideation, but there are laid down as innate certain spatial perceptions.[3]

In his biography of Helmholtz, Koenigsberger says that it was 'Kant who had already perceived that the qualities of our sensation must be determined by the idiosyncrasies of our perception (which was first established as unquestionable by modern physiology), but apprehended space and time in the same way, since we can perceive nothing in the external [!] world without its happening at a given time and occurring at a given place' (p. 264).

The influence of Kant was thus felt mainly through his psychological or quasi-physiological idiom. As a further example, Lotze was led to look for the antecedents of spatial representation in non-spatial 'local signs'. Unfortunately, he pretty soon discovered (as closer attention to the critical aspects of Kant would have predicted) that the antecedents of spatial impressions were extremely space-like. This was the general result of scientific investigations that tried to take Kant seriously. No believing scientist can base a theory of perception on the proposal that the causes of perception are unintelligible 'things in themselves'. He is bound to provide an intelligible account and it is the essence of Kant's position that such an account must be in terms of space and time. We cannot consider space a representation in the same way as we consider a colour. The best that can be done, if we believe that perceptions are representations, is to distinguish *subjective space*, the representation, from *objective* space which it represents. But we have to admit that there are considerable similarities between these two spaces, and the question arises how far these similarities extend.

Geometry would form the basis of the most searching comparison. At first sight it is difficult to see how geometry, or the science of 'earth measurement', could be applied to a purely subjective or phenomenal space. However, the idea has often been advanced that there is such a thing as a phenomenal geometry, and that it makes sense to compare it with the geometry of fields, stars and so on. Here, too, the influence of Kant has been decisive. Kant held that geometry, by which he was bound to understand at his time Euclidean geometry,[4] is known by us to be true because it describes the rules of our spatial intuition. Geometry is a prime example of the kind of knowledge referred to by Kant in his terms as '*a priori synthetic*'. The existence of this kind of knowledge of geometry was supposed to be one of the main proofs that our knowledge of space is not gathered from experience, but rather is necessary for any experience to take place at all. By an *a priori* proposition Kant means one that does not depend upon experience for its verification. The most obvious examples are pure definitions such as 'all vegetables are plants'. This is an example of an *analytic* proposition in which the predicate assigned to the subject is part of the definition of the subject anyway. A *synthetic* proposition, on the other hand, assigns to the subject a predicate that is not contained by definition in the subject: for example, 'all vegetables contain chlorophyl'. (Not all plants have chlorophyl.) Now, in this scheme the question arises as to the status of propositions in physics such as 'A body free from external forces will move in a straight line', and in geometry such as 'A line bisecting one angle of a triangle will necessarily intersect the opposite side of the triangle.' One account of these statements is that they are merely definitions, therefore *analytic*. But Kant was not able to accept this view of geometry. It is indeed a little difficult to see at first sight how a mere set of definitions, if this is all that there is to

Euclidean geometry, can be used to deduce consequences about lengths and distances, as in Pythagoras' theorem. Therefore Kant argued that the truths of geometry are synthetic. At the same time, he would not allow that they were discovered by experience, since no actual experience in measuring triangles is required to convince one that Pythagoras' theorem is correct. Thus Kant concluded that there exists a class of propositions that are both synthetic and *a priori*, a class of which the axioms and theorems of Euclidean geometry are a clear example.

Kant's position on this is expressed in the following example, which could not make it clearer to a positivist (who draws a sharp distinction between what can be learned from experience and from unaided logic) where he has gone wrong:

> That the straight line between two points is the shortest is a synthetic proposition. For my concept of *straight* contains nothing of quantity, but only of quality. The concept of the shortest is wholly an addition, and cannot be derived, through any process of analysis, from the concept of the straight line. Intuition, therefore, must be called in; only by its aid is the synthesis possible. (B 17)

Now, by any standards, this is a very odd way of illustrating the supposedly synthetic nature of geometrical propositions. What else do we mean by calling a line 'straight' other than that it is the shortest distance between two points? The idea that it has some extra *quality* is very unsatisfactory, and Kant nowhere tries to say what this elusive quality is. It is tempting, therefore, to agree with the positivists that the statement in question is purely analytic, and that it owes its 'apodictic certainty' simply to the fact that it is a definition.

But this is too simple, as may be seen immediately from the fact that Euclid himself defined the straight line in quite a different way, namely as 'a line which lies evenly with the points on itself'. Euclid's straight lines, subject to constraints which we shall examine presently, make up triangles of which the angle sum is two right angles and of which the sides obey the Pythagorean formula. Can it not be argued that there is something more than definition here in the fact that the lines, of which these metrical propositions hold true, are those which present themselves to our intuition as being 'straight'?

But it is still not obvious what kind of quality Kant thought a straight line had. His claim that 'intuition ... must be called in' suggests visual imagination might be involved. Perhaps the *a priori* character of certain geometrical propositions arises because they describe constructions that we can visualize, and perhaps our visualization is systematically limited by precisely the rules of Euclidean geometry. This interpretation is encouraged by passages like the following:

> Thus I construct a triangle by representing the object which corresponds to this concept either in imagination alone, in pure intuition, or in accordance therewith also on paper, in empirical intuition – in both cases completely *a priori*, without having borrowed the pattern from any experience. (A 714, B 742)

Two aspects of Kant's theory of geometry can be distinguished: (1) his apparently psychological argument that EG describes the rules of our spatial intuition, and (2) his epistemological argument that EG is known to be true of the world because our only knowledge of the world is through our spatial intuition. The second argument is now almost universally discredited, but the first has very wide acceptance. Thus David Hilbert gave a lecture course on the foundations of geometry entitled *Anschaunglische Geometrie* (Intuitive Geometry), and it is especially significant that his great work *Foundations of Geometry* begins with a quotation from the *Critique of Pure Reason*. Frege (quoted by Hopkins) claimed that '... the truths of EG govern all that is spatially intuitable, whether actual or product of our fancy.' Johnson followed up the emphasis of Kant upon the constructive aspects of spatial intuition:

> We may ... by a rapid act of ocular movement represent a line revolving through 360 deg. from any one direction to which it returns. In this imaginative representation the entire range of variation, covering an infinite number of values, can be exhaustively visualized because of the continuity that characterizes the movement. It is only if such a process of imagery is possible that we can say that the axiom in its universality presents to us a self-evident truth.[5]

An extended argument to the effect that Kant was right about the Euclidean nature of our spatial intuition was made by Strawson. In the final part of *The Bounds of Sense* Strawson argued not only that Kant was correct about the application of EG to our spatial intuition, but in addition, and more importantly from his (Strawson's) point of view that this minor merit of Kant's theory vitiates the more central claim that the propositions of geometry and physics are *a priori* synthetic truths. The argument here is difficult, but for our purposes important. We have already seen how Strawson distinguishes Kant's psychological idiom, which appears to concern the innate faculties of the (human) mind, from his austere and critical idiom in which he attempts to discern the *a priori* characteristics of any experience whatsoever. According to Strawson, Kant irrelevantly clouded the latter investigation by persistently dragging in observations of the former kind, namely psychological facts. This is what Kant does with geometry. He claims to describe what a geometry of space *must* be, but succeeds only in describing what it *is for us* because of our peculiar intuition. Thus, according to Strawson, Kant is right about phenomenal geometry, but that is all:

> If we can make sense of this notion of a phenomenal interpretation for Euclidean geometry, then perhaps Kant's theory of pure intuition and of the construction of concepts in pure intuition can be seen, at least up to a point, as a perfectly reasonable philosophical account of it. To bring out the status of the propositions of such a geometry, it is best to take an example. Consider the proposition that not more than one straight line can be drawn between any two points. The natural way to satisfy ourselves of the truth of this axiom of phenomenal geometry is to consider an actual or imagined figure. When we do this, it becomes evident that we cannot, either in imagination or on paper, give ourselves a picture such that we are prepared to say of it both that it shows two distinct straight lines and that it shows both these lines as drawn through the same two points. (p. 282–3)

Strawson has been widely quoted on this point, but the more one considers this argument the more mysterious it starts to appear. What can be meant by a 'straight line' in a purely phenomenal sense? We can apply all sorts of tests to a physical line, such as the edge of a brick, to determine whether it is straight or not, but what tests can we apply to a phenomenal line? If someone claimed to visualize what Strawson asserts to be impossible, we might be tempted to say that they were misusing the expression 'straight line', but how could we prove it? Powerful doubts about the existence of a purely phenomenal geometry have been voiced by Nagel, amongst others. 'When we perform experiments in imagination upon straight lines', Nagel puts it, 'in what manner are these lines envisaged? We cannot employ any arbitrary images of lines in the experiment.' (p. 225) Similarly, Craig in his essay 'Phenomenal Geometry' points out that in the case of phenomenal figures, 'We have at best one sense, one viewpoint, one observer, and such evidence, in the case of a physical object, could certainly not establish its shape.' This problem of how to assign a meaning to a phenomenal straight line or curve raises the whole question of the interpretation of the terms in a geometry. The problem has a long history, which it will be necessary to consider in some detail before tackling the specific issue of phenomenal geometry. It arose in the first instance from the discovery that EG is not the only self-consistent axiomatization of geometry.

The story of the discovery of non-Euclidean geometries has been told many times, and I shall repeat here no more than is necessary for what follows. We need to distinguish first between the *axioms* of a geometry, which are stated without proof, and the *theorems* which are deduced logically from these axioms. In an acceptable axiomatic system the axioms should be self-consistent, and none of them should be derived as a theorem from the others. Euclid's 5th Axiom stated: 'Given 3 straight lines p, q, r one of which p intersects the other two, then if the sum of the interior angles of intersection on the same side of p is less than two right angles, then if r and q are produced indefinitely they will meet on that side of p.' This differs from the remaining axioms in having little immediate intuitive appeal, and it says much for Euclid's standards of rigour, whatever shortcoming they may have had in other respects, that he realized the necessity of stating it as an axiom. The historians sometimes say that mathematicians were offended by the arbitrariness of the axiom and therefore set out to show that it was not an axiom at all, but a theorem. Indeed, it did arouse passion. Wolfgang Bolyai wrote to his son Johann: 'It is unbelievable that this stubborn darkness, this eternal eclipse, this flaw in geometry, this eternal cloud on virgin truth can be endured.'[6] But the lack of intuitive appeal of the axiom was not long at issue. Very early on in the debate it was shown that the axiom could be replaced by one stating that the perpendicular distance between lines that do not intersect is the same wherever it is measured, and this is obvious if nothing else is. Moreover, the really maddening thing about the famous parallel axiom is that the other axioms could quite readily be used to demonstrate its converse, namely: 'Consider a line falling on two intersecting lines. Then the sum of exactly one pair of interior angles on the same side is less than two right angles.'

What on earth is lacking in the axiom that one cannot seem to prove the converse of this, namely the parallel axiom itself? It turns out to be an axiom that was stated by David Hilbert as follows: 'Let a be a line and A a point not on it. Then there is at most one line in the plane,

determined by *a* and A, that passes through A and does not intersect *a*.'
From this and the basic axioms of congruence Euclid's parallel
postulate can be derived, and also the theorem that the angles of a
triangle add up to two right angles, the theorem which carries the basic
metrical implications of EG. The fundamental principles of measuring
length by first determining its projections upon independent spatial
axes (Pythagoras' theorem) also follows.

So far the main aim has been to establish that Euclid's parallel
axiom, although not particularly intuitive in the way he states it, can
be replaced by several others with powerful intuitive appeal, such as
Hilbert's axiom of parallels. We now consider the intuitive status of
geometries in which the parallel axiom is replaced.

These geometries arose from attempts to show the dependence of the
parallel axiom of Euclid upon the others, using the device of *reductio
ad absurdum*. It was reasoned that if the axioms are not independent,
then a contradiction should show up if one of them is replaced by a
different version. The Jesuit priest Saccheri in his work *Euclides ab omni
naevo vindicatus* (Milan, 1733) tried replacing the Euclidean triangle
sum of two right angles (which is cognate with the parallel axiom) by
either (a) an angle sum of less than two right angles, or (b) an angle
sum greater than two right angles. He tried to show that the resulting
geometries were not self-consistent. In the case of (a) he failed
completely, and later on a self-consistent geometry of this kind was
developed by Lobachewsky, by Bolyai and by Gauss, all working
independently. This geometry, in which there are two lines through
a given point parallel to a given line in the same plane as the point,
and in which the angle sum of a triangle is less than two right angles
by an amount proportional to its area, is termed *hyperbolic*. It will be
noted that in this geometry the angle sum of a triangle is not constant;
in fact, it is characteristic of EG alone that the angle sum of all
triangles is the same, and the parallel postulate can be dispensed with if
instead one asserts that all triangles have the same angle sum.
Alternatively, one can characterize EG by the axiom that there exists
a single triangle with the angle sum of two right angles (Saccheri's discovery; Legendre's second theorem).

The status of the geometry with an angle sum for triangles of more
than two right angles was less clear. Saccheri could show that it did
indeed produce contradiction with the remaining axiom set of EG.
Subsequent work by Legendre showed that contradiction arose
because of conflict with the very basic 'Archimedian axiom of continuity':'If AB and CD are any segments then there exists a number *n*

such that n segments CD constructed contiguously from A along the ray from A through B, will pass beyond the point B.' If this axiom is sacrificed along with the parallel postulate, then an angle sum greater than two right angles for a triangle does not produce contradiction. As in the case of hyperbolic geometry, the resulting class of geometries have triangles with different angle sums depending on their area.

The controversy about the parallel axiom was finally settled when Klein established a method for proving that the non-Euclidean geometries are at least as consistent as EG. Klein's method is important for our treatment of phenomenal geometry, and may be stated as follows. EG makes reference to a number of primitive entities such as *point and line,* and to a number of primitive relations between these elements such as *joining on, lying on, contained in,* and so forth. Considered together these entities and relations form the *primitive elements* of the axiomatic system. Put aside for the moment the intuitive interpretation of these primitive elements in EG and consider replacing them by abstract symbols, such as a, x, & and (*). In principle the self-consistency and independence of the axioms can now be established using formal logic alone, without bothering about what a, x, etc. might actually mean. Suppose now, however, we wish to *interpret* the primitive elements, that is, assign meanings to them. The mere fact that the axiom set is consistent does not mean that any arbitrary interpretation can be chosen. To establish this point, consider an attempted arithmetic interpretation. Let the primitive term *points* in EG be interpreted as the field of arithmetic integers. Let a *line* be interpreted as a ratio between two integers and let *contain* mean that the line so defined is itself an integer. In this interpretation at least one of the Euclidean axioms is not upheld, namely: 'For every two points A, B there exists a line a that contains each of the points A, B' (Hilbert's first axiom of incidence). A related arithmetical example is given by Nagel.

So EG is not consistent with every possible interpretation of its elements in terms of numbers and the arithmetic operations of addition, subtraction and multiplication. But as Hilbert was able to show, there exists at least one interpretation of the primitives of EG in arithmetical terms that is not inconsistent with the rules of arithmetic. This means that the axioms of EG *can* be just as consistent with an interpretation in terms of arithmetic as they are in their geometrical interpretation. In other words we have a choice of interpretations. Now consider this method of interpretation applied to a non-

Euclidean geometry. There is nothing to stop us interpreting a term such as 'straight line' in this geometry with a geometrical entity that would not be called a straight line in the usual interpretation of EG, but which would be called something else: for example, a point. The interpreted theorems of such a geometry will state results of which we can ask whether they are true or false in EG, since they use only interpretations which also exist in EG. Our previous arithmetic example shows that the interpreted theorems are by no means necessarily consistent with EG, any more than they are necessarily true of every arbitrary arithmetic interpretation. But what Klein showed was that it is in fact possible to choose a particular interpretation of a non-Euclidean geometry in the domain of interpreted elements covered by EG, such that every theorem stated a result that was also a theorem in EG. This proved that the non-Euclidean axiomatic system was at least as consistent as the Euclidean axiom system. Klein's model of hyperbolic geometry is too complex to consider here, but its essence can be grasped by considering a well-known Euclidean model of elliptic or Riemannian geometry. If the primitive element 'straight line' in this geometry is interpreted as a 'great circle on a sphere' in EG, then the axiom 'there are no parallels' is seen to result in theorems that are also theorems in EG, such as 'the angle sum of the triangle composed of three straight lines is greater than two right angles' (this being true of a spherical triangle in EG).

As a result of such interpretations of non-Euclidean geometries by Klein, Hilbert and Poincaré, it is now accepted by mathematicians that a sharp distinction must be drawn between the logical consistency of EG considered as an axiomatic system of inference, and the truth of EG when it is interpreted in terms of real-world elements such as straight lines. As an axiomatic system *per se* EG is no more or less consistent than several rival versions. As a statement about facts it can only be tested when its primitive elements have been interpreted and unambiguously correlated with observables. As soon as a 'straight line', for example, is defined as the path taken by a light ray, we can ask whether it is true or false that the angle sum of a triangle is equal to two right angles. Gauss seems to have been the first to suggest an empirical test of this kind with stellar triangles, and his suggestion was followed up by his successor Schwartzchild at Göttingen. Observations logically related to this one have in fact led some physicists to prefer a Riemannian to an Euclidean geometry for astronomical purposes.

There is much less agreement amongst mathematicians, as I understand it, about the extent to which any set of observations could *compel* one to abandon a faith in EG. Poincaré pointed out that one could always alter one's interpretation of the Euclidean primitives so as to stay one jump ahead of refutation. If light rays, for example, fail to provide data congenial to a Euclidean theorist he could simply decide that light rays are not straight lines. This so-called 'conventionalist' solution is widely despised by working scientists, for obvious reasons, but is more easily reviled than refuted. Since this particular problem is still debated by mathematicians and physicists, it would be a brave psychologist or philosopher who volunteered an opinion. It does not seem to me to matter very much in any case for our present purposes. It is enough to have established the agreed point that no claim for truth of EG can be legitimized without first fulfilling the obligation to interpret its primitives in some unambiguous way, and to note that this is quite distinct from establishing its logical consistency. From here we are poised to ask how we might back up the claim that EG is a true account of 'phenomenal geometry'.

Is phenomenal geometry Euclidean?

Although it may seem a bit perverse, I want to tackle this question initially by considering how we might establish that phenomenal geometry is actually non-Euclidean. This is in point of fact a live issue, for experimental psychologists (and I must include myself as a guilty party: Morgan, 1969, pp. 380–4) have sometimes tried to show that EG is a poor account of perception. I shall now try to show that the alleged demonstrations of a phenomenal non-Euclidean geometry rest upon two major fallacies. Consider, for example, the claim that 'acute angles look larger than they really are' which is based upon illustrations such as that in Figure 4.1. If this statement is taken seriously, and if it be further allowed that the angle sum of a *real* triangle be two right angles, then it has seemed to some theorists to follow that the *phenomenal* angle sum of a triangle composed of three physical acute angles would be greater than two right angles, so that the sides would be bowed. Thus Fisher (1969) argued:

> The statement '*All acute angles are overestimated*' must necessarily be false ... If the sizes of all acute angles were to be overestimated it would follow that triangular figures are distorted, so that their sides assume a bowed appearance.

This seems to me an example of a mistake that I shall refer to as the

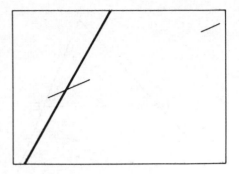

Fig. 4.1   One of many figures used to show that acute angles tend to be expanded in visual perception. The two thinly drawn segments are actually colinear, but the proximity of the left-hand one to the thick line makes it appear as if it points to a point below the right-hand thin line. Taken from N. K. Humphrey (1973) Les illusions visuelles, *La Recherche 3*: 631–8.

'fallacy of swopping horses'. The idea seems to be as follows. If we take a physical triangle and bend its sides outwards from the centre, we obviously end up with a figure that has bent sides, a bit like a planar projection of a spherical triangle. There is reasoned to be a psychological process that bends the phenomenal sides of a figure in this way. Therefore the phenomenal figure is a bit like the physical figure just described. But here we have swopped horses mid-stream between the physical and the phenomenal figure. If we expand a physical angle of, say, 30 deg. we obviously have an angle that is greater than 30 deg. But if we expand the phenomenal representation of a physical angle of 30 deg. precisely nothing follows about the size of this phenomenal angle, since the size was unassigned to start with. All the phenomenal angles in the representation of an acute angled triangle could be expanded as much as we wish, and the sum still be two right angles. The fact that expansion of the angles in a physical triangle would disqualify the figure from being an Euclidean triangle does not help us to decide what happens in the phenomenal case. It would do so only if we assumed the same geometry for physical and phenomenal figures to start with, which would be to rule out the very conclusion which the demonstration is attempting to justify.

Consider Blank's triangle as another example. In EG the line *d*

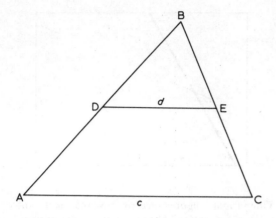

Fig. 4.2   Figure used by Blank to show departures of visual perception from Euclidean geometry. The line *d* joins the midpoints of sides AB and BC, and in Euclidean geometry *d* is one half the length of the third side, *c*. However, some subjects underestimate the length of *d* relative to *c*.

joining the midpoints of two sides of a triangle is equal in length to half the third side, *c* (see Figure 4.2). In hyperbolic geometry *c* is greater than 2*d*, and in elliptic geometry 2*d* is greater than *c*. Blank required subjects to mark off on side *c* of a physical triangle a distance corresponding to the phenomenal distance '*d*'. Six subjects marked off a distance less than *d* and were held to have a hyperbolic geometry. We may note that this conclusion is inconsistent with the one derived from the phenomenal expansion of acute triangles, a disagreement not to be wondered at given the dubious nature of the reasoning in both cases. Because the subjects have marked off a physical distance on *c* that is less than the physical distance *d* they have been accused of having a non-Euclidean geometry. But if the subjects did what they were told, it is a safe bet that the phenomenal distance they marked off along *c* is equal to the phenomenal distance *d*. It is simply swopping horses to complain that the *physical* distance they mark off is not equal to the *physical* distance *d*.

But, it may be replied, surely the subjects can *see* directly that the distance they mark off along *c* is not equal to one half of *c*? Now we seem to have an inconsistency with EG based entirely upon 'looks' and thus upon phenomenal considerations. This introduces a more funda-mental, and perhaps more controversial fallacy, for which I have unfortunately been able to find no more memorable designation than the 'fallacy of determinate phenomenal congruence'. The fallacy consists in supposing that the equality or inequality of lengths in a phenomenal domain can somehow be directly appreciated, without laying down any criteria for the judgement, and that only a single judgement of congruence can be made in a given set of circumstances. This issue of congruence is fundamental to all the metrical geometries. The point has been laboured already that the primitive terms of a geometry need to be interpreted before the geometry can be used to make measurements. Amongst the primitive elements of Euclidean, hyperbolic and elliptic geometries is the term 'congruent or equal to' – which is why these geometries are termed collectively congruence geometries. For example, Hilbert's Axiom III.1 reads:

> If A,B are two points on a line a, and if A′ is a point on the same or on another line a', then it is always possible to find a point B′ on a given side of the line a' through A′ such that the segment AB is *congruent or equal to* the segment A′B′.

In the relevant definition it is merely explained that 'congruent or equal to' means 'standing in a certain relation to'. Before carrying out tests between the different geometries we evidently have to interpret this term 'standing in relation to'. For example, we could agree that a line which marks off two given points on a ruler is congruent to a line in a different place which marks off the same two points on the same ruler. Armed with this interpretation we could then test the Euclidean claim that the perpendicular distance between two parallel lines at a given position is equal or congruent to the distance measured at a different position.

How is congruence to be established in the phenomenal domain? It is tempting, but I think quite pointless, to say that 'congruent' means 'looking the same length as'. Pointless, because we still do not know from this definition the criteria by which it is decided whether two lengths are judged to 'look the same'. Translations such as 'looking *as if* the lengths could be superimposed' or 'looking *as if* they would mark off the same two points on the same rule' give the game away, because of the telling 'as if' phrase which informs us that an appeal is made to a further operation. Without such an appeal it just is not obvious what it means to say that two lengths 'look the same', or why we apply the concept of congruence to the 'look'. Whitehead asked the right question: 'When we say that two stretches match in respect to length, what do we mean?'[7] But his answer is surely unacceptable when he tells us that there is some completely un-analysable sensation that tells us so. He says: '... there will be a class of qualities, one and only one of which attaches to any stretch on a straight line or on a point, such that matching in respect to this quality is what we mean by congruence....' According to this thesis we can just *see* that two lengths are congruent in the same way that we can smell a pickled onion, and no more can be said about the matter. Whitehead believes that this perception of congruence is not only independent of physical criteria of measurement, but is actually logically and historically prior to them. The difficulty here is to see why we should ever come to apply the same phrase 'congruent or equal to' when speaking of a certain relation between physical figures, and when speaking of an unanalysable simple sensation. They have nothing obvious in common. As Grünbaum says: 'For when pressed as to what it is about two congruent-*looking* physical intervals that enables them to sustain the relation of spatial equality, our answer will inevitably have to be: the fact of their capacity to coincide successively with a transported solid rod' (p. 61).

The mistake of presupposing that there is some unique congruence relation between phenomenal entities seems to me to arise from a very common habit in psychology, that of ignoring basic problems because they are superficially not problems, and concentrating on complex and entertaining phenomena instead. In this case the basic fact that we can judge lengths as equal or unequal is taken for granted, without wondering how we do it. Return to Figure 4.2 for a moment and consider how we actually set about marking off a length equal to d upon c. It will soon appear that we can adopt a variety of strategies for doing this, and that there is no unique and determinate 'congruence' sensation. There is a temptation in the first instance to solve the problem by imagining a perpendicular from E to AC and consider-ing the segment to the left of the intersection of this perpendicular with c to mark off the distance equal to d. This, of course, gives a gross error in the direction of Blank's 'hyperbolic' subjects. How do we know that they did not succumb, at least partially, to this temptation? A more likely way to succeed is to run the eyes along DE and then to program the same eye movement to mark off the equivalent distance along c. A danger here is that when moving the eyes along DE there will be a tendency to overshoot and include a part of the segment EC. Just such a tendency has been revealed in studies of the Müller-Lyer illusion figure, in which subjects scanning the line with the outgoing fins tend to overshoot the end of the figure. It will be noted that in the quadrilateral DECA, the segment DE is a Müller-Lyer figure with outgoing arrows on one side, while AC is a line with ingoing arrows on one side. This is a second reason why DE might be overestimated relative to AC.

Yet another way to solve the problem is to construct a line from C to meet AC at a point M, and to make this construction such that the angle EMC is congruent to the angle DAC. The point M is now the midpoint of AC and AC will be equal to DE, as required. I find that I can make pretty accurate judgements of the midpoint of AC in this way. Of course, this leaves completely unanswered the question of how to judge the congruence of angles EMC and DAC. But the only point I wish to make from this example is that there is more than one way to skin the cat, and we get different answers according to the strategies we adopt in making the measurement. These strategies correspond to different ways in which we might set about making the measurements on a physical triangle. There is not, *pace* Whitehead, a single God-given and unambiguous method of determining whether or not two lines are congruent in a figure. The fact that different strategies are available presumably ·explains why different experimental investigations of figures such as Blank's triangle have given such different results. Blank found that his subjects were predominantly 'hyperbolic', but in a different study Battro et al. (1976) found a mixture of Euclidean, hyperbolic and elliptical subjects. Some strategies for judging congruence may be expected to be better than others. If subjects happen on some occasions to perform the task badly it is being far too polite to say that their geometry is non-Euclidean. A surveyor who uses feeble instruments will make mistakes also, even if he tries to apply the methods of EG as well as possible. His mistakes are not non-Euclidean, they are just mistakes.

I have just pointed out that the different strategies one can use in judging phenomenal congruence correspond to the different measurements one might wish to make on a physical figure. This will make it obvious that I am trying to support what amounts to a behavioural solution to the problem of phenomenal geometry. For the reasons stated, it is hard to see how a 'geometry' is possible on the basis of 'pure looks' and mysterious qualitative sensations of congruence. An axiomatic system which defines 'congruent or equal to' as 'looking congruent or equal to' simply has not interpreted its primitive elements, and it remains an axiomatic system, not a geometry at all.

Why should we apply the terminology of congruence to simple 'looks' if they are unanalysable sensations? Surely we do so only because the 'looks' are able to anticipate, to a certain extent, the results of measurements to which the congruence terminology is meaningfully applied. When we say 'these two lines look congruent' we mean that they look as if they are physically congruent. If we mean only that they have 'an unanalysable look of having the relation x' it is not at all clear why we should ever be tempted to translate x by 'congruent or equal to'. Why apply the same term that we apply to the physical relation between objects, unless in fact the same relation is referred to in both cases? And if the same thing is meant, the case for a separate phenomenal geometry collapses. The working of a phenomenal congruence is incomprehensible unless it is the anticipation of a physical measurement, carried out by some operation that correctly (more or less) reproduces the results of a physical congruence measurement. And this, I suggest, is exactly what phenomenal geometry is at its best, that is, when it is a geometry at all.

As noted earlier in relation to arithmetic interpretations, one cannot hope to coordinate primitive elements in an axiomatic geometry willy-nilly with interpreted elements in an arbitrary domain. The results will not necessarily constitute anything like a metrical geometry. This applies to congruence as well. Someone might lay down the operation that AB is congruent with BC if a stone of a given weight can be thrown from A to B with maximum effort, and a stone of half that weight thrown from A to C. In a fully axiomatized congruence geometry it needs to be stated, or deduced from more elementary axioms of order, that a segment AB is congruent with BA. But the stonethrower will assent to this only in the very unlikely event of throwing-distance being a linear function of weight. If it is not then an axiom common to all congruence geometries will not hold for him, and the question can hardly arise whether his 'geometry' is or is not Euclidean. Thus it is unlikely that an arbitrary quality in our sensation could give a work-able interpretation of 'congruent or equal to'. It would have to satisfy at least some of the requirements that are set by a physical measure of congruence.

The relationship between phenomenal geometry and geometry I would now conceive to be something like the following. When we move our eyes around the outline of a figure; or when we copy a figure with a drawing; or when we walk along a straight line from A to B, we are carrying out geometrical operations in the physical world, since it is movements of our body that are occurring. But we are also able, to a certain extent, to make plans for such movements and to antici- pate the results of carrying them out. Thus, to give an example, three straight lines drawn on a sheet of paper could activate the motor programme necessary to move the eyes in a straight line along them or to draw a straight line with hand and pencil. This is what is meant by saying that the line is 'phenomenally straight'. It is not that there is some mysterious inner line distinct from the line on the paper, and on which we make some internal measurement. A phenomenal line joining a set of points is the line we plan to draw to connect up the points. This means that we can ask a person to show what he means by a phenomenal straight line by drawing it, moving his eyes along one, or by pressing buttons with his feet to make a spot move in a straight line on an oscilloscope screen. The objects of this phenomenal geometry cease to be private and indescribable 'looks' of things, but instead programmes for action that can be fully com- municated to another person.

If this account is right, then the geometry of our phenomenal space is precisely the geometry of our actions. Its rules will state neither more nor less than the conditions under which our actions are organized and the rules according to which they are made. The powerful hold of EG over our intuition arises from the fact that our actions in space turn out to be permissible interpretations of the primitive terms in the congruence and other axioms of EG.

This argument derives from Helmholtz, and a particular version of it has been recently worked out in some detail by Lucas in his book *A Treatise on Time and Space*. Lucas suggests that 'We like Euclidean geometry because we are men, and have eyes and hands, and need to operate a concept of size that will be independent of orientation, distance and size' (p. 185). In non-Euclidean geometries, it will be recalled, there are no congruent figures of different sizes. If this were the geometry to which our actions had to conform, then, for example, if we tried to move our eyes around the boundaries of a shape such as a triangle, we should have to move through different angles at the corners of the figure depending on its distance from us. Quite different eye movement programmes would thus be necessary for scanning the same shape at different distances. In point of fact, however, the angle through which the eyes must turn at the corners of the figure is invariant with distance, and this could be useful in extracting in- variances from the shape. It is a bit difficult to follow Lucas' argument that things just have to be like this if we are to have any perception of shape at all. Nothing logically would prevent one from establishing equivalences between shapes based upon much more complex invariance properties than those of EG. Undeniably these would be much more complex than the Euclidean equivalences, but the convenience of the Euclidean solution does not make it necessary. Lucas is attempting to produce a Kantian proof that EG has to be true if we are to perceive. It seems simpler to say that it is, in point of fact, an accurate description of our actions.

Indeed, similar reasoning to that of Lucas led Helmholtz (in his beautiful essay 'On the origin and significance of geometrical axioms', 1870) to conclude that EG is learned from our experience of equivalences. This conclusion seems no more logical than Lucas' Kantian argument. If it is useful to organize our actions according to the principles of EG, as seems to be the case, then there is every reason why these principles should be built into the design of the motor system, rather than having to be acquired painfully by trial and error.

Conclusion

I began by explaining the reasons why a 'two spaces' theory has so often been advanced. Dissatisfaction with the theory arises because if there are separate physical and phenomenal spaces, it is not at all clear why phenomenal space has the puzzling feature, which is not shared by other representations such as colours and smells, that it bears a considerable isomorphic similarity to the object of its representation. We can overcome this puzzle by agreeing with Kant that there are not two spaces at all, and that space and geometry are not representations such as colour and smell. There is a single set of spatial relations in the world. Kant argued that they are entirely phenomenal. I have tried to argue that they may just as easily be viewed as entirely physical. So called phenomenal representations of spatial relations are in fact just actions, which are a part of the physical world. The arguments advanced here may not convince a reader who prefers the Kantian solution, but I hope that they are at least sufficient to raise doubts about the theory that there are two space-like worlds, one for minds and the other for bodies.

Notes

1 I gratefully acknowledge my debt to the authoritative texts of Grünbaum, Reichenbach and Nagel; to Strawson's *The Bounds of Sense*; to Lucas'

Treatise; and to the very clear and readable articles by Craig and Hopkins. These and other sources are listed in the references.

2 Kant, *Critique of Pure Reason*. Pages numbered A refer to the first edition (1781) and those numbered B to the second edition (1787).
3 Quoted in Boring, *A History of Experimental Psychology*, p. 305.
4 Abbreviated in the rest of the chapter to EG.
5 Quoted in Nagel, *The Structure of Science*, p. 224.
6 Quoted in Meschkowski, *Noneuclidean Geometry*, p. 31.
7 See Grünbaum, *Philosophical Problems of Space and Time*, for a critical account of Whitehead's theory (pp. 48–65).

References

Battro, A. M., Netto, S. and Rozestraten, R. J. A. (1976) *Perception*, pp. 5, 1–122.
Bell, E. T. (1937) *Men of Mathematics*. New York: Simon and Schuster.
Boring, E. (1957) *A History of Experimental Psychology*, New York: Appleton–Century–Crofts.
Craig, E. J. (1969) Phenomenal geometry. *British Journal of the Philosophy of Science 20*: 121–34.
Fisher, G. H. (1969) *Quarterly Journal of Experimental Psychology 21*: 356–66.
Grünbaum, A. (1973) *Philosophical Problems of Space and Time*. Boston Studies in the Philosophy of Science, Volume XII. Boston: D. Reidel.
Helmholtz, H. von. (1960) On the origin and significance of geometrical axioms. In J. R. Newman (ed.) *The World of Mathematics*, Vol. 1. London: George Allen and Unwin, pp. 647–88.
Hilbert, D. (1971) *Foundations of Geometry*. (*Grundlagen der geometrie*, second edition; Translated by L. Unger and revised by P. Bernays.) La Salle, Illinois: Open Court.
Hopkins, J. (1973) Visual geometry. *Philosophical Review 82*: 3–34.
Kant, I. (1929) *Critique of Pure Reason* (trans. N. Kemp-Smith). London: Macmillan.
Koenigsberger, L. (1965) *Hermann von Helmholtz* (trans. F. A. Welby, with a preface by Lord Kelvin). New York: Dover Publications. First published by Clarendon Press, Oxford in 1905.
Lucas, J. R. (1973) *A Treatise on Time and Space*. London: Methuen.
Meschkowski, H. (1964) *Noneuclidean Geometry*. London: Academic Press.
Morgan, M. J. (1969) Estimates of length in a modified Müller-Lyer figure. *American Journal of Psychology 82*: 380–4.
Nagel, E. (1961) *The Structure of Science*. London: Routledge and Kegan Paul.
Piaget, J. (1950) *Épistémologie génétique*, I. *Pensée mathematique*. Paris: Presses Universitaires de France.
Reichenbach, H. (1957) *The Philosophy of Space and Time* (trans. by M. Reichenbach and J. Freund, with introduction by R. Carnap). New York: Dover Publications.

Robertson, H. P. (1964) Geometry as a branch of physics. In J. J. C. Smart (ed.) *Problems of Space and Time*. New York: Macmillan.

Strawson, P. F. (1966) *The Bounds of Sense*. London: Methuen.

5 The foundations of psychology

N. E. Wetherick

Sigmund Koch opens his contribution to the 1975 Nebraska Symposium on 'Conceptual Foundations of Psychology' by pointing out that the letter of invitation to participants refers to the 'current "crisis" with respect to alternate paradigms in psychology'. He goes on, 'If one were to try to establish the date of the letter on the basis of that phrase alone, it could have been written on any of the 36,500 days in the century-long history of "scientific" psychology'. 'Crisis' is, in his view (Koch, 1976), endemic to psychology as a consequence of the assumption that psychology can be a single conceptually coherent discipline. Koch believes that it cannot and invariably refers to 'psychological studies' not to 'psychology'. He is not alone in this view; in the same symposium Royce (1976) entitles his contribution 'Psychology is multi-: methodological, variate, epistemic, world-view, systemic, paradigmatic, theoretic and disciplinary'. But the crisis persists! The belief that psychology ought, in principle, to be capable of the same degree of conceptual coherence as physics or chemistry or biology has not been abandoned, although agreement on a basis for this coherence seems as far away as ever.

'The grandiose nature of the very claim to be a psychologist' (Bannister, 1977) cannot easily be denied. If there is a unified science of psychology then human nature falls within its purview, and the psychologist must offer an account of his behaviour qua psychologist as well as qua human being. Moreover, there is a class of human beings that deny the possibility of a science of psychology on what appear to be rational grounds and the psychologist must account for them too. Clearly psychology is not an appropriate discipline for the modestly inclined! A new attempt to establish that a unified science of psychology is possible in principle, despite the fact that no agreement has yet been reached on the subject, may fail. However, such an attempt may at least have the useful side effect of shedding light on the relationship between the different paradigms for psychology whose mutually incompatible claims to unique and often self-evident validity now threaten to swamp the serious but uncommitted student of the subject. Such an attempt will be made in this chapter and must necessarily touch on areas that have often been regarded as the prerogative of the philosopher. The fact is that any psychological theory constitutes, or at least implies possession of, a view of human nature, human knowledge and the relationship between human and non-human reality, and this fact remains whether or not the theorist chooses to consider implications.

It seems to me that ordinary men and women who have never seriously considered the issue hold something like the following view of reality. (The justification for an appeal to the view of the ordinary man lies in the fact that the object is to secure a foundation for the science of psychology, which must cover laymen, scientists and philosophers alike and in the likelihood that the philosophers' more sophisticated views originated from a consideration of contradictions which are, as we shall see, inherent in the ordinary man's view.)

For the ordinary man, then, there is on the one hand external reality (matter) and on the other internal reality (mind). External reality (matter) is law-governed, the object of investigation of the sciences, but it would still be there governed by the same laws even if we were not. Internal reality (mind) differs from external reality in at least two important respects: it involves conscious awareness (and consciousness appears to have no analogue in matter) and it does not appear to be governed by laws.

My assertion that this is the ordinary man's view is unsupported. It is difficult to see how evidence on the subject could be obtained since the ordinary man is not accustomed to employ terms like 'real' and 'exist' in the necessary technical sense and it is almost impossible to introduce the technical sense briefly without at the same time determining the kind of answer likely to be given. If the reader is prepared to grant for the moment that my personal intuitions on the subject may be correct it must immediately be apparent that what I have characterized as the ordinary man's view does not survive the most cursory rational scrutiny.

It is widely agreed that we are dependent on the evidence of our senses. But our senses can mislead us, we sometimes see or hear things that are not there and fail to see or hear things that are. What right have we to assume that there is a real external world corresponding to the evidence provided by our senses? Berkeleyan idealism suggests that there is no such real external world, all that exist are 'ideas' whose mutual coherence is guaranteed by a beneficent deity. This is an ontological doctrine – it expresses a view about what exists; 'ideas' exist but not 'material objects'. Humean empiricism is an epistemological doctrine – it expresses a view about what can be known rather than about what exists. Of the real external world nothing can be known to us except 'impressions of sense'. We may derive laws of nature from the 'constant conjunctions' we experience between different 'impressions of sense', but we have no basis for speculation about any corresponding material reality. Kantian idealism suggests that we may go further, indeed must do so. We may postulate models to explain the 'constant conjunctions' in our experience. But the models we postulate are as dependent on the knower as the 'impressions of sense' themselves; what, if anything, exists beyond these impressions cannot become the object of our knowledge.

Psychology in an empiricist framework

There can be no question here of doing justice to the immense sophistication with which these alternative views have been developed over the last 250 years. For our present purpose the bare outline is sufficient for we are primarily concerned with science and the science of psychology in particular. Science developed mainly under the influence of Humean empiricism but *all* these views commit what Bhaskar (1975) calls the epistemic fallacy. They direct attention to what can be known (epistemology) rather than to what exists (ontology). They have all rejected half the ordinary man's reality but retained the other (mental) half more or less on the ordinary man's terms. The consequences for the development of physical and biological science have not been serious. Scientists customarily write as if the scientific laws they propound governed some kind of external reality but the laws can, to all appearance, be reformulated in terms of 'constant conjunctions of sense impressions' that are acceptable to an empiricist philosopher.

The consequences for psychology are more serious, for there appears in short to be no possibility of a science of psychology. 'Laws of association' by cause and effect or by contiguity of time or place can be propounded but they specify merely how the mind operates in deriving laws in the non-psychological sciences. From retaining the ordinary man's conception of mind, it follows that the whole enterprise of empiricist *psychology* is misconceived. When Watson (1913) expressed the hope that consciousness (i.e. mental reality) would in future play only the same role in psychology that it played in chemistry and physics he came near to admitting as much. For the function of consciousness in chemistry and physics is (in empiricist terms) to register the 'constant conjunctions of sense impressions' that constitute the laws governing chemical and physical events. But it can perform no such function in psychology, because the laws would have to govern events in which it participated. Even if it succeeded in deriving such laws it would be able to override their effects and the laws would consequently not be laws in the full sense. It is not plausible to argue that we might, without knowing it, be impotent spectators of our own behaviour! Patients undergoing brain surgery can distinguish very easily between limb movements initiated by themselves and movements evoked by direct stimulation of the motor cortex of which they are 'impotent spectators'. In empiricist terms a science of psychology would only be possible if the individuals whose behaviour formed the subject matter of the science were incapable of becoming aware of the laws constituting the science. A visiting extra-terrestrial intelligence (to whom the laws did not apply) might succeed in developing such a science. As a genuine science of behaviour, behaviourism seems to be ruled out. (That is not of course to deny that in a particular case some aspects of an individual's behaviour may be governed by laws of which he is not aware. Psychotherapy may then be able to bring the laws into awareness where they can be overridden by the individual; behaviour therapy may be able, so to speak, to repeal the laws, with or without the conscious participation of the subject.)

In an empiricist intellectual framework we may have all the sciences except psychology much as they are at present. The majority of British and American philosophers were brought up to accept this framework, flourish in it, and have no desire to change it. Moreover there is no process of rational argument by which they could be compelled to do so. It seems eminently reasonable to rely on the evidence of one's senses, and if one so chooses there are at the least strict limits to what can be predicated of the ordinary man's external reality. The ordinary man's internal reality must however be accepted as it stands, and problems like the nature of consciousness and the grounds of human freedom become susceptible of discussion but not of solution. Attempts at solution usually end in what may be termed logically demonstrable incomprehensibilities. On the question of consciousness, for example, what is sometimes known as Australian materialism is a widely held view (e.g. Place, 1956). This asserts that states of consciousness are as a matter of fact identical with patterns of activity in the brain even though there is no logically necessary connection between such states and such patterns (many such patterns are not identical with any state of consciousness known to us). The overriding objection to this view is that the experience of consciousness is irreducibly different from the experience of any pattern of brain activity. My consciousness is of sights, sounds, smells, real or imaginary, and these are categorically different from patterns of brain activity. This argument is held by some philosophers to show the necessity of mind/body dualism, body being material and mind non-material. The philosopher is not troubled by the impossibility of understanding what the nature of a non-material substance might be, or how such a substance might be supposed to exchange information with material substance. A valid chain of argument requires the conclusion that this is the way things are. Scientists, however, tend to assume that if a chain of argument leads to a logically necessary incomprehensibility, it must contain a flaw. For them there can be no such thing as a necessary incomprehensibility. To admit such a possibility would be destructive of science itself.

Malcolm (1977) is a recent example of the philosopher's approach to a problem (memory) which also concerns many psychologists. In his book the author sets out to show that any theory holding that memory involves some kind (any kind) of representation of what is remembered or some kind (any kind) of neural 'trace' or storage mechanism is necessarily false. For a psychologist the question immediately arises 'What can Malcolm possibly be for, being against so much?' but this is a question that the philosopher is not bound to answer. If he has shown that it is logically impossible for an object to be both green and red simultaneously, there is simply no point in the Royal Society awarding a research grant to a man who proposes to look for one! A passage quoted with approval (p. 166) from

Wittgenstein indicates what Malcolm may be for: 'Why should there not be a psychological regularity to which no physiological regularity corresponds.'

In an empiricist intellectual framework there is no reason why not; since transcendental deduction to what may lie beyond our sense impressions is in any case ruled out as illegitimate speculation. It is doubtful whether Bhaskar is entitled to characterize this attitude as strictly *fallacious* but it must be remembered that it is not the only attitude that can be adopted. Shortly we shall proceed to consider the consequences of adopting other attitudes, but before doing so there are attempts to preserve a place for psychology in an empiricist framework which demand notice.

Rescue operations

Gauld and Shotter (1977) present an argument to show that accounts of human actions are not, even in principle, reducible to mechanistic terms; they do this by showing that a 'generalized machine' (in which by definition any mechanistic theory can be embodied in a program of finite length) cannot be programmed to behave as if it possessed the concepts, intentions and so forth characteristic of a human agent. Their proof is introduced by considering stimulus-neutral concepts (like 'honesty') where, since the instances exemplifying the concept may have no perceptual properties in common, there is no 'physically delimitable class of input classes' to which output can be linked and no program can be written. Gauld and Shotter go on to show that as much is true of concepts that are not stimulus-neutral, though a slightly more complex argument is required. The generalized machine in short contributes nothing of its own, its behaviour is entirely dependent on inputs, which are linked directly to outputs. It is widely accepted that a mechanistic psychology of this kind can provide no adequate account of human behaviour. I am not sure that Gauld and Shotter take us any farther than the general argument we have considered that while behaviour may be governed by 'laws' linking stimuli and responses, any individual who becomes aware of such a law may choose to override its effects as they apply to him. The argument formally rules out any purportedly scientific psychology that can be developed within an mechanist framework, but has no necessary application to a psychology developed in a different framework.

What Gauld and Shotter propose as an alternative is a non-mechanistic 'hermeneutical' psychology. Hermeneutics was originally a term in textual criticism meaning the effort to understand what an author meant by the words he used, by reference to the author's own characteristic ways of using language and the linguistic and other conventions applying in his time. Thus when Milton's shepherd 'tells his tale' it is to be understood that he is counting sheep not recounting an anecdote. More recently the term has been applied to a similar kind of effort to understand 'text-analogues'; in particular, sequences of behaviour. Psychology should, according to Gauld and Shotter, apply itself to understanding human behaviour by the application of hermeneutical analyses; the psychologist should in effect be a specialist in the practise of an activity undertaken more or less skilfully by every human being qua human being. It is not clear to what extent the individual is, for Gauld and Shotter, the final arbiter of the validity of a hermeneutical analysis of his behaviour; this may not be the case if, for example, he is mentally disturbed. There is a moral issue here which is in part avoided by placing main emphasis on the value of the technique for the investigation of patterns of mother/infant interaction.

While ruling out other kinds of psychological explanation, Gauld and Shotter do not rule out the possibility of a physiological explanation of human behaviour. The physiology, however, would have to be non-mechanistic in character. I am not clear what they think a non-mechanistic physiology would be like; it is however interesting that the authors are prepared to allow the possible reduction of psychology to physiology.

That psychology will never prosper without a proper theory, that the only possible 'proper theory' is physiological in nature, and that consequently adoption of a proper theory will destroy psychology, is the theme of Joynson's dilemma (Joynson, 1970). Harré (1971) tried to show how the dilemma could be resolved and his views are elaborated in Harré and Secord (1972) and Harré (1976). Harré holds that Joynson was wrong in supposing that psychology would ultimately disappear without trace. He distinguishes three levels of theory about the nature of science. At the level of positive empiricism only the actual observations ('impressions of sense') are allowed existential status. Science comprises the observed 'constant conjunctions' holding between these observations. This level is represented in psychology by Skinnerian behaviourism. At the level of empiricism proper, existential status may be allowed to a substrate of the actual observations as well as to the observations themselves. In the context of psychology the obvious substrate is physiological, leading directly to Joynson's dilemma. Harré however advocates a three-level concept of psychological science. There are observations, there is a substrate, but there are also intermediate theoretical entities. These form an indispensible bridge between substrate and observations. In psychology the substrate is physiological, the observations are of behaviour, the intermediate theoretical entities are mental states and access to them is available through the medium of language. Psychology has therefore scope for independent existence, taking as its object of study mental states made accessible by language. Harré subscribes to Australian materialism. Mental states are likely to be 'system features of the mode of organization of the nervous system'. He also explicitly allows the human being's capacity to become aware of laws governing his behaviour and to override such laws if he so decides, which he calls 'monitoring the monitoring of actions'.

Malcolm, as we have seen, allowed no possibility of either psychological or physiological understanding of the mental process. Gauld and Shotter allow hope for an eventual physiological understanding if and when a suitable non-mechanistic physiology is developed. Harré insists on an independent status for psychology. In his 1971 paper he seemed to be concerned with all aspects of behaviour but since then he has restricted himself to social behaviour, developing a discipline to which he has given the name 'ethogenics' in which 'that part of social action which is directed towards the creation, maintenance and orderly change of fragments of social order is conceived as fundamentally ritualistic, intelligible on a "liturgical" model and mediated by shared meanings' (Harré, 1976). It is not clear what status he now allows the rest of psychology. Within his own field of interest his reliance on ordinary language accounts as data is, if anything, more uncompromising than Gauld and Shotter's, who allow the possibility that the hermeneutical analysis of a behavioural text-analogue may yet be valid in face of the agent's denial.

There is an established tradition in philosophy of 'phenomenological analysis' in which the immediate data of consciousness are subjected to 'reductions' in order to uncover 'presuppositions' which may be subtly and secretly influencing them. There is evidence that this process of analysis can be at least partially successful and verbal accounts subsequent to such an analysis ought surely to be more valuable as data than immediate introspections. There is also a mass of empirical evidence that verbal reports of mental processes may be wildly inaccurate. Nisbett and DeCamp Wilson (1977) conclude that introspective reports are not usually based on any 'true introspection' but on *a priori* implicit causal theories, or on judgements about the extent to which a particular stimulus is a plausible cause of a given response. This evidence would seem to indicate that Harré's accounts might be perfectly self-consistent (if there is general agreement within the group on what 'implicit causal theories' are valid and what stimuli are 'plausible causes' of a given response) and yet misrepresent what is actually happening in the individual. Harré is of course correct in asserting that 'some statements are not a *sign* of a state of mind but themselves constitute that state of mind'. From such statements it is possible to deduce 'shared meanings' (i.e. implicit causal theories generally accepted in a given social group) but this activity seems more akin to social anthropology or sociology than to social *psychology*.

Alternative frameworks: Marxism

While no one has sole rights to the use of the term 'psychology' in a specific limited sense it seems clear that what Harré and Gauld and Shotter are concerned with is not psychology as it is commonly understood by most psychologists. The status of psychology as it is commonly understood remains in question and it appears that no favourable answer is likely within an empiricist framework. What alternative frameworks are there?

In the sense of the term we have employed there is a psychology implicit or explicit in every framework. Marxism is no exception. Since Marxism attributes all the negative aspects of human nature to distortions arising from the capitalist structure of society and holds that they will disappear in a genuinely socialist society, a view of human nature as wholly determined by social structure is implicit in it. Marx himself wrote 'It is not the consciousness of men that determines their being, on the contrary it is their social being that determines their consciousness.' Some Marxists (e.g. Gramsci) have asserted that 'there is no such thing as human nature' and a recent consideration of the Marxist attitude to psychology (Adlam et al., 1977) concludes that there can be no such thing as (Marxist) materialist psychology. 'It is an impossibility, a contradiction in terms' because the individual subject, the object of study in psychology, has no central place in the Marxist analysis. From the fact that the absolute plasticity of human nature is an essential pre-condition of the validity of the Marxist world-view, follows the need to oppose by all means any suggestion that, for example, general intelligence (a

necessary component of human nature) may be genetically determined, while being prepared to allow that particular mental abilities
(not, individually, necessary components of human nature) may be so
(Kamin, 1977). No final determination of this question will be possible
until a genuinely socialist society has been established. But it is
important to remember that whether or not human nature is wholly
determined by social structure is a matter of fact not stipulation.

The conclusion that there can be no such thing as Marxist
psychology has been seized upon eagerly by Marxist sociologists, but
as Adlam et al. (1977) point out 'A psychology that stresses man
cannot be countered, in the name of Marxism, with a sociology
that stresses society' because 'man' and 'society' are mutually defining.
This is not in any case the conclusion that was drawn in the USSR.
To see why not it is necessary to look briefly at the history of
Marxism in pre-revolutionary Russia. Lenin published *Materialism and
Empirio-Criticism*, his most important philosophical work, in 1909 as a
contribution to a debate within Russian Marxism. (Relevant extracts
from this book are reprinted in Marx et al., 1972) At that time a form
of positive empiricism known as 'empirio-criticism' in Central Europe
and associated with Mach and Avenarius had become influential, and
a strong body of Russian Marxists believed that it was possible to
reconcile this position with Marxism. Lenin disagreed. He held that
'materialism in general recognizes objectively real being [matter] as
independent of the consciousness, sensation, experience, etc. of
humanity. Historical materialism recognizes social being as independent of the social consciousness of humanity. In both cases
consciousness is only the reflection of being. At best an approximately
true [adequate, perfectly exact] reflection of it.' To deviate in the
slightest degree from this position was to fall prey to 'bourgeois
reactionary falsehood'.

Lenin makes quite clear his reasons for holding that the issue was
of vital importance. We earlier distinguished between Berkeleyan
idealism which holds that 'ideas' are the only existents (an ontological
position) and Humean empiricism (from which empirio-criticism
ultimately derives) which holds that 'impressions of sense' are the
form in which knowledge is available to us (an epistemological
position). It requires considerable subtlety of argument to distinguish
the ontological from the epistemological position and, for Lenin,
empirio-criticism simply opened the door to ontological idealism
which he regarded as absolutely incompatible with Marxist materialism, as indeed it is. Idealism allowed a place for religion and denied

historical determinism in the development of social structure. Nothing smacking of idealism could be tolerated however fashionable it might be.

The ritual denunciations of positivism which preface every account of so-called 'radical' psychology (e.g. Heather, 1976) may derive in part from this source, though the objection is in part also to positivist 'reification' (treating persons as things, as suitable objects of 'scientific' study). Holzkamp's 'critical emancipatory' psychology (Graumann, 1970) suggests that psychology should be concerned with 'the presuppositions, the implications and the consequences of the traditional research practice, enquiring into the social, economic and political dependencies of scientific psychology'. Holzkamp believes that at present psychology merely bolsters up the existing social and economic order. Kvale (1973) goes further, holding that the experimental paradigm in psychology derives directly from the exploitative capital/labour relationship and that the only purpose of experimental psychology is to accustom students to 'treat persons as things', which capitalism requires them to do!

Soviet psychology has not taken this line. It derives from two sources, one philosophical (Marxism/Leninism) and one physiological (principally the work of Seçenov, Bechterev and Pavlov). The latter source was monist, materialist but also mechanist in outlook (though Pavlov's work is currently regarded as materialist but not mechanist!). A form of mechanism analogous to behaviourism was in fact dominant in the USSR in the late 1920s, but because Marxism/Leninism had always emphasized the importance of 'consciousness', and mechanism (like behaviourism) had no place for consciousness, it was obliged to give way. This is the only case I know of where scientists were obliged to defer to a philosophical view regarded as authoritative, with useful results. In the West the same beneficial change did not come about in experimental psychology till the 1960s and has not yet achieved universal acceptance.

The insistence that psychology must be materialist but not mechanist led to the development of a sophisticated theory of human consciousness and activity deriving from Lenin, in which matter and consciousness become correlative terms. Consciousness is a reflection of matter, matter is what consciousness is consciousness of. Payne (1968) discusses in detail the work of the principal Russian theorist, S. L. Rubinsteyn (whose books have been translated into German but not into English). Rubinsteyn emphasizes psychophysical unity, the importance of individual and species development and educability,

but his main effort is directed towards explaining how psychological phenomena can be simultaneously 'reflections of material
reality' and physiological processes. As we have seen, Western
philosophers struggle with the same problem. Ivanova (1967–8)
reports a symposium on consciousness held in Moscow in 1966 which
was much concerned with the concept of 'goal' and how it could
be reconciled with Pavlovian theory. (This is by no means impossible
in the theory as it is interpreted, i.e. non-mechanistically, in the
USSR). Leontiev (1974–5) is also concerned with goals and emphasizes the necessity of avoiding the reduction of psychology to either
physiology or sociology, since psychology is concerned with 'activity'
and activity involves 'a reciprocal transformation between the subject/
object poles'.

Marxist psychology is represented in North America by the work of
Riegel and his associates (e.g. Riegel, 1976). It is known there as
'dialectical psychology' but makes no serious attempt to disguise its
affiliations. (Riegel, 1975, is a 'manifesto for dialectical psychology'
which echoes the Communist Manifesto of 1848!) Riegel's emphasis is
on the social embeddedness of activity, whether at the level of
mother/child interaction or later. His dialectic is neither materialist
nor idealist but methodological; he does not share the Russian
compulsion towards materialism and away from idealism. He was
perhaps not so much interested in the foundations of psychology
as in new and better ways of collecting developmental data.

Alternative frameworks: phenomenology

We have briefly outlined the psychologies implicit in empiricism and
in Marxism; phenomenology remains to be considered. Phenomenology has been concerned from the beginning with the nature of
conscious experience. Each conscious experience is regarded as having
a noetic aspect (the experience belongs to an 'ego') and a noematic
aspect (it is an experience of something; a 'cogitatum', an object of
awareness). The question of the real physical existence or non-
existence of objects of experience is initially put aside as unanswerable
(which is not, of course, the same thing as to answer it in the
negative).

Phenomenology, starting from conscious experience, can move in
either of two directions. By an inward movement it can seek to
uncover the presuppositions implicit in experience, the (unattainable)
ideal objective being complete presuppositionlessness. The data cited

in Nisbett and DeCamp Wilson (1977) come as no surprise to a phenomenologist, since he will have assumed that awareness is subject to distortion by implicit presuppositions (in Nisbett and DeCamp Wilson's terms, that we subscribe to 'implicit causal theories' which may or may not be true). The phenomenologist believes however that, by analysis of the conscious process, he can bring into awareness some at least of these presuppositions and thus discount their effects and come nearer to experiencing the 'things themselves', as they really are.

By an outward movement from conscious experience, transcendental phenomenology seeks to answer questions about what, if anything, lies beyond our conscious experience. Husserl (the first and most important of the phenomenologists) believed, towards the end of his career, that he could deduce a transcendental ego as the ultimate 'centre' of the individual's conscious experience and has consequently been accused of relapsing into absolute idealism. It would be possible in principle, to move towards a transcendental realism of the objects of which objects of experience are in some sense representations but this move has not so far as I know been made within phenomenology. In any case transcendental phenomenology has no direct relevance to psychology. It is the 'inward movement' with which psychologists are or should be concerned. Husserl's own views of the relationship between phenomenology and psychology are to be found in his *Encyclopaedia Britannica* article (Husserl, 1971), where he adopts as an expository device the idea of a progression from psychology considered as a natural science (which he calls *psychophysics*), to *phenomenological psychology* whose function is to establish the foundations in experience of psychophysics, to *transcendental phenomenology*. Analyses in phenomenological psychology (called in the phenomenologist's technical language 'reductions') can in principle reveal the structures that have to be explained by natural scientific psychology. For this purpose neither ordinary introspection nor the 'expert' introspection practised at the turn of the century by the Wurzburgers will do. The former reveals conscious processes tainted to an unknown degree by 'presuppositions'. The expertise involved in the latter is merely in placing conscious awarenesses in categories established on what phenomenologists regard as irrelevant *a priori* grounds.

Two lines of development have been followed in phenomenological psychology. One has been concerned with the elucidation of the structure of conscious experience as an end in itself and emphasizes description, leading to a kind of understanding that does not involve either precise prediction or control; that is, in short, an extension to the kind of understanding we all employ in our everyday dealings with each other. The resemblance to the psychologies advocated by Harré and Gauld and Shotter is obvious; though phenomenological psychology is, in my view, in the right in its insistence that verbal reports are not necessarily to be taken at face value. The close connection between this approach to phenomenological psychology and humanistic 'third-force' psychology is brought out by Giorgi (1970). He is at pains to point out that although humanistic psychology has its main strength in the area of clinical psychology and personality, it represents a possible approach to the whole of psychology; an approach which is not necessarily less scientific for trying to take account of the phenomenon of man as a whole. Giorgi (1976) and Rychlak (1976) share the desire to extend the range of acceptable theory and investigatory practice in psychology, with the object of constructing a genuinely human science. As Giorgi (1970) points out, the fundamental question is 'can the world view of the natural sciences comprehend fully and adequately the phenomenon of man as a person?' In principle, Giorgi is willing to accept either a 'yes' or a 'no' answer to this question. However, 'it seems [to Giorgi] that the bulk of the evidence both within and outside of psychology indicates a negative answer'.

The second line of development is less ambitious in scope and seeks (following Husserl) to bring the technique of phenomenological analysis to bear on natural science psychology as it has been brought to bear on the other sciences. Every psychologist is capable of functioning, has functioned as a subject in a psychological experiment. This makes it possible in principle for him to determine how a task is likely to appear to the subject. This type of analysis can be applied to existing psychological investigations but is better employed in advance to refine the investigatory process before the subject is approached. Thinès (1977) considers the relationship between phenomenology and natural science psychology from this point of view. (His book also includes much valuable material on the history of the relationship drawn from Continental sources that are largely inaccessible to British and American workers.) One of Husserl's main preoccupations was, as we have seen, with founding the sciences in experience. He believed that what he saw as the 'Crisis of the European Sciences' arose from a loss of contact between human conscious experience and the subject matter of science, that contact between the two ought as a matter of urgency to be restored, and that only phenomenological analysis could heal the breach. For reasons that Thinès considers at length the breach is more apparent in psychology than elsewhere, but it is not unique to psychology. He presents (p. 18) some basic propositions concerned with the fact that 'the subject matter of psychology differs fundamentally from that of the traditional scientific disciplines' and with the consequences that follow. He concludes (p. 153) that 'psychologists and other human scientists [now] appreciate better the relationship between epistemological analysis and the methodological requirements of their own discipline'. Let us hope he is right, for this would appear to be an essential precondition for any significant advance.

Psychology and transcendental realism

We earlier characterized the ordinary man's view of reality as a rationally indefensible simultaneous acceptance of free, conscious minds and determined, non-conscious matter, independent of minds. In an effort to achieve a view of reality that was rationally defensible the empiricists dropped the ordinary man's conception of matter while retaining his conception of mind.

Marxism insists on what it calls 'materialism' (which is close to the ordinary man's view of material reality) but vigorously opposes the ordinary man's view of mental reality as tending to 'idealism'. Marxism has therefore to offer its own account of 'freedom' and 'consciousness', to account for which the ordinary man postulates 'mind'. 'Freedom' poses no problem for the Marxist. The ordinary man's conception of freedom is based on 'false consciousness', the freedom is apparent not real. Real freedom is held to involve behaviour in accordance with the laws of historical materialism (the argument much resembles the theologians' argument for a God 'whose service is perfect freedom'). Consciousness is more difficult to deal with. Marx's use of the term obliged Soviet psychologists to incorporate it in a none the less materialist psychology and Rubinsteyn, Leontiev and others have made heroic efforts to do so, starting out from Lenin's conception of consciousness as reflection.

Phenomenology from the beginning took an independent line which ignored the idealist/materialist dichotomy. For phenomenology the question was, starting from the data of consciousness and bearing in mind that it may be unreliable: how may one maximize the reliability of the data and what may legitimately be concluded from it! Phenomenology could be represented as consistent with either idealism or materialism if it chose to take a stand on this metaphysical issue, though it seems to ally more naturally with the former.

Reference has already been made to Bhaskar (1975). He advocates what he calls 'transcendental realism'. In his view the empiricist attempt to treat laws of science as directly derived from 'constant conjunctions of impressions of sense', even as elaborated by Kant, ultimately fails. The possibility of experimental physical science demands the supposition that the laws of science apply to a reality existing independently of the scientist. The existence of a physical reality corresponding to our sense impressions and in some sense causally responsible for them is assumed by the ordinary man and by the physical scientist in his laboratory. It is important to remember that this assumption is denied by empiricism. Bhaskar's case is that although scientific knowledge once obtained can be presented in empiricist terms, empiricism can offer no account of how such knowledge is obtained. The possibility of establishing a natural law by means of a scientific investigation depends on there being a real, independent, law-governed structure which is the object of the investigation. The structure is real because it exists independently of us as observers and transcendental in the sense that its existence is 'on the other side of' our sense impressions.

Bhaskar has little to say of psychology. For him, experimental activity is at the very least 'devoid of the same significance in psychology as it possesses in chemistry and physics'. The problem is to devise a procedure of 'enquiry and selectively empirical confirmation [and falsification]' analogous to experimental activity in natural (i.e. physical) science. The only suggestion he has to offer is reliance on the 'agent's capacity to give a commentary on intentional action'. Bhaskar's characterization of psychology seems to me inadequate. His concept of transcendental realism is, however, potentially much more important for the psychologist than for any other variety of natural scientist. If Bhaskar had grappled with the problem of psychology he would have had to specify his conception of mind. What he says is consistent with full-blown dualist interactionism but it can also be given a monist interpretation and, in a monist interpretation, transcendental realism is close to Marxist materialism, consistent with a version of phenomenology and echoes (and owes something to) Polanyi (Polanyi, 1966).[1]

In psychology, this version of transcendental realism implies that the object of study is a real existent structure, as in the other natural sciences. However, the structure with which psychology is concerned has a special characteristic: it has the capacity to model other structures with a view to predicting their future states (the advent of programmable computers has made this idea widely acceptable). Empiricism can make nothing of such a structure, since there will be no 'constant conjunctions of impressions of sense' from which to derive laws except what the organism embodying the structure chooses to present. Empiricist psychology has in fact spent its time 'persuading' human and other organisms to adopt a consistent model in the laboratory and pretended that the laws derived resemble those derived in the other sciences; in fact the constant conjunctions observed were contingent on the decision of the organism to cooperate, made freely or as a consequence of *force majeure*! The reality in psychology is more complicated. The object of investigation is a model-making structure. The models it makes are the business of philosophy, social anthropology, sociology, etc., and of everyday life, not of psychology. (The structure may in principle be reducible to neurophysiology but its complexity and inner interrelatedness is such as to preclude elucidation by any neurophysiological technique at present conceivable.)

Since the object of study in psychology is a model-making structure like the experimenter himself, the variety of data potentially available is literally infinite. Any model an experimenter can hypothesize, a subject can detect in the experimental task and conform to if he chooses. In physical science, if the experimenter asks questions based on a false model he may be unlucky and get what appears to be support for his model but more likely he will get no interpretable result at all (as the alchemists found). The latter eventuality is very much less likely to arise in psychology simply because the object of study makes models for itself (can operate in no other way at the psychological level), instead of merely exemplifying a model. In trying to model the model-making structure, the psychologist has to employ a form of phenomenological analysis to establish what the task is from the subject's point of view and what light if any his performance on the task can throw on the nature of the model-making structure. He has also to make his hypotheses consistent with what is known of the neurophysiological substrate in which the structure is embodied. The greatest obstacle to progress in psychology is the ease with which data of great variety and interest may be collected by investigating the models made by the structure, instead of the structure itself.

Kelly's (1963) theory of constructive alternativism is the only psychological theory that shows any real grasp of what is required, though it is inadequately developed and applied only to personality formation. Kelly could in my opinion have been convinced that he was a transcendental realist at heart, though that is not what he says he is. He characterizes man as 'man the scientist' in his everyday life interactions and Bhaskar's arguments, directed to 'man the scientist' in the laboratory, apply *pari passu*.

My conclusion is that in the general intellectual framework of transcendental realism psychology can aspire to the status of a science like other sciences. Every science has special characteristics of its own determined by the nature of its object of study and this will certainly be true of psychology because its object of study is infinitely more complex than that of any other science. The important point is that psychology requires no special pleading. It may hope to discover laws governing the structure exhibited by its objects of study as other sciences do. These laws will have nothing to do with the prediction and control of behaviour because they will not be about behaviour. They will be about the model-making structure, whereas behaviour depends on the models that the model-making structure makes, which in turn depend on the selection the individual organism makes and made in the past among items of potential information impinging on its sense receptors (i.e. on its experience).

In order to justify their claim to be scientists some psychologists have felt obliged to assert that they could or would in due course be able to predict and control behaviour. This assertion is, as we have seen, false. The exercise of such a capacity would be morally indefensible if it were possible, but fortunately the question does not arise. In revulsion against 'prediction and control' it has however, recently become fashionable to claim that the psychologist is somehow specially expert at doing the kind of thing that human beings do qua human being. This claim seems to me to be as indefensible as the other. Neither is entailed or justified by the claim to be a scientific psychologist.

It may be accepted that different assumptions will lead some individuals to conclude (legitimately) for a more restricted framework than transcendental realism; empiricism, Marxism, phenomenology, etc. Occasionally such an assumption may be demonstrably false (eliminating, for example, behaviourism). In other cases (e.g. assumptions leading to an empiricism which asserts that no science of psychology is possible) attention may be drawn to the implications these assumptions have for the other sciences as well as psychology, which may or may not be acceptable. The assumptions of transcendental realism have fewer unpalatable implications and lead to a framework of greater generality. In such a framework scientific psychology has a secure place, not as yet earned by any substantial body of results it has obtained. Many of the activities now practised under the name of psychology also remain legitimate. All that need be contested is their several claims to unique and self-evident validity and their denial of validity to natural scientific psychology.

A transcendental realist psychology retains the ordinary man's external reality (matter) but denies his internal reality (mind). My own feeling is that the ordinary man is unhappy about the non-material aspects of mind and would willingly sacrifice them if he thought a satisfactory account could be offered of freedom and consciousness without them. The possibility of such an account seems to me to exist. In the case of freedom the argument has been developed largely by Mackay (e.g. 1967, 1973). Mackay's argument is complex; broadly it asserts that even though all human choices are part of a causal 'chainmesh of events', the agent is nevertheless correct in his belief that at the time of making his decision it is in no sense determined – though it is not uncaused either. It is not determined (from the point of view of the agent or anybody else) because there is no 'unalterably fixed specification of the future which is already true'. If the agent were presented with what purported to be such a specification he could, if he chose, falsify it by his decision; there can therefore be no such specification. His decision is not uncaused (the purported specification may become part of the cause) but it is undetermined. To be free to decide on the basis of what seem to the decider to be factors relevant to the decision is to be as free as it is possible to be. The decision is none the less part of the causal 'chainmesh of events'.

The argument on consciousness is due to Globus (1973). The problem here is that so-called 'Australian' materialism does not go far enough. The argument that a state of consciousness may be contingently identical with a process in the brain, while acceptable, offers no explanation of the crude 'feel' of consciousness – which is not at all like 'electro-chemical activity in a set of neurons'. Globus's argument is that a pattern of activity in a set of neurons which form part of the organism which constitutes me (and thus constitutes a state of consciousness for me) will have been triggered by an event at the 'transformation boundary' constituted by my sense receptors. If I wish to experience the pattern of neural activity as 'electro-chemical activity in a set of neurons' I have to arrange for the activity to impinge on my sense receptors in that form (by the use of some kind of 'autocerebroscope') and the pattern then constitutes a triggering event for another 'pattern of activity/state of consciousness'. The feeling of discontinuity between 'consciousness' and 'brain process' arises from the change of stance involved and is not therefore an argument for dualism. One would expect a pattern of activity in the brain of an organism that has not qua pattern crossed the transformation boundary of that organism to 'feel' different from a pattern that has, and that different 'feel' is consciousness.

The adoption of a transcendental realist frame of reference will do no more than bring psychology into line with what has always been the practice of the other sciences. Psychology got off on the wrong foot by trying to do what philosophers *said* was done in science. Books on physics, chemistry, biology, etc. do not contain statements about sequences of sense impressions which happen to present themselves to us in that order (after Hume), nor do they contain theories designed only to relate sense impressions to each other in the order in which they regularly appear (after Kant). They contain theories, more or less well established, about real, law-governed structures which are held to be causally responsible for our sense impressions; theories which are generated by acts of imaginative modelling and tested by setting up situations in which an entailed sense impression may or may not be experienced.

In the case of psychology the act of imaginative modelling has to take account of the fact that the structure to be modelled has the capacity to model other structures. Other sciences contend only with objects of study that exemplify a structure and challenge the investigator to find it out; the task of the psychologist is more difficult because his only access to the structure to be modelled is via the models that exemplars of that structure make, as a basis for their behaviour in the world. The task would be impossibly difficult were it not for the fact that each of us *is* an exemplar of the structure that the psychologist seeks to elucidate, and can communicate (via language) with other exemplars. Psychologists already know more than enough about experimental method, they need now to learn how to use their status as objects of study of their own science to enable them to design relevant experiments.

Note

1 In *Behind the Mirror* (London: Methuen, 1977) Lorenz advocates what he calls 'hypothetical realism'. His use of the term 'hypothetical' is unfortunate

since 'hypothetical' tends, in English, to mean something like 'imaginary', making 'hypothetical realism' look like a self-contradiction. What Lorenz intends by 'hypothetical realism' appears to be closely parallel to what I have called 'transcendental realism'; see, for example, his assumption (p. 1) 'that all human knowledge derives from a process of interaction between man as a physical entity, an active, perceiving subject, and the realities of an equally physical external world, the object of man's perception' and his rejection (p. 9) of the Kantian *a priori*.

References

Adlam, D., Henriques, J., Rose, N., Salfield, A., Venn, C. and Walkerdine, V. (1977) Psychology, ideology and the human subject. *Ideology and Consciousness 1*: 5–56.

Bannister, D. (1977) On the absurdity of being a psychologist. *Bulletin of the British Psychological Society 30*: 211.

Bhaskar, R. (1975) *A Realist Theory of Science*. Leeds: Leeds Books.

Cole, J. K. and Arnold, W. J. (eds) (1976) *Conceptual Foundations of Psychology*. Nebraska Symposium on Motivation, 1975. Lincoln/London: University of Nebraska Press.

Gauld, A. and Shotter, J. (1977) *Human Action and its Psychological Investigation*. London: Routledge and Kegan Paul.

Giorgi, A. (1970) *Psychology as a Human Science*. New York: Harper and Row.

Giorgi, A. (1976) Phenomenology and the foundations of psychology. In *Cole and Arnold*.

Globus, G. G. (1973) Unexpected symmetries in the world knot. *Science 180* (4091): 1129–36.

Graumann, C. F. (1970) Conflicting and convergent trends in psychological theory. *Journal of Phenomenological Psychology 1*: 51–61.

Harré, R. (1971) Joynson's dilemma. *Bulletin of the British Psychological Society 24* (83): 115–19.

Harré, R. (ed.) (1976) *Life Sentences*. London: John Wiley and Sons.

Harré, R. and Secord, P. F. (1972) *The Explanation of Social Behaviour*. Oxford: Basil Blackwell.

Heather, N. (1976) *Radical Perspectives in Psychology*. London: Methuen.

Husserl, E. (1971) 'Phenomenology', Edmund Husserl's article for the *Encyclopaedia Britannica*; a new complete translation by R. E. Palmer, *Journal of the British Society for Phenomenology 2*: 77–90.

Ivanova, I. I. (1967–8) Symposium on Consciousness (Moscow, 1966). *Soviet Psychology 6*: 57–60.

Joynson, R. B. (1970) The breakdown of modern psychology. *Bulletin of the British Psychological Society 23* (81): 261–9.

Kamin, L. J. (1977) *The Science and Politics of I.Q.* Harmondsworth: Penguin Books. (First published by Lawrence Erlbaum Associates, 1974.)

Kelly, G. A. (1963) *A Theory of Personality*. New York: W. W. Norton.

Koch, S. (1976) Language communities, search cells and the psychological studies. In *Cole and Arnold*.

Kvale, S. (1973) The technological paradigm of psychological research. *Journal of Phenomenological Psychology 3*: 143–59.

Leontiev, A. N. (1974–5) The problem of activity in psychology. *Soviet Psychology 13*: 4–33.

Mackay, D. M. (1967) *Freedom of Action in a Mechanistic Universe*, Eddington Memorial Lecture. Cambridge: Cambridge University Press.

Mackay, D. M. (1973) The logical indeterminateness of human choices. *British Journal for the Philosophy of Science 24*: 405–8.

Malcolm, N. (1977) *Memory and Mind*. New York: Cornell University Press.

Marx, K., Engels, F. and Lenin, V. (1972) *On Historical Materialism*. Moscow: Progress Publishers.

Nisbett, R. E. and DeCamp Wilson, T. (1977) Telling more than we can know; verbal reports on mental processes. *Psychological Review 84*: 231–59.

Payne, T. R. (1968) *S. L. Rubinsteyn and the Philosophical Foundations of Soviet Psychology*. Dordrecht: D. Reidel.

Place, U. T. (1956) Is consciousness a brain process? *British Journal of Psychology 47*: 44–51.

Polanyi, M. (1966) *The Tacit Dimension*. London: Routledge and Kegan Paul.

Riegel, K. F. (1975) A manifesto for dialectical psychology. In K. F. Riegel (ed.) *The Development of Dialectical Operations*. Basle: S. Karger.

Riegel, K. F. (1976) From traits and equilibrium towards developmental dialectics. In *Cole and Arnold*.

Royce, J. R. (1976) Psychology is multi-: methodological, variate, epistemic, world-view, systemic, paradigmatic, theoretic and disciplinary. In *Cole and Arnold*.

Rychlak, J. F. (1976) Psychological science as a humanist views it. In *Cole and Arnold*.

Thinès, G. (1977) *Phenomenology and the Science of Behaviour*. London: George Allen and Unwin.

Watson, J. B. (1913) Psychology as the behaviorist views it. *Psychological Review 20*: 158–77.

6 The computational metaphor in psychology

Margaret A. Boden

Introduction

The past twenty years have seen an increasing use of computational concepts in theoretical psychology, and of computer programs as models of psychological processes. This has happened most noticeably within cognitive psychology, but social, dynamic and psychopathological issues have been addressed in these terms also. The seminal book *Plans and the Structure of Behavior*[1] introduced programming analogies into discussion of a wide range of psychological topics, and professionals within psychology and artificial intelligence (AI) have since then explored such analogies in increasing detail.[2] The philosophy of mind, too, has seen growing use[3] – and concomitant criticism[4] – of the computational metaphor.

The computational metaphor can aid in the generation and the rigorous formulation and testing of psychological hypotheses about the mind's contents and functions. These hypotheses form part of a distinctive theoretical approach that takes account of the complex structures and interacting processes that make thought and action possible. From the philosophical point of view, computational insights enable us to understand how it is possible for the immaterial mind and the material body to be closely related, and in particular how it is possible for the mind to act on the body during purposive action and voluntary choice. The nature of human subjectivity (the idio-syncratic interpretation of the individual's experiential world) also is illuminated by this approach.

Clearly, then, it is a mistake to regard the computational metaphor as essentially 'dehumanizing'. A psychology that looks to machines for some of its central concepts need not be crudely mechanistic in character, nor inhumanly reductionist in type. On the contrary, the computational approach to psychology stresses (and helps explain) important features of the human mind, such as purpose and sub-jectivity, which many psychological theories have ignored – or even denied.

The computational metaphor and scientific explanation

Someone employing the computational metaphor for the mind uses the concepts and insights of computer science and artificial intelligence in describing and explaining psychological phenomena. The mind is seen as an information-processing or symbol-manipulating system, and the psychologist's task is to clarify the content, structure, trans-formation and use of the person's (or the animal's) mental representa-tions of the world. In general, the theoretical emphasis is on mental *processes*; this of course does not exclude reference to mental structures (such as conceptual systems, for example), but the theorist tries to specify what processes build or transform a given structure, and what (inferential) processes can have access to the structure so making use of the knowledge stored in it. The concepts of artificial intelligence (the science of making machines do things that would require intelligence if done by people) are helpful in this regard since they are concerned with these very questions. Within artificial intelligence, such questions are asked in relation to a programmed system (a computer program) wherein every item of information and every process for manipulating that information can be rigorously specified.

The many computational concepts that may usefully be applied to natural psychological phenomena as well as to artificial information-processing systems include the following: subroutine; bug; recursive procedure; hierarchical organization; heterarchical control; compiler and interpreter programs; top-down and bottom-up processing; depth-first and breadth-first search; locally and globally bound variables; cue and schema; demon; antecedent and consequent theorems; iteration; mini-mixing; plan; linear and parallel processing;

procedural v. declarative representation of knowledge; content-addressable memory.

A proponent of the computational metaphor need not claim (though many would) that *all* psychological phenomena can in principle be fruitfully discussed in such terms as these. Nor need such a person believe (though many do) that actually writing computer programs to simulate psychological processes – or, better, to model psychological theories – is the best way of employing the computational metaphor in psychology. Least of all need such a person assert that complete simulation of all human knowledge and abilities will ever in practice be achieved. This would be equivalent to saying that one day some psychological theory will exist that accounts for every least detail of someone's knowledge, action and experience. (One might well doubt whether biochemistry will ever be able to explain *all* the metabolic processes occurring within the human body – but it does not follow that biochemistry has nothing of significance to say about these processes.)

The use of metaphors is widespread in scientific theorizing. Examples include Harvey's hydraulic metaphor for the circulation of the blood, Rutherford's planetary metaphor for the atom, and the Sherringtonian 'telephone exchange' metaphor for the central nervous system. In all such cases, the metaphor provides an interlinked set of familiar concepts that bear some analogy to the phenomena requiring explanation. In exploring this analogy, the theorist is led to discover new phenomena, or newly noticed features of known phenomena, which are intelligible in so far as they can be assimilated to the more familiar pole of the analogy.

Every metaphor or analogy has its limits, and the scientist should ideally know what these are. But it is not always possible to predict – or even sensible to ask – what these limits are at the early stages of employment of a theoretical metaphor in science. The planetary and telephone exchange metaphors just mentioned, for instance, are now known to be misleading in important ways; but this knowledge has been gained only by way of the physical and neurophysiological investigations guided by these seminal metaphors. To have hoped to show their limitations before extensive exploration of their implications would not have been sensible. At most, various possible limitations might have been suggested (Sherrington himself suggested some) which later studies might confirm as significant.

In this chapter, then, I shall not discuss the question of what (if anything) no computer, in principle, could ever do. It will be enough for my purposes that they can already do some things that are sufficiently similar to human mental processes to make them useful as theoretical analogies of the mind. Doubtless they will be able to do more such things in future: *how many* more is uncertain, and both the theoretical psychologist and the 'pure' philosopher would be wise to leave this question open pending fuller experience with AI systems than anyone has at present. Suffice it to say that programs already exist that can do things – or, at the very least, appear to be beginning to do things – which ill-informed critics have asserted *a priori* to be impossible. Examples include: perceiving in a holistic as opposed to an atomistic manner; using language creatively; translating sensibly from one language to another by way of a language-neutral semantic representation; planning action in a broad and sketchy fashion, the details being decided only in execution; distinguishing between different species of emotional reaction according to the psychological context of the subject.

Nor does use of the computational metaphor commit one to saying (though some proponents would be happy to do so) that psychological terms may in principle be applied *literally* to any current or future AI program. You probably noticed that the list of 'computational' concepts given earlier included seemingly psychological items such as *control, search, cue, plan* and *memory*; and many other everyday psychological words are commonly used in describing programs. There are two reasons why one might feel bound to admit that all psychological terms applied to programs are being used in an analogical rather than a literal sense. First (and incontrovertible), the computational abilities of existing programs are puny as compared with those of the human mind, so that even words like 'deduce' and 'infer' – never mind 'know' and 'want' – are not used with the full range of implications implicit in their ordinary meaning. Second (and philosophically more controversial), it is often claimed that the possession of intrinsic interests – that is, interests whose existence cannot be explained by reference to the purposes of some other individual or agent – is essential to any creature that can merit the literal application of psychological terms, and that no imaginable computer program could possibly possess such interests. On such a view, terms like 'intelligent' (or even 'stupid') could never be applied in their full sense to any program, no matter how impressive its 'thinking' abilities.

But from the theoretical psychologist's point of view, the important point is that one may reasonably make use of words like 'plan', 'goal', 'represent', 'reason', 'deduce', 'ask', 'infer', 'choose', ... and so on, in describing what programs do and how they manage to do it. Provided that these words are selected carefully, bearing in mind the precise functional details of the program concerned, their use is justified in that it leads to fruitful theoretical insights into and questions about how analogous processes might be carried out in the human case.

The use of psychological words in computational contexts even aids development of the programs themselves, for it highlights not only similarities but also differences between program and person that suggest dimensions along which the program's thinking could be improved. In other words, the psychological metaphor is useful to the study of computation much as the computational metaphor is helpful in the study of psychology. For instance, use of the word 'belief' for data-items in a program's data-base readily suggests – which the more technical 'data-item' does not – that one consider how one might provide the program with various degrees, or strengths, of belief; how one might allow for the program to recognize and correct its false beliefs; how the program should be enabled to generalize and make use of its beliefs; how it might suit the program, for certain purposes, to hold specific (perhaps erroneous) beliefs; and how one could represent the evidential relations between this and other items that might be thought to be relevant to the item in question. It is no accident that to label a sentence a 'data-item' makes it sound less interesting than if one were to label it a 'belief'. In general, sterile technical terms synthesized in the laboratory may be less heuristically useful to the scientist than a borrowed vocabulary that is already richly infected with implicit logical relations.

The technical vocabulary, however, has its own advantages, of which the chief are non-ambiguity and precision. In addition, if computational concepts can be embodied in a functioning computer program that can be run on a machine, then one *knows* that the programmed theory in question is sufficiently powerful to generate the performance evinced by the machine. Since the meaning of ordinary language terms – and also the technical terms of 'verbal' psychologies – is largely implicit rather than fully explicit, it is not usually clear just which phenomena they cover and which they do not. (What *is* cognitive dissonance, or denial, or frustration, or aggression, or ...?) The explanatory power of verbally expressed theories is thus intuitively sensed rather than rigorously articulated, and there is considerable room for disagreement over whether or not a given theory explains a certain phenomenon, let alone whether some other theory might not explain it better.

The comparative assessment or validation of psychological theories, as of any scientific theory, requires more than clear expression of the theories: it requires their testing by being matched against empirical facts. Since most of what goes on during thinking is neither introspected nor even introspectible, this matching necessarily has to be indirect. Rather than thinking of it as a testing of the *predictions* made by a programmed theory, one should think of this matching as a testing of the range of observed phenomena against the range of phenomena whose descriptions can be generated by the theory. The theory expresses and integrates a range of possibilities, and makes them intelligible in so far as it explains how they may be generated within the mind. To the extent that observed phenomena fall within that range, they are explicable in terms of the theory. But it does not follow that the theory can (or should attempt to) predict precisely *which* possibilities will be realized on a particular occasion. Analogously, one might say of Freudian interpretative theory that it shows how it is possible for someone to dream of a crumpled giraffe as a symbolic representation of the person's mother, even if it can neither predict that a specific child will experience this manifest dream-content next Saturday night nor prove (when he does) that the relevant latent dream-content is in fact 'mother'. In short, testing the explanatory power of a theory is not the same thing as testing its predictive power, positivist philosophies of science to the contrary. (Even non-psychological sciences may employ non-predictive explanatory theories, as the example of evolutionary theory in biology shows.)

The question whether one or another putative explanation is *the* (or *the best*) explanation of something is even more difficult than the question whether it *might* be the explanation. With respect to theories expressed as programs, it boils down to the question whether a human performance that is simulated by a program is carried out in our minds *in the same way*. This is not an all-or-none question, since two systems may think in the same way when their thought is represented at one level of detail, but in different ways when it is described at another level. Some of the functional levels involved in playing chess, for instance, may be common to all players of good chess (whether programs or people), whereas others may differ as between people and programs or even between one program and another. One must specify the aspect of thought concerned before one can ask whether the thinking is done in the same way; and for this specification one will require computational concepts that distinguish carefully between different aspects of the use, content and organization of thought.

Some workers have tried to write programs simulating human behaviour to a fair degree of detail. For example, their programs simulating cryptarithmetic problem-solving,[5] or young children's seriation behaviour,[6] predict the order of steps (and the nature of mistakes) taken by the human subject in the situation concerned. Such workers typically pay attention to detailed experimental evidence, and often generate more such evidence themselves. Assessing the importance of a match or mismatch between program and human performance, however, is not a straightforward matter. For instance, the programmer may attempt to incorporate processes modelling the person's 'protocols', or thinking aloud, while doing the task assigned. Suppose a certain program-process has no equivalent protocol: given that not all the significant thinking processes going on in the human mind are going to be introspected – or introspectible – one cannot hastily assume that the process is a mere programming artefact. Conversely, suppose the human's protocol differs radically from the program-process (the person might even say 'I didn't do it *like that!*'): since these protocols themselves (which are not normally produced outside the experimental situation) may involve a large element of rationalization, of unwittingly but misleadingly saying what the person's implicit theory of mind suggests *must* have been happening, they cannot be accepted at face value. There is long-standing evidence within cognitive psychology showing that people do not necessarily know how it is that they are managing to think (perceive, reason, remember ...) on any given occasion.

Other workers regard it as premature to attempt a detailed matching with human performance, and unnecessary to generate new programmes of experimental investigation. For many visual, reasoning or language-understanding programs, for example, quite clearly cannot do many things which people can do; no further experimentation is needed to show this. Such experimentation will only be needed when the programs concerned are powerful enough to give a close approximation to human behaviour, so close as to make discriminatory experimental tests appropriate. As has been pointed out with respect to the experimental psychology of vision,[7] psychologists as yet have no clear idea of how most of the things we do (or the things that animals do) might or could be done, so there is no question of picking and choosing between different programs all capable of doing them. Rather, computational concepts and programmed models should be used to highlight the lacunae in current theories, and help formulate others more nearly adequate to the task of explaining mental processes.

Largely because of the non-introspectible nature of many thought-processes, methodological problems of validation will of course remain. But these plague the 'verbal' psychologist no less than his computational colleague – and some of them are common to the scientific enterprise in general, not just to psychological enquiries. Critics of the computational approach should take care to distinguish methodological difficulties specifically associated with computational theorizing from difficulties inherent in any psychological, or even scientific, investigation.

People, programs and positivism

The positivist approach to psychology, characterized by stimulus-response and physiological theories of animal and human behaviour, is criticized elsewhere in this book. I shall not repeat those criticisms, but shall show that, contrary to common belief, the computational approach is itself radically antipositivist in nature.

A central characteristic of positivism is its incapability of expressing subjectivity, its avoidance of concepts incorporating the distinction between the psychological subject and the object of thought. These concepts are termed 'intentional' concepts, and only they can express the meaning attributed to the world by a mind, as opposed to the intrinsic features of the world considered independently of any inter-pretation or representation of it. All the psychological terms of ordinary language – and of non-positivist psychologies – are inten-tional (as is the concept of *representation* itself). Antipositivists regard such concepts as indispensable in any adequate psychology, and as irreducible to behaviourist or physiological terms.

Psychologists who employ intentional concepts in their theories include many groups, from the cognitive psychologists (who in general have some sympathy with the computational approach), through ethogenic and ethnomethodological groups within social psychology (who tend to ignore computational methodologies), to self-styled 'humanists' within clinical and personality theory (who often criticize 'mechanistic' models of man in general, and have no patience for the AI context of theorizing in particular). Despite their many differences, these psychologists agree that thought and behaviour must be conceptualized as meaningful action on the part of a subjective agent rather than as causal process in the natural world.

This concern with semantic rather than causal issues, with hermeneutic interpretation rather than objective process and prediction, is shared by workers in AI and by psychologists making use of the computational metaphor. To study representations (whether in natural or artificial systems) is to concern oneself with intentional matters, with the way in which meanings are constructed, organized, transformed and utilized by the system in question. And to explain the performance of their machines, AI workers need to specify the information-processing or symbol-manipulating properties of the program (which might have been very different in an alternative program running on the same physical machine).

For example, many scene analysis programs exist[8] which can interpret Figure 6.1 as a picture of a scene containing a cube – and some programs[9] can similarly interpret Figure 6.2. But there is an important sense in which these programs see different things in the pictures or, in other words, *see different pictures.* For some, these pictures contain lines and regions, for others lines and vertices; some see Figure 6.2 as consisting of a greater number of lines than do others; while only some programs are capable of seeing Figure 6.2 'meaningfully' as a solid object at all, instead of regarding it as an insignificant muddle of lines. These differences arise because the details of the interpretative process differ from one program to another, so that one and the same picture is 'experienced' in different ways.

In general, the interpretative process relates picture and scene (the representational and the target domains) by way of a conceptual schema embodying the system's knowledge of the 'mapping' relation between them. This procedure requires an analysis or structural description of the picture in terms that are relevant to the particular representational system, or theory of mapping, concerned. That is, the 'parts' of the picture must be *cues* that relate to the target domain in ways defined by the inner conceptual scheme. It follows that 'parts' (like 'cues') is a subjective, or intentional, notion and is not equivalent to purely physical features of the picture. (A microscopic examination of these two pictures would not show the straight lines we see, but much more complex and messy structures: even the lines are not objectively there *as lines*, and have to be interpreted by the observer.) From a strictly objective point of view, a picture just *is* marks on

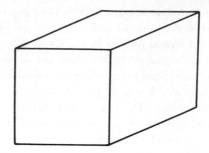

Fig. 6.1

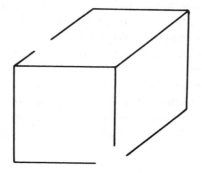

Fig. 6.2

paper – and wholly meaningless, or uninformative, to boot. From a subjective (interpretative) point of view, however, it may or may not contain lines, or coloured regions, or angles of various sorts.

If the conceptual models of solid objects that are used by a visual system (whether program or person) in recognizing objects include no reference to colour, no way of mapping colour onto the objects concerned, then a colour photograph of them has *no* coloured parts *from the point of view of the object-recognizing section of the system,* even though other subsections may already have seen it as coloured. Similarly, sentences contain *no* grammatical parts, such as noun phrases, for systems (programs, babies or chimps) having no knowledge of syntax. Again, the behaviour of people in an alien culture will appear meaning*less* to an observer in so far as he does not share their implicit and explicit knowledge of the rules structuring the behaviour; and a neurotic's obsessional actions may equally seem meaningless to someone unable – or unwilling – to posit a set of mental schemata that could generate and so account for the neurotic 'symptoms'.

There are indefinitely many representational schemata one might employ in making sense, of one sort or another, out of a phenomenon. But any such interpretative schema requires an analysis of the phenomenon into the parts that it takes to be significant, and different questions may require reference to different parts, or cues. Whatever the specific details the parts of a picture – as of a sentence, or of any human action – are subjectively projected onto the picture (taking due account of the physical input provided to the eyes, or to the TV camera used by a program) rather than found objectively in it. Cues thus have to be defined intentionally, by reference to the method of representation assumed in the interpretative schema. It follows that *cue* is a concept that cannot occur within a strictly positivist psychology, and that cannot be straightforwardly identified with the behaviourist's *stimulus*.

Psychologists investigating animal and human, individual and social, or normal and pathological psychology have discovered many of the cues we take to be salient, many of the concepts we use in interpreting our world and acting accordingly. But they have in general been less successful in specifying how these cues are used, how these concepts are accessed and employed in everyday thinking. Even theorists who make some attempt to ask about the function of memory as well as its structure (for instance, Bartlett, Freud and Piaget) leave most of these questions unasked, and still more unanswered. They rely on intuitive inferences suggesting that such and such a thought process is possible (taking a policeman to be an analogue of one's father, for example), while saying very little, if anything, about just how this process is effected.

By contrast, theorizing in a programming mode forces the theorist to specify, not merely that a particular cue-schema pair is activated in a given psychological context, but how the cue is identified as such, how the potentially relevant schemata are accessed by it, how the most appropriate of these is identified in face of the essential ambiguity of the cue, and how the conceptual schema is used to mediate 'appropriate' thought and action. Many of the admittedly vague Gestalt notions, for example (such as the whole's being greater than the sum of its parts) can be more clearly (and more richly) formulated in computational terms. Programs already exist with an ability to pass from bottom-up to top-down processing and back again in the

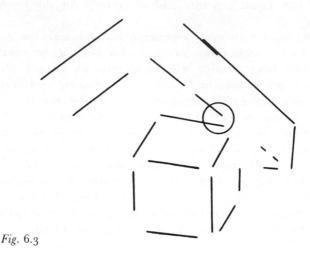

Fig. 6.3

interpretation of highly ambiguous material, which are well suited to illuminating the sort of epistemological 'chicken or egg?' phenomena highlighted by the Gestalt psychologists.

For example, a program which uses light-intensity gradients to construct line drawings on the basis of its input grey-scale TV picture may construct the lines shown in Figure 6.3. In trying to interpret this line drawing, it may first come across the two lines circled in Figure 6.3, and, quite reasonably, provisionally decide that they represent part of a corner of a wedge. On following these lines leftwards through the picture, it will even find some confirmatory evidence for this hypothesis. However, on consideration of the group of nine lines at the bottom-right of Figure 6.3 it will decide (as you doubtless do also) that these represent the sides of a cube. It follows that the two circled lines do not constitute a genuine vertex (or corner-image) at all – a conclusion that can be confirmed by noticing the two tiny little marks representing the continuation of the upper circled line. Further confirmation can be attained if the program accordingly directs its line-finder to look again at the original TV input, adjusting the physical parameters of its light-intensity measures so that the expected lines and corners are 'filled in' by faint evidence that was previously not noticed. This resolution of ambiguity is effected by the program's sensible alternation between examination of low-level details and interpretation by way of higher-level schemata: cube and wedge are high-level with respect to line and vertex, which are each high-level with respect to the grey-scale image that is actually input to the program's visual sensors. In much the same way, one and the same curve may 'be' a nose or a chin in an ambiguous (old-young woman) picture of the type studied by the Gestalt psychologists.[10]

It should be clear from these examples that a computational model of man is radically antipositivist, in that it not only has a place for subjectivity but gives intentional concepts pride of place in its theoretical lexicon. Explaining why one program sees Figure 6.2 as a cube, whereas another (untroubled by Figure 6.1) does not, necessitates appeal to the representations and interpretative processes specified by the programs involved. To be sure, in order to function at all the program has to be run on (embodied in) a physical machine. But the important point is that the electronic 'physiology' of the computer is not a prime concern of the AI worker who wishes to design or understand programs capable of seeing Figures 6.1 and 6.2 as pictures of cubes. Computational accounts cannot be replaced by electronic accounts without losing sight of the intentional powers and properties of the system.

The irreducibility of psychology

It is often assumed, by positivists and antipositivists alike, that any basically mechanistic account of psychology must be inhumanly reductionist in character. On this view, neurophysiology is interpreted as implying that psychological phenomena are nothing but brain processes, and the computational metaphor as implying that people are nothing but machines – albeit machines fashioned out of flesh and blood instead of tin-cannery. Supposedly, both these approaches involve a commitment to the notion that psychological explanations are in principle dispensable, that everything that can be said in the 'human' vocabulary of values, purposes, beliefs, actions and perceptions could in principle be less misleadingly stated in terms of bodily mechanisms. Psychological language and theory, apparently, is at best a useful shorthand for neurophysiological matters (of which we are still largely ignorant, and which would take too long to state fully even if we had the knowledge) and at worst a mystifying illusion. Mechanism and reductionism are assumed to go hand-in-hand: and what could be more 'mechanistic' than an approach seeking to compare psychological phenomena to the computations carried out by electronic machines?

Despite the prevalence of these views, the previous section should have suggested that the computational metaphor does not view psychological terminology as dispensable. On the contrary, psychological vocabulary is deliberately imported into computational contexts to describe and explain what computer programs do. (Analogously, computational concepts are imported into neurophysiology in order to specify the functions which the brain is effecting, so that the physiologist may be in a position to ask how it is that the cerebral mechanism effects them.[11]) Philosophical justification of this *anti*-reductionist interpretation of the computational approach requires discussion of the concepts of reduction and mechanism, and of the relation between psychology and physiology.

The crucial point is that each of the key terms 'reduction' and 'mechanism' has two different senses. Given these distinctions, it is possible wholeheartedly to endorse the humanist stress on subjectivity in psychology without thereby jeopardizing the mechanist's firm insistence that psychological phenomena depend ultimately on causal processes within the brain.

One of the important senses of 'reductionism' in psychology is the (mistaken) view that psychological descriptions and explanations are mere shorthand for complicated sets of non-psychological statements about the brain, so that psychological statements could be translated into physiological ones without loss of meaning. This view is mistaken because intentional sentences, whose meaning involves the notion of subjectivity, have a very different pattern of logical implications from sentences that do not involve these notions. In technical terms, the logical peculiarities of intentional sentences include indeterminacy, referential opacity, failure of existential generalization, no implication of any embedded clause (or its negation), and non-extensional occurrence of embedded clauses.[12] More plainly, the intentional object (the object of thought that is mentioned in the sentence) can be described only by reference to the subject's thoughts (purposes, beliefs, expectations, desires). There may be no actual thing with which the object of thought can be sensibly identified; and even if there is, the identification will seem sensible on the basis of only *some* descriptions of the real thing, and the intentional object may be indeterminate in a way that no actual object can be.

For example, it does not follow from 'Hamlet intended to stab the man behind the arras' that 'Hamlet intended to stab Polonius', even though Polonius and the man behind the arras were one and the

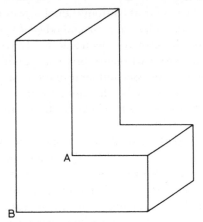

Fig. 6.4

same, for Hamlet *did not know* that Polonius was behind the arras. Similarly, from the fact that someone sees pink elephants it does not follow that there are any actual pink elephants (or even grey ones) to be seen. These all-too-human examples may be compared with the scene analysis programs mentioned in the section 'People, programs and positivism'. The more 'intelligent' visual programs can see an arrow-shaped vertex at the lower right-hand corner of both diagrams: but only in Figure 6.1 is there actually a vertex there. And even an intelligent scene analysis program may jump to mistaken conclusions, for instance in hallucinating a line joining points A and B in the L-beam of Figure 6.4.[13] Since intelligence is largely a matter of jumping sensibly to conclusions on the basis of the incomplete evidence which is all we ever have in a complex and rapidly changing world, making programs more intelligent will never exclude the possibility of their making mistakes.[14] Simply, like human beings, they may be expected to avoid the really stupid mistakes. But, stupid or not, illusory or veridical, the beliefs of programs must be described in basically intentional terms that share the range of logical peculiarities attributed to psychological vocabulary used in describing people.

Another reason why psychological language cannot be reduced to physiological terms (in the sense of *translation* into such terms) is that this language is basically computational in character.[15] It ascribes computational or symbol-manipulating processes (which are not so closely or rigorously specified as in the case of programs, but which are computational processes none the less) to the psychological system, saying nothing whatever about their physiological embodiment. It may not even be the case that computational processes falling clearly into one and the same class are all embodied by way of one and the same bodily mechanism (or electronic hardware): in fact, there are various reasons why this one-to-one correspondence between a class of computational processes and some unitary class of physiological events is highly unlikely to be the case. Each individual instance of computation, however, will of course be carried out by some particular series of cerebral events.

This raises the second sense of 'reductionism' to be distinguished: the view that subjective psychological phenomena are totally dependent on cerebral mechanisms, much as the information-processing functions of a program are grounded in the engineering details of the computer on which it happens to be being run. One can be a reductionist in this (second) sense without being a reductionist in the first sense. As the third section showed, proponents of the computational approach – whether in 'straight' psychology or in AI – in fact espouse this combination of views, which might be called an 'anti-reductionist reductionism'. (Essentially comparable views characterize philosophical debate concerning the relation between other pairs of sciences, such as molecular biology and quantum mechanics.[16])

Passing from reductionism to mechanism, a 'mechanistic' psychology is sometimes defined as one that abandons conceptual schemes employing the subject–object distinction, and that refuses to interpret (or explain) behaviour in terms of meaning, phenomenology or purposive action. Psychologists who are 'mechanists' in this sense avoid subjective concepts if they can, and if they cannot they at least insist on their dispensability in principle: according to them, subjective or intentional concepts are mere convenient shorthand, and could be replaced by a purely objective (non-intentional) vocabulary. It will already be apparent that computational theorists in general are not mechanists in this sense.

The second sense of 'mechanism' covers any psychology which allows that subjective psychological phenomena can be generated – and in a manner explained – by bodily processes. This is not to say that psychological processes are identical with neural processes (so this type of mechanism is not 'nothing-buttery'), nor even that they are the effects of bodily causes. Rather, the crucial notion in understanding how subjectivity can be grounded in objective causal mechanism is the concept of an internal model or representation; a concept which we have seen to be central to the computational approach. It is possible for the categories of subjectivity to be properly attributed to human beings because bodily processes in our brains function as models, or representations, of the world – and of hypothetical worlds – for the individual concerned. Since the 1940s, these cerebral models have featured in neurophysiological theory, and much brain research has focussed on asking how they are built up (or built in) in the nervous system and how they are organized so as to influence bodily action. (The way in which programs influence computers, by contrast, is already understood.)

To identify or describe the neural processes concerned *as* models is itself to ascribe meaning, or intentionality, to them. They could alternatively be described, at least in principle, at the level of 'objective' physiological events occurring at particular neuroanatomical locations (such as the 'edge-finders' or 'bug-detectors' within the visual systems of animals that have been discovered by single-cell neurophysiology). At this level, however, their meaning cannot be expressed and so their (psychological) function in the life of the individual is lost to view. Even so simple a neurophysiological concept as a 'bug-detector', for example, is implicitly psychological in so far as it identifies a functional relation within the animal's intentional world. Consequently, the categories of meaning, subjectivity and purpose would still be required to describe a person as a psychological being even if full neurophysiological knowledge were available. Indeed, a large part of 'physiological' data would be expressed in intentional terms. To forbid the use of such intentional language would be to omit all mention of mental phenomena, since there is no possibility of saying anything about the mind using only the language of the body.

Correlatively, there is no possibility of specifying a computation, or of explaining it in terms of other computational processes, if one limits oneself to electronic descriptions of the engineering of the computer. The explanation of a program's seeing Figure 6.2 *as* a cube, if it does, would require reference to the program's inner model of, or expectations about, cubes – including the ways in which cubes can appear to the eyes, considered as mere physical transducers. The knowledge that a (real) line can appear as an (actual) gap is a *computational* insight, having nothing essentially to do with either electronics or biochemistry.

It follows from all this that reductionism and mechanism do not necessarily go hand-in-hand. It is characteristic of the computational approach that it is reductionist only in the second sense defined above, and mechanistic only in the second sense also. Moreover, the complexity of the 'machines' (digital computers running complex AI programs) used as its tools and metaphorical exemplars is vastly greater – and significantly richer – than that of any previous machine. Likening a man to a machine was indeed insulting and basically dehumanizing in previous centuries, when this metaphor had to rely on relatively simple and inflexible (and non-representational) mechanisms such as the clock or the steam-engine. Even the cybernetic metaphor of the guided missile is not adequate to guide theoretical exploration of the computational nature of thinking, although it is closer to genuinely purposive behaviour than were the earlier mechanistic metaphors. With the advent of machines that store, transform and use complex and subtly structured inner models of their world, however, the psychologist has a metaphor for the mind that can do it considerably more justice than could any heretofore. Whether or not this metaphor will eventually elucidate *all* aspects of the human mind, it offers the psychologist an anti-reductionist version of mechanism that avoids the dehumanizing implications often mistakenly attributed to it.

In sum, the image of 'machine' provided by current computer science renders it intuitively less inconceivable that mental phenomena may be grounded in a mechanistic physiological base while also having a characteristically psychological guiding influence on bodily behaviour. The computational metaphor therefore contributes not only to theoretical psychology but to the philosophy of mind also, in that it illuminates the mind–body problem by suggesting *how it is possible* for an immaterial, computational process to direct bodily events. Associated problems concerning human purpose, self, consciousness, freedom and moral choice can each be clarified by this metaphor.[18] By this I do not mean that terms like 'free', for instance, can plausibly be applied to any computer example. But the computational distinctions that can be clearly made as between particular programs help one to suggest what may be the complex functional bases of the contrast between 'free' and 'involuntary' behaviour that each of us makes in daily life. Similarly, computational insights can make sense of some of the strange dissociations and the non-reciprocal coconsciousness between the different 'selves' that are observed in clinical cases of so-called split personality. For example, the well-known case[19] of Eve White and Eve Black involved two alternating personalities – demure and vulgar respectively – in the same body, such that Eve White had no knowledge of the experience or even the existence of Eve Black, but Eve Black knew everything that Eve White thought and experienced while the latter was temporarily in control of the shared body, and gleefully reported on it later to the psychiatrist. These phenomena are much less perplexing if we think of the two 'personalities' as different subroutines or modules of the same overall computational system, alternately using the same motor facilities and sensory apparatus, and having different degrees of access to each other's information or data-store. Not least, such insights can help clarify the way in which a person's aspirations and self-image can play a central role in the determination of action: persons and programs are not so different as they may seem.

Conclusion

The computational metaphor can help psychologists seeking a scientific understanding of the mind. Science can delight and fascinate because scientific metaphors and theories have their own kind of beauty. But, as Spinoza remarked three centuries ago, 'everything which is beautiful is as difficult as it is rare'.

Some of the difficulties facing proponents of the computational approach have already been mentioned. The difficulties of validation include some that are general to all scientific enquiry, some that bedevil all psychological theories, and some that are specific to theories based on a programming methodology. The difficulties of implementing powerful computational theories lie less in the limitations of current hardware (though advances in hardware availability will undoubtedly contribute to theoretical progress), than in still unsolved theoretical problems concerning the expression and efficient use of large amounts of heterogeneous knowledge. The intuitive knowledge continually accessed by human minds must first be made explicit, and then – what is even more taxing – it must be organized and indexed in such a way (or multiplicity of ways) that the inferential processes of thinking can recognize when a particular aspect of the total knowledge is relevant, can find it when it is needed, and can use it sensibly, given the constraints of the situation in mind.[20] In addition, the computational approach has to face a political difficulty, or philosophical prejudice, based on the popular view that to use machines of any sort as metaphors for the mind must be essentially dehumanizing. This difficulty can only be overcome to the extent that people can be made aware of the antipositivist and antireductionist features of the computational metaphor.

However, one often-cited 'difficulty' is not a difficulty at all. It is commonly claimed that no sense whatever can be made of talk about computers 'seeing', 'wanting', 'feeling', or even 'knowing'. The conclusion is drawn that computers are therefore useless as tools in the psychologist's search for scientific insight into *real* seeing, wanting, feeling and knowing. But this conclusion does not follow, even if one grants the truth of the premise (which in any event is philosophically controversial). Computational theories of the mind are no more than that: theories. One would not ask of a chemical theory that it fizz if put into a test-tube. Why, then, should one demand of a psychological theory that it see, or feel, if put into a computer? Psychologists try to understand human action and experience, not to mimic it; accordingly, their 'failure' to mimic it is irrelevant to their aims. In short, psychologists who espouse the computational metaphor are engaged not in science fiction, but in science.

Notes & references

1   G. A. Miller, Eugene Galanter and K. H. Pribram (1960) *Plans and the Structure of Behavior*. New York: Holt.
2   A comprehensive discussion of recent work in this field is in M. A. Boden (1977) *Artificial Intelligence and Natural Man*, Hassocks, Sussex: Harvester Press. The early history of AI is described in a forthcoming book by Pamela McCorduck, to be published by Freeman Inc. Representative discussions by AI workers include: M. L. Minsky and Seymour Papert (1973) *Artificial Intelligence*, Eugene, Oregon: Condon Lecture Publications; Bertram Raphael (1976) *The Thinking Computer: Mind Inside Matter*, San Francisco: Freeman; P. H. Winston (1977) *Artificial Intelligence*, London: Addison-Wesley. Collections of relevant papers are in: R. C. Schank and K. M. Colby (eds) (1973) *Computer Models of Thought and Language*, San Franciso: Freeman; D. G. Bobrow and Allan Collins (eds) (1975) *Representation and Understanding: Studies in Cognitive Science*, New York: Academic Press. Many references to relevant psychological work are given in the notes to chapter 13 of my *Artificial Intelligence and Natural Man*.
3   M. A. Boden (1972) *Purposive Explanation in Psychology*, Cambridge, Mass.: Harvard University Press (to be published in paperback by Harvester Press); J. A. Fodor (1968) *Psychological Explanation: An Introduction to the Philosophy of Psychology*, New York: Random House; J. A. Fodor (1976) *The Language of Thought*, Hassocks, Sussex: Harvester Press; D. C. Dennett (1969) *Content and Consciousness*, London: Routledge and Kegan Paul; Aaron Sloman (1978) *The Computer Revolution in Philosophy: Philosophy, Science, and Models of Mind*, Hassocks, Sussex: Harvester Press; Allen Newell (1973) Artificial intelligence and the concept of mind, in R. C. Schank and K. M. Colby (eds) *Computer Models of Thought and Language*, San Francisco: Freeman, p. 160.

4 H. L. Dreyfus (1972) *What Computers Can't Do: A Critique of Artificial Reason*, New York: Harper and Row; Joseph Weizenbaum (1976) *Computer Power and Human Reason: From Judgement to Calculation*, San Francisco: Freeman; Alan Gauld and John Shotter (1977) *Human Action and its Psychological Investigation*, London: Routledge and Kegan Paul.

5 Allen Newell and H. A. Simon (1972) *Human Problem Solving*, Englewood Cliffs, N.J.: Prentice-Hall; Allen Newell (1973) You can't play 20 questions with nature and win, in W. G. Chase (ed.) *Visual Information Processing*, New York: Academic Press; pp. 283–310.

6 R. M. Young (1976) *Seriation by Children: An Artificial Intelligence Analysis of a Piagetian Task*. Basel: Birkhauser.

7 N. S. Sutherland (in press) Intelligent picture processing. In N. S. Sutherland (ed.) *Tutorial Essays in Psychology*, Vol. 2. Hillsdale, N.J.: Erlbaum.

8 M. B. Clowes (1971) On seeing things, *Artificial Intelligence 2*: 79–116; M. B. Clowes (1973) Man the creative machine: a perspective from artificial intelligence research, in Jonathan Benthall (ed.) *The Limits of Human Nature*, London: Allen Lane pp. 192–207; Yoshiaki Shirai (1973) A context sensitive line finder for recognition of polyhedra. *Artificial Intelligence 4*: 95–120 (also available as pp. 93–114 of P. H. Winston (ed.) (1975) *The Psychology of Computer Vision*, New York: McGraw-Hill); L. G. Roberts (1965) Machine perception of three-dimensional solids. In J. T. Tippett et al. (eds) *Optical and Electro-Optical Information Processing*, Cambridge, Mass.: MIT Press, pp. 159–98.

9 Gilbert Falk (1972) Interpretation of imperfect line data as a three-dimensional scene. *Artificial Intelligence 3*: 101–44.

10 G. R. Grape (1969) *Computer Vision Through Sequential Abstractions*. Stanford University AI Department.

11 David Marr (1976) Early processing of visual information. *Phil. Trans. Royal Society B 275*: 483–524.

12 R. M. Chisholm (1967) Intentionality. In Paul Edwards (ed.) *The Encyclopedia of Philosophy*, Vol. 4. New York: Macmillan, pp. 201–4. Cf. M. A. Boden (1970) Intentionality and physical systems. *Philosophy of Science 37*: 200–14.

13 G. Falk. Interpretation of imperfect line data. Cf. A. K. Mackworth (1977) How to see a simple world: An exegesis of some computer programs for scene analysis. In E. W. Elcock and Donald Michie (eds) *Machine Intelligence 8*, esp. p. 524. Chichester: Ellis Horwood.

14 R. L. Gregory (1977) *Eye and Brain*, 3rd revised edn, London: Weidenfeld and Nicolson; R. L. Gregory (1967) Will seeing machines have illusions? In N. L. Collins and Donald Michie (eds) *Machine Intelligence 1*, Edinburgh: Edinburgh University Press, pp. 169–80.

15 J. A. Fodor (1976) *The Language of Thought*, esp. introductory section.

16 H. C. Longuet-Higgins (1970) The seat of the soul. In C. H. Waddington (ed.) *Towards a Theoretical Biology: 3. Drafts*. Edinburgh: Edinburgh University Press, pp. 236–41.

17 K. J. W. Craik (1943) *The Nature of Explanation*. Cambridge: Cambridge University Press.

18 M. A. Boden (1978) Human values in a mechanistic universe. In
    G. A. Vesey (ed.) *Human Values (Royal Institute of Philosophy Lectures, 1976–7)*,
    Hassocks, Sussex: Harvester Press.
19 C. H. Thigpen and H. M. Cleckley (1957) *The Three Faces of Eve*. London:
    Secker and Warburg. An even more complex case is described in Morton
    Prince (1905) *The Dissociation of a Personality: A Biographical Study in
    Abnormal Psychology*. New York: Longman.
20 M. L. Minsky (1975) A framework for representing knowledge. In
    Winston (ed.), *The Psychology of Computer Vision*, pp. 211–77.

Part III
The context of action

7 Perception and representation

Arthur Still

Introduction

In this paper two theories of perception are considered. The first, which I shall call the constructionist theory, has dominated psychology at least since Descartes, and because it takes many different forms amongst psychologists, I quote here a non-psychologist's attempt to capture the essence of the theory in a few sentences:

> As perceivers we select from all the stimuli falling on our senses only those which interest us, and our interests are governed by a pattern making tendency, sometimes called *schema*. In a chaos of shifting impressions, each of us constructs a stable world in which objects have recognizable shapes, are located in depth, and have permanence. In perceiving we are building, taking some cues and rejecting others. (Douglas, 1970, p. 49)

The second theory, which is a form of realism, supposes that in some form the stable world is out there waiting for us, and does not have to be constructed. The difference between the two theories may be brought out by means of historical parallels: 'What, then, differentiates the Aristotelian view from Descartes' view that secondary qualities are "powers that objects have"? For Descartes the power was to set our nerves in motion; for Aquinas it was to produce likenesses of themselves.' (Kenny, 1968, p. 219; Aquinas follows the Aristotelian view.) Obviously, if an object *produces* a likeness of itself, it does not have to be constructed by the mind. A modern version of this theory, in which the 'likeness' is produced by a combination of the object and an information seeking (but not processing) organism, is due to Gibson (1966).

My argument proceeds by examining an important consequence of the constructionist theory, namely the necessity of supposing that the brain or mind constructs a *representation* of objects and the environment. Logical objections to the possibility of such a representation are considered and it is concluded that conclusive logical or empirical refutation of the theory is in principle impossible. Choice between the constructionist and realist theories, like the choice between the Ptolemaic and Copernican theories of astronomy, must be on other grounds.[1]

The constructionist theory

In its modern form, the constructionist theory is information processing or cognitive psychology (Neisser, 1967). The raw materials out of which the world is constructed are not (as they have been in past versions of the theory) sense-data, or sensations, or 'shifting impressions', but the sensory input. The physical energies impinging upon us are transduced by the sense organs into patterns of nerve impulses which travel to the brain and are there interpreted in the process of construction. An essential part of the theory is that the information contained in the input is relatively impoverished, and cannot account for the richness of experience. The evidence that this is so comes from experiments which show what Bartlett called an 'effort after meaning' (Bartlett, 1932). As Blakemore says:

> Nowadays we look upon visual perception as a piecemeal affair; our seemingly unified view of the world around us is really only a plausible hypothesis on the basis of fragmentary evidence. The transformations that go on in the retinae and visual pathways are not merely reproductions, in high fidelity, of the visual image. At every stage a censor is at work, cutting with its scissors, and deleting with a red pencil, the unwanted visual messages. (Blakemore, 1973, p. 51)

The two points that seem essential to a constructionist theory of vision are that there is something called a retinal image (which is presumably what Blakemore means by 'visual image'), which is a static, momentary unit of visual contact between organism and world; and that the world is a hypothesis based on such units of contact. It seems likely that there are formidable logical difficulties with this point of view (see, for instance, Anscombe's (1974) criticism of Gregory's (1974) statement of the constructionist theory); but nowadays cognitive psychologists do not feel obliged to take these difficulties seriously. For it is possible to sweep them all away with a simple 'existence' argument; the existence, real or imagined, of a suitably programmed digital computer, which provides a kind of embodiment of the constructionist theory.

Such computers, or their programs, receive inputs, perform operations on these inputs by making use of knowledge which is stored or represented in the form of memories, and produce outputs which are the results of these operations. They can make inferences, form hypotheses, interpret data, use deductive and inductive logic, and, it is even claimed, create music and poetry; in short they can, one might say, think. These words for various intelligent human activities are used about computer programs by workers in artificial intelligence (AI), which is the attempt to formalize the intelligent activities of the human mind in a form which can be realized on a digital computer.[2] Each word has a fairly precise meaning within the language of AI because it refers to some definite process or result in the workings of computer programs. This has given enormous freedom to cognitive psychologists, since they can now use terms like 'memory' and 'knowledge', in the belief that their terms are soundly embedded in a suitable theoretical framework, and that their task is to map these terms onto the workings of the human mind. The resulting confidence has led to a proliferation of experiments and theories in cognitive psychology, and if there is at present any influence between psychology and philosophy it is from psychology to philosophy.[3]

All this sounds very healthy, but the surface bloom may be misleading; it depends upon the soundness of analogy between computers and mind. Theoretical psychology has few of the technological achievements to its credit that help to make the physical sciences seem, to an outsider, so safe and assured. The output of experimental research and the confidence of psychologists are not in themselves guarantees of truth; and the hypothetico-deductive method, which is used in one form or another by most psychologists, is not obviously a self-correcting system. A theory stated within the information processing or computer analogy framework may be genuinely tested by the risk of falsification at the hands of carefully designed experiments, but it does not follow that the framework itself is tested in the same way.

Constructionism entails representation

At present then, constructionism rests heavily on the computer analogy. Recent work in AI has stressed the importance of finding suitable *representations* of the input (Amarel, 1968), and representation seems equally to be a necessary part of a constructionist psychology. For if a construction of the world is to exist in the way proposed by constructionists, it must exist in the form of a representation in the brain or mind. Before considering the consequences of this it is necessary to have before us the several shades of meaning contained in the concept of representation.

As Goodman (1969) has pointed out, physical resemblance is neither a necessary nor a sufficient condition for representation. Not sufficient, since identical twins do not represent each other, and however much you look like a portrait of Henry VIII the portrait represents Henry VIII and not you. And nòt necessary, since a symbol on a map may look nothing like the object represented, and a salt cellar may represent Napoleon in a dinner-table discussion of military strategy. If *A* is to be a representation of *B*, *A* must either be *used* as a representation or substitute for *B*, or a representation must be intended, for instance by the painter of a portrait. A weathered rock that happened to look like Socrates would not thereby be a representation of Socrates, but it could be *used* as, and therefore become, a representation of Socrates in a new board game. But if the rock had in fact been successfully sculptured to look like Socrates, this alone would make it a representation of Socrates. Goodman sees representation as a kind of denotation, which probably includes these two ways in which *A* could represent *B*. There is also a mathematical definition of representation (Suppes and Zinnes, 1963) which supposes only a similarity of structure or relational similarity between *A* and *B*, and which does not involve denotation. It is in the first sense, in which *A* is *used as* a representation of *B*, that the constructionist theory may be said to require an internal representation of the external world. Relational similarity is not sufficient, though some kind of relational similarity may be necessary for this kind of internal representation to take place.

The consequences of a need for representation are explored by Fodor (1975) who sees the constructionist theory of perception as a necessary partner of his view that thought is computational, and that therefore the digital computer provides an adequate model of thought. The important conclusion from our point of view is that in thinking and making decisions an agent must have the means for internally representing different actions and their consequences. Perception is regarded by Fodor as analogous to concept learning. It involves hypothesis formation and confirmation, and the sensory data which confirm a given perceptual hypothesis are typically internally represented in a vocabulary that is impoverished compared with the vocabulary in which the hypotheses themselves are couched: '. . . what must go on in perception is that a description of the environment that is *not* couched in a vocabulary whose terms designate values of physical variables is somehow computed on the basis of a description that *is* couched in such a vocabulary.' (Fodor, 1975, p. 47) 'Perception must involve hypothesis formation and confirmation because the organism must somehow manage to infer the appropriate task-relevant description of the environment from its physical description . . . together with background information.' (Fodor, 1975, p. 50) A perceptual description of the environment is a representation of the environment, and a representation presupposes a medium of representation; but since there is no symbolization without symbols, there can be no internal representation without an internal language. This internal language, at least in some form, must be innate, and must be prior to the learning of a natural language (from which Fodor concludes that Wittgenstein was wrong to think that St Augustine was mistaken in thinking that learning a first language is like learning a foreign language; on the contrary, St Augustine was 'precisely and demonstrably right'). The internal language does not itself require interpretation by a further language, which would lead to an infinite regress of internal languages. This is because it is a kind of computer machine language, whose 'formulae can be paired directly with the computationally relevant physical states of the machine in such fashion that the operations the machine performs respect the semantic constraints on formulae in the machine code.' (Fodor, 1975, p. 67)

This notion of an internal *language* of representation leads to some remarkable but (I think) shaky conclusions. Fodor begins his book by arguing convincingly for a non-reductionist physicalism, which is possible since physicalism 'does not imply a correspondence between the kind predicates of the reduced and the reducing science' (Fodor, 1975, p. 22; kind predicates are predicates which are part of the descriptive vocabulary of the science). But surely reductionism has crept in with an internal language of representation whose formulae can be paired directly with the computationally relevant physical states of the machine. If it is argued that the 'computationally relevant physical states' cannot be paired directly with what might be called natural kind physical states, then a further internal language *is* necessary to mediate between the computationally relevant physical states and the natural kind physical states, so an infinite regress of internal languages is not avoided.

In fact it seems strange to call the internal language of representation a language at all if it is similar to a machine language. In effect a machine language is a means of representing the states of the machine, and would be unnecessary if there were not a community of computer engineers who needed the language to make computations and to communicate with each other and with the machines. The machines themselves do not need the language. Similarly, there is no need for an internal language of representation that can be paired directly with the computationally relevant physical states of the brain, since the physical states of the brain are sufficient to serve our purposes (*qua* people rather than psychologists). Fodor might argue that the psychologist, like the computer engineer with his machine language, might need such a language, but he has not yet got one, and it is not clear why it would not be better to talk explicitly about the physical states themselves. In any case it is at best misleading to call it a language, and although Fodor says that he does not much mind whether it is called a language or not, if we did not it would take much of the interest out of his startling conclusion that '... no one learns L (a natural language) unless he already knows some language different from L *but rich enough to express* extensions of the predicates of L' (Fodor, 1975, p. 72).

But even if we do not agree that an internal representation entails a language of representation, a weaker conclusion seems acceptable. The representation must have a propositional form in that it must be possible to translate it into a set of propositions that could be embodied in a digital computer.[4] Such a representation will be referred to as a propositional representation (a usage that is wider than that of Pylyshyn (1973); it includes all Pylyshyn's senses of representation).

A propositional representation is always a selective representation of the environment, or what Fodor calls a task-relevant description. 'Of all the indefinitely many properties the stimulus *does* have, only those can be behaviourally salient which the organism *represents* the stimulus as having.' (Fodor, 1975, p. 55)

Can the demands of psychological theory always be met by an internal propositional representation? To answer this question we turn to some specific uses of the concept of representation (and cognate concepts) in psychology, and consider the adequacy of these uses for psychological theory.

The use of the concept of internal representation in psychology

Representation as model of the world

Craik (1943) argued that the function of thought is to model reality, a point which was made in very similar terms many years before by Hertz: 'The relation of a dynamical model to the system of which it is regarded as the model, is precisely the same as the relation of the images which our mind forms of things to the things themselves. For if we regard the condition of the model as the representation of the condition of the system, then the consequents of this representation, which according to the laws of this representation must appear, are also the representation of the consequents which must proceed from the original object according to the laws of this original object. The agreement between mind and nature may therefore be likened to the agreement between two systems which are models of one another, and we can even account for this agreement by assuming that the mind is capable of making actual dynamical models of things, and of working with them.' (Hertz, 1956, p. 177) Perhaps Wittgenstein had this passage in mind when he wrote: 'In the terminology of Hertz we might say: Only uniform or lawlike connexions are *thinkable*' (Wittgenstein, 1922, p. 177). Certainly it seems to follow from what Hertz writes that, in so far as the mind makes dynamical models of things, thought processes might be constrained to follow the possible laws that those things obey. The importance of such a representation or model is that 'If the organism carries a "small scale model" of external reality and of its own possible actions within its head, it is able to try out various alternatives, conclude which is the best of them, react to future situations before they arise, utilize the knowledge of past events in dealing with the present and future, and in every way to react in a much fuller, safer, and more competent manner to the emergencies which face it' (Craik, 1943, p. 61). Craik is even more explicit than Wittgenstein in trying to pin down the *a priori* possibilities of thought. The brain is a mechanism which 'has the power to represent, or parallel, certain phenomena in the external world as a calculating machine can parallel the development of strains in a bridge. It follows that this machine will parallel ... processes where the classical laws of mechanics are true' but will not be able to 'represent in itself' microscopic phenomena obeying different laws' (Craik, 1943, p. 95).

It is instructive to compare the first passage from Craik with a superficially similar passage from William James:

> The towering importance for human life of this kind of knowing lies in the fact that an experience that knows another can figure as its *representative*, not in any quasi-miraculous (epistemological) sense, but in the definite practical sense of being its *substitute* in various operations, sometimes physical and sometimes mental, which lead us to its associates and results. By experimenting on our idea of reality, we may save ourselves the trouble of experimenting on the real experience which they severally mean. The ideas form related systems, corresponding point to point to the systems which the realities form. (James, 1912, p. 61)

In spite of the similarity, James and Craik (or Hertz) mean very different things. For Craik gives no account of the difference between thinking about something in that thing's absence, and experiencing the thing directly, as when we see it in front of us. In both cases, for Craik, there will be some kind of representation or model of the thing, and it is clear that he is very much a constructionist; he is indeed often regarded as one of the founders of the information processing approach to psychology. James, on the other hand (*pace* the penultimate word in the above quotation) is writing about a 'world of pure experience', and it is one experience which represents another, by being its 'substitute in various operations'.

In Craik's use of the concept of representation, aspects of the environment relevant to desired predictions are selected for modelling. Since the model is a repository of physical laws a propositional representation must obviously be possible.

Representation as selection of an appropriate structure

In representation as model, the problem for a designer of a brain must be *what* to represent: what parts of physical reality, and what physical laws, are going to be extracted for successful and useful predictions. In representation as appropriate structure, the problem is that of finding the *best* of several logically similar representations. Thus a newspaper photograph may be coded into a sequence of binary digits, which can be useful for transmitting, but useless as a representation which could be used by somebody to recognize the scene depicted. But the two representations are similar in that they can be mapped (in a mathematical sense) onto each other (and are therefore iso-morphic); for recognition, however, the representation in the form of a photograph is the *best* representation.

Consider the following game. There are nine cards, marked as follows: A1, A3, B2, B3, C1, C3, A2, B1, C2. The cards are laid out face up, and two players alternately select a card until there are no more cards on the table. The winner is the first player to pick up a 'run', where a run is a set of three cards which contain the same letter, or the same number, or which contain all different numbers and letters in such a way that the ordering by letters is either the same as the ordering by numbers, or it is the reverse: i.e. A1, B2, C3, or A3, B2, C1.

This game is in fact noughts and crosses (tic-tac-toe), or at least one way of representing the game, and one that makes it seem, to us, more difficult than it really is. We prefer a spatial representation, and the game seems much easier once it is mentally translated into the familiar spatial form.

The problem of finding the best or most suitable mode of representation is one of great importance in artificial intelligence, as Amarel (1968) shows by considering the effect upon ease of solution by a computer program of different ways of representing the 'brain-twister' known as the missionaries and cannibals problem. It is also current in experimental psychology where, for instance, a subject might be asked to 'code' material either in the form of visual images, or in a verbal form, and his performance on some task is then compared under the two conditions. In the computer case, however, the representations are likely to be isomorphic in a mathematical sense, whereas this is not obviously so in the case of different forms of 'coding' in human subjects.

If we take representation in the mathematical sense, it is clear that propositional representation of an appropriate structure is possible, as it is in a computer program. But it may be that the best representation in the mind of someone playing noughts and crosses is not merely isomorphic with a simple propositional statement of the rules of the game. Something more may be necessary, perhaps some form of visual image. But even so, as Pylyshyn (1973) argues, a propositional representation may still be possible. In particular we may note again that if a visual image is regarded as an analogue representation, this may be translated, to any desired degree of accuracy, into a propositional or digital representation.

The use of alternative representations in the resolutions of ambiguity

Consider an ambiguous figure such as Boring's young woman/old woman figure or a Necker cube (Gregory, 1966). These are themselves representations, but ambiguous, since they may be seen in one of two ways. Thus Boring's figure may be seen either as a young woman or as an old woman, and a possible explanation of this is that the picture activates or is a stimulus for one of two alternative internal representations; one being a possible representation of a young woman, the other of an old woman. Either we can say that these internal representations are representations of what the picture represents; or they are representations of the picture itself, which make explicit what is ambiguous in the picture. The concept of representation in this sense may also be used when the presented picture is unclear, as it may be when presented for a very brief period in a tachistoscope, or in a cartoon sketch where the representation is very schematic; in both cases the representation by the brain or mind seems to be of greater clarity than is justified by the information contained in the picture.

Another example of this use of representation comes from Chomsky's distinction between deep and surface structure (Chomsky, 1965). In a sentence like 'They are flying planes', the ambiguity may be resolved by showing the alternative ways of parsing the sentence; in one sense the verb phrase is 'are', in the other it is 'are flying'. In a sentence like 'The shooting of the hunters was terrible', the ambiguity cannot be resolved by parsing, but only by rephrasing the sentence to bring out the alternative meanings, as: 'The hunters could not shoot straight' and 'It was tragic that the hunters were shot'. In the second case of ambiguity Chomsky appeals to a deep structure which contains, in some form, these alternative renderings, which may be regarded as alternative representations of the sentence, or of what the sentences themselves represent.

The use of this kind of representation in a constructionist theory is brought out by Oldfield's (1954) attempt to translate Bartlett's concept of the schema into information theory terms. Consider a device which classifies inputs, consisting of sequences of eight binary digits, into one of several classes, Alternation (10101010), Mirror

Image (e.g. 11011011), etc. Sometimes the inputs are imperfect, or truncated, and do not correspond exactly to any of the class instances which are contained within the device. The device then looks for the closest fit, and in this way the device may be said to 'fill in gaps' or 'ignore minor discrepancies' in its effort to fit the input to one of the classes. We might even say that the device shows an 'effort after meaning'.

The illustrations of this kind of representation usually involve stimulus material that is itself a kind of representation (often a picture), and mapping the input onto an internal representation may be regarded as an interpretation of the input. Since the internal space which contains alternative representations is linked to the memory and knowledge of the system, selection of an appropriate representation will be based on prior knowledge, as well as on the input itself. Thus if, in a conversation about the fate of some hunters who accidentally strayed onto an army firing range, someone says 'the shooting of the hunters was terrible', there will be no doubt about what is meant; while a subject's perception of the ambiguous figure can be determined by prior presentation of a series of pictures of one type (e.g. old woman pictures) or the other (young woman pictures).

If the constructionist view (implicit in this use of the concept of representation) is to have any general validity it must be argued that this type of perception, which can be described as a mapping onto a representation, provides a paradigm for perception in general. What one sees, in the real world (i.e. outside the laboratory), is in some sense interpreted by being mapped onto an internal representation. But what if this description is only plausible in the experimental situation in which the stimulus is itself some kind of representation, so that the notion of interpretation is applicable? After all, what, in the real world, does the stimulus represent?

Representation of 'field of consciousness' and the frame problem

In a recent paper Shaw (1971) proposed a hypothesis of 'what the brain does', which he sets out by means of what he calls a simple phenomenological demonstration:

Look around you. Now close your eyes and describe aloud what you saw. Open your eyes and check to see how accurate your recall was. Although your recall of detail was by no means total, you probably ceased your description from boredom, rather than from lack of recall. (Shaw, 1971)

Shaw then suggests further questions to ask yourself, such as where are you located in the world, what is your present body posture, what is the weather like, who are you, how did you get here? These seem simple questions, but they are very difficult to answer by any imaginable computational process, and Shaw suggests that 'the basic psychological function is ... involved in this exercise'. He goes on to quote Minsky: 'To an observer B, an object A* is a model of an object A to the extent that B can use A* to answer questions that interest him about A', and continues: 'The significant question for cognitive theory concerns the nature and the organization of the 'object' that is neurologically instantiated and that allows man to answer questions which interest him about the current state of history of his environment, of himself and the relation between the two.' (Shaw, 1971) Shaw appears to be talking about what is sometimes called the field of consciousness, which is defined by Gurwitsch (1964) as 'the totality of co-present data'. Implicit in the field of consciousness is not only the ability to answer questions about it, but also the possibility of the diverse actions that are in fact possible to me at any moment in the world I see. One aspect of this last possibility (and one involved in answering Shaw's question about present body posture), was the concern of the neurologist Henry Head.

On the basis of clinical observations on brain-damaged patients Head (1920) developed his concept of the schema. The schema is a model of the body upon which movements are recorded so that the subject is always able to tell the position of his limbs, and to make movements (i.e. send out motor commands) appropriate to the present position. It is similar to an inertial navigation system, in which present position is determined in relation to some starting point by means of a continuous record of changes in position upon some map (cf. Oldfield and Zangwill, 1942). The schema is 'physiological' in that the input to consciousness is the present state of the schema, and not sensations of movement and position, which require interpretation. This relationship between sensations and schema reoccurs when Head talks about more general visual schema, in which a sensation is not associated with an object, nor is it the basis of an hypothesis, but it is from the beginning projected onto the schema of surrounding space. 'Every recognizable change enters into consciousness already charged with its relation to something that has gone before, just as on a taximeter the distance is presented to us already transformed into shillings and pence' (Head, 1920, p. 605). Here Head is writing of the postural schema, but what he writes applies equally to the visual schema. Schemata may be enlarged by introjection, in which a postural schema is extended by means of a 'tool': 'Anything which participates in the conscious movements of our bodies is added to the model of ourselves and becomes part of these schemata.' (Head, 1920, p. 606) Polanyi describes a similar process in *The Tacit Dimension* (Polanyi, 1967).

It would seem that, in a similar way, the visual schema, which 'centres' us in visual space and provides the visual part of the field of consciousness, must, as it were, become more and more penetrating, extending further around corners, as a place becomes more familiar, so that we can anticipate the visual consequences of our movements. To continue the quotation from Gurwitsch:

> Co-presence is understood in a broad sense so as to comprise not only data which are experienced as simultaneous but also those which are simultaneously experienced, though not as simultaneous. For instance, suppose that a musical note no longer resounds but is still retained as just having resounded. The note thus retained belongs to the total field of consciousness experienced at the moment under consideration. Correspondingly, the same holds, in the case of a still resounding note, for we expect the note to continue resounding or to stop. (Gurwitsch, 1964, p. 2)

In this way the clock past and the clock future are contained within the clock present, and must be included within any auditory or visual schema. These properties of a schema may have something in common with the visual icon (Neisser, 1967) investigated by cognitive psychologists as a first stage in the constructive process, and with the expectancies of learning theorists. Closer still is the notion of a 'cognitive map' (Tolman, 1948; Neisser, 1976), but the term 'map' is not a happy one here. In using a map one looks away from the environment to consult the map, which is not like finding one's way in a familiar environment. Of course one *might* have an image of a place, and use it when absent from the place, or even, when one is in the place, close one's eyes and consult the image to try to remember what lies around the corner. Then one might reasonably be said to be using an internal map, but the atypicality of this case, the fact that one usually looks *more closely* at an environment to find the desired direction, suggests the inadequacy of the term in the normal case.

Part of this inadequacy stems from an ambiguity in the modern use of the terms 'schema' and 'cognitive map'. Neisser (1976) appears to mean by 'schema' both that which underlies my present field of consciousness, and that which underlies my knowledge of an environment from which I am absent.

> A schema is that portion of the entire perceptual cycle which is internal to the perceiver, modifiable by experience, and somehow specific to what is being perceived. The schema accepts information as it becomes available at sensory surfaces and is changed by that information; it directs movements and exploratory activities that make more information available, by which it is further modified. (Neisser, 1976, p. 54)

A schema which is modifiable by experience seems to correspond to knowledge of an environment that I carry away with me. While one that is 'somehow specific to what is being perceived', and which 'directs movements and exploratory activities' seems to correspond to my present field of consciousness. The two senses of schema are obviously closely related, and we might talk of a schematic framework into which my present field of consciousness is fitted. There is no map, but a skeleton plan which is completed by the environment itself.

Representation of the 'behaviourally salient aspects' of the field of consciousness presents problems of propositional representation that are not present in the other senses of representation considered. These problems are recognized by workers in AI, where it is called the 'frame problem', which 'arises in attempts to formalize problem-solving processes involving interactions with a complex world. It concerns the difficulty of keeping track of the consequences of the performance of an action in, or more generally of the making of some alteration to, a representation of the world' (Hayes, 1973, p. 45). Some of the implications of the frame problem are outlined by Minsky (1975) who offers some informal solutions from an AI point of view.

> When we move about a room, the shape of things change. How can these changes be anticipated, or compensated, without complete reprocessing? The results of eye and head rotation are simple: things move in the visual field but keep their shapes; but changing place causes large shape changes that depend both on angle and on distance relations between the object and observer. The problem is particularly important for fast-moving animals because a model

of the scene must be built up from different, partially analysed views. Perhaps the need to do this, even in a relatively primitive fashion, was a major evolutionary stimulus to develop frame systems, and later, other symbolic mechanisms. (Minsky, 1975, p. 224)

Minsky's account of the problem here is similar to that of Gibson (1958, 1966), but whereas Gibson is led to conclude that a cognitive or constructionist approach cannot provide a solution, Minsky sees it as a difficult but not insurmountable challenge for the cognitive approach. Both recognize that any adequate solution must go a long way towards determining one's account of the traditional cognitive problems of memory, problem-solving, language, etc. So Minsky applies his theory of frames to these problems, while Gibson rejects the cognitive approach altogether. If Gibson is correct, the implications for the constuctionist theory are devastating, since the existence argument (based on the validity of the computer analogy) collapses. Furthermore, if the frame problem contains within itself, as Minsky seems to argue, the key to the problems of memory and knowledge that are home ground to the constructionists, and if the frame problem is insoluble within a constructionist framework, then the problems of memory and knowledge should also be insoluble within a constructionist framework.

This leads to three questions which may be equivalent: Is the frame problem soluble in principle? Is a propositional representation possible for what is behaviourally salient in the field of consciousness? Is a propositional representation possible for the field of consciousness? Some characteristic attempts to prove that the answer must be 'no' are considered briefly below.

Attempts to prove the impossibility of representing the field of consciousness

(a) It has been argued that the information involved in the field of consciousness is unlimited, and therefore cannot be represented by a finite set of propositions; 'our phenomenal field has always a richness that no finite series of statements can do justice to' (Kullman and Taylor, 1958, p. 126). But the size of 'a finite propositional representation' is also unlimited and therefore could always, in principle, be expanded in order to converge upon an adequate representation, just as an analogue device, which has an unlimited number of potential states, can be represented to any degree of accuracy by a suitable digital device.

(b) Godel's theorem has been used to argue that for any given digital device there will always be theorems that human beings can recognize as true, but which cannot be derived by the device (Lucas, 1961). Humans thus remain one step ahead of machines. But again it is possible to converge upon an equivalence of humans and machines in this respect, since one can always, in principle, build a more powerful digital device that will derive the theorem in question.

The same argument may be applied against Godel's own argument that 'Either the human mind surpasses all machines (to be more precise: it can decide more number theoretical questions than any machine) or else there exist number theoretical questions undecidable for the human mind' (Wang, 1973, p. 324). Godel rejected the second alternative, and so accepted the first. But it is presumably possible, if knowledge can be represented in propositional form, and person A is fully cognisant of the internal propositional representation of person B, for A to decide a number theoretical question that cannot be decided by B. He can then inform B of this, thereby changing his propositional representations so that B can now decide that number theoretical question. But the same applies if B is a computer.

(c) Thinking cannot be divorced from being human in other ways, in particular having a body (Dreyfus, 1972). This argument stems from a phenomenological analysis of the field of consciousness. The argument has force against the existence argument for constructionism only if the processes studied by cognitive psychologists cannot be understood without first understanding what it is to have a body in the world. In some respects this seems to be equivalent to Minsky's (1975) version of the frame problem. If so, Dreyfus's argument is no more than a restatement of the frame problem, with the conclusion that it is insoluble by means of propositional representations. But once the differences between the machine mind and the embodied mind are spelled out in propositional form (if they can be) simulation to any degree of approximation should, in principle, be possible.

(d) Experiences cannot be represented in propositional form (and the field of consciousness is an experience). This is argued by Gunderson (1971), although he talks of particular experiences (e.g. pains, after-images) rather than experiences in general. He develops his argument by distinguishing between program receptive aspects of the mental, which are task-oriented, protocol-possible, and projective; and program resistant aspects which are none of these things, and which seem to be equivalent to experiences in their non-projective aspect. The trouble with this argument is that it concerns experiences, and not the 'behaviourally salient' aspects of experience. In spite of disclaimers to the contrary, cognitive psychologists are behaviourists in that the subject matter of psychology (i.e. that which is to be explained) is behaviour and there is no reason why pain *behaviour*, or the *reports* of after images, cannot be explained by a theory based upon propositional representations. Once again, it should be possible to converge on a solution.

(e) The processes involved in thinking, perceiving, etc. are not the same as the processes gone through by a computer in simulating these processes (Dreyfus, 1972). Attempts have been made to get computers to print out 'protocols' during problem solving, and to compare these with the protocols of human subjects given the same problems (Newell and Simon, 1971). The similarities are often striking, though perhaps a similar attempt for computer 'perception' would not produce such similarities. But Minsky recognizes this in his formulation of the frame problem as that of simulating an ability to answer questions about the environment. And again there seems no limit in principle to the closeness with which specified human performance can be simulated.

Thus these and other attempts to prove the impossibility of a propositional representation of the field of consciousness, which would be a solution to the frame problem, fall to the convergence argument. Once the consequences for behaviour of a field of consciousness are made explicit (as in a statement of the frame problem) propositional representation becomes in principle possible. Perhaps the consequences for behaviour can never fully be made explicit, but there is no limit on how close an approximation can be made, and therefore convergence upon a solution is always possible. More generally, nothing can be proved or disproved about the field of consciousness until the notion of a field of consciousness is put into a propositional form suitable for logical manipulation. But once it is put into this form (and there is no apparent limit to the accuracy with which this may be done) no proof is necessary, since propositional representation is now possible.

Not only is it impossible to refute the constructionist theory on logical grounds, it is also impossible to refute it on empirical grounds, and by the same argument. For an appropriate propositional representation is possible for any behaviour or scene that can be described. A particular theory within the constructionist framework might be refutable, but not the framework itself.

But these arguments should not bring comfort to the constructionist. For the geocentric or Ptolomaic theory of astronomy could also be said to converge upon an explanation of the planetary motions. But it is the very fact that it merely converges upon a solution, by adding to the already complex system of epicycles, that makes the theory so unsatisfactory beside the heliocentric or Copernican theory, which seems to provide a direct description of the structures underlying the phenomena to be explained. Perhaps a similar point (as applied to constructionism) was being made by Von Neumann when he wrote that 'There is a good deal in formal logic to indicate that the description of the functions of an automaton is simpler than the automaton itself, as long as the automaton is not very complicated, but that when you get to high complications, the actual object is simpler than the literary description' (quoted by Shaw, 1971, p. 32).

The 'actual object' in the case of psychology is the organism and its environment regarded as a single system. Although this may be approximated by a theory which starts from an organism which constructs its own environment from limited materials, an alternative description, not requiring the same kinds of approximation, may be more satisfactory. Such an alternative description has been attempted by Gibson.

The alternative theory

The constructionist theory starts with the idea of physical energies striking the sense organs, being transduced into nerve impulses, and giving rise to perception and behaviour by means of a constructive process. The stimulus therefore is described in the terms of physics, and is regarded as an almost instantaneous affair, so that successive stimuli must be held together by memory. In these terms it seems very reasonable to study static two-dimensional images as a kind of stimulus unit, like retinal images, out of which experience is built. There is thus a cognitive problem involved in binding together the successive images that occur during movement through the world.

Let us consider instead an organism that is adapted to accept as stimuli precisely the successive 'images' that pose a cognitive problem for the constructionist's organism. There *is* no succession of stimuli bound together by memory, for the constructionist's 'succession of stimuli' is the single stimulus to which the organism will respond. The stimulus for perceiving oneself as moving in a straight line is a certain kind of continuous perspective transformation, the stimulus for a table is another kind of perspective transformation, an invariant which is contained in any time slice of the continuous transformation of a table projected as a retinal image. Movements of eyes and the head or body will be geared to pick up invariants of this kind, so that we should think of the eye, not in isolation, but as part of a system which includes the means of coordinating these movements with the perspective transformations. Furthermore, there is no clear limit to the time over which the transformations involved in the detection of an invariant can extend; movement around this table, across the room, through this house will all involve their characteristic invariants contained within the perspective transformations, and these invariants are independent of the particular routes through the house that are taken. At no point are we *required* to break up the transforming array into separate stimuli, and therefore we do not have to invoke memory, in the sense in which it is used in cognitive psychology.

In a way this account of perception is merely an alternative *description*, which sees the aspects of behaviour dealt with by the constructionist's frame problem not as a problem for a cognitive theory but as the point from which a cognitive theory can start. At this starting point we are already given the vertebrate's ability to find its way in the world; or, in phenomenological terms, we *start* with the field of consciousness or being-in-the-world, 'just as on a taximeter the distance is presented to us already transformed into shillings and pence'.

But the cognitive theory that starts from this point cannot develop independently of the precognitive process. For already there is the possibility of picking up in the transforming array the visual invariants that define, for instance, that object by the tree as a moving animal, and a potential prey. Now if the moving animal disappears from sight, and the predator, using his visual system, goes in search of it, there is still no need to break up the transforming array into separate stimuli (Gibson et al., 1969, have shown that there are invariants associated with disappearing objects). But if we do do this we have memory and the beginning of a cognitive theory, which thus does not start where the precognitive process ends, but emerges out of the precognitive process.

Although the theory may be an 'alternative description' it is not *merely* this since it has far-reaching implications. The study of perception of static two-dimensional stimuli will now be of little interest, for these are no longer 'units' of perception, but involve rather complex and unnatural transformations; simple and natural transformations will be difficult to create artificially, which means that theoretically interesting illusions will be hard to set up. The theoretical emphasis will not be on how the nervous system constructs representations, but on developing a language (which Gibson calls ecological optics) for describing the invariants in the environment. Thus Fodor's physicalism without reductionism is now applied to the external world, and the problem is not how to construct mental structures out of the physical brain and its inputs, but how to describe the structures or invariants that are embodied in the world. And for the physiologist the problem will be not one of construction, but one of how the sense organs and the nervous system *preserve* the information that is available in, and actively picked up from the environment. It is in this sense that it is like a scholastic theory, in that objects produce likenesses of themselves, instead of representations that have to be constructed by the mind. This is a reversal of Descartes' view:

> We can very well conceive how the movement of one body can be caused by that of another, and diversified by the size, figure and situation of its parts, but we can in no wise understand how these same things (viz. size, figure and motion) can produce something entirely different in nature from themselves, such are those substantial forms and qualities which many suppose to exist in bodies. (Quoted in Kenny, 1968, p. 223)

For Fodor the problem is to show how the nervous system constructs a psychologically meaningful world from a description that is couched in the terms of physics. The alternative now being considered, by treating the stimulus as extending indefinitely over time, puts the structure in the world itself. Thus, if this structure can be said to contain 'substantial forms' a successful ecological optics would provide the understanding that Descartes thought was lacking.

A realist account of error

The supposed difficulty of dealing with perceptual error has often been used as an argument against realist theories such as Gibson's, and therefore this paper concludes with a brief and speculative account of error within the framework of a realist theory.

Some of Gibson's experimental work has involved the artificial setting up of invariants which give rise to non-veridical perception. An example is the looming shadow which produces avoidant reactions in individuals of a number of species (Schiff, 1965). These experiments enable us to describe particular invariants, but such isolation is not representative of normal perception (though more so than the tachistoscopic experiments of constructionists). For normally the invariants that are abstracted by these experiments form part of higher order invariants. This argument leads to a hierarchy of higher order invariants, for which there is no clearcut end point, although the spatial field or visual field of consciousness provides us with a convenient resting place. As Wittgenstein (1969) recognized, I cannot in the ordinary sense make perceptual errors about objects in the centre of my visual field of consciousness. If I have doubts about the reality of this table on which I am writing, the doubts are, as it were, referred to the higher order invariants in which the table is embedded, and ultimately to the field of consciousness itself. And real doubts about *that* (which *may* be justified) are akin to madness, which is a far cry from the illusions of perceptual psychologists. On the other hand, in the periphery of my field of consciousness, when an object is some distance away, or glimpsed out of the corner of the eye, ordinary errors occur. For in these cases the invariants which are picked up are only loosely embedded within higher order invariants, which are not therefore brought down by the non-veracity of their subordinates (it is indeed the higher order invariants which may be said to detect the non-veracity). These invariants which are picked up from the periphery of the field correspond to the 'cues' of constructionists, upon the basis of which inferences are made. But cues in this sense are not required for perceptions in the centre of the field. The distance and shape of an object are not given by cues but are determined by the space which it fills within the field. This implies the existence of a spatial schema within which objects are fitted. But this schema is not now part of a constructionist theory, and therefore does not require representation in a propositional form, nor need it exist as an independent structure. Instead it is defined (like Head's schema) by the part it plays in the account given of the constitution of experience and the explanation of behaviour.

Notes

1 Theories which are in principle irrefutable should perhaps be called 'frameworks' or 'paradigms'. However, I shall generally continue to refer to the constructionist and realist 'theories'.
2 Distinctions are sometimes made between artificial intelligence, computer simulation and robotology, but nowadays AI seems to be used to cover

all approaches. A recent hybrid is 'cognitive science' which is defined in the SRC Bulletin for 1977 as 'The attempt to understand the information processing mechanisms which underlie perception, memory, reasoning, language and related activities in computational or other equally precise terms.' This begs many of the questions we are trying to ask.

3 It is interesting that a similar process occurred after Watson launched behaviourism. Before Watson psychologists were given a thorough grounding in philosophy which enabled them to steer a way through the tortuous logic of the mind. Watson, impatient with this, and making use of ideas current amongst his more subtle but timid colleagues, broke away from philosophy by denying mind a place in psychology. Philosophers were then influenced by behaviourism.

4 It has been argued that although some form of representation may be necessary it does not have to be propositional. The usual alternative suggested is an analogue representation, but this can be represented, to any degree of accuracy, in a digital or propositional form. The possible weaknesses of this argument against the significance of analogue representation are discussed in general terms below.

References

Amarel, S. (1968) On representations of problems of reasoning about actions. In D. Michie (ed.) *Machine Intelligence*, vol. 3. Edinburgh: Edinburgh University Press, pp. 131–72.

Anscombe, G. E. M. (1974) Comment on Professor R. L. Gregory's paper. In S. C. Brown (ed.) *Philosophy of Psychology*. London: Macmillan, 211–20.

Bartlett, F. C. (1932) *Remembering*. Cambridge: Cambridge University Press.

Blakemore, C. (1973) Environmental constraints on development in the visual system. In R. A. Hinde and J. Stevenson-Hinde (eds) *Constraints on Learning*. New York: Academic Press, pp. 51–73.

Chomsky, N. (1965) *Aspects of the Theory of Syntax*. Cambridge, Mass.: MIT Press.

Craik, K. J. W. (1943) *The Nature of Explanation*. Cambridge: Cambridge University Press.

Douglas, M. (1970) *Purity and Danger*. Harmondsworth: Penguin Books.

Dreyfus, H. L. (1972) *What Computers Can't Do: A Critique of Artificial Reason*. New York: Harper and Row.

Fodor, J. A. (1975) *The Language of Thought*. New York: Crowell.

Gibson, J. J. (1958) Visually controlled locomotion and visual orientation in animals. *British Journal of Psychology* 49: 182–94.

Gibson, J. J. (1966) *The Senses Considered as Perceptual Systems*. London: Allen and Unwin.

Gibson, J. J., Kaplan, G. A., Reynolds, H. N. and Wheeler, K. (1969) The change from visible to invisible: a study of optical transition. *Perception and Psychophysics* 5: 113–16.

Goodman, N. (1969) *Languages of Art*. London: Oxford University Press.

Gregory, R. L. (1966) *Eye and Brain*. London: Weidenfeld and Nicolson.

Gregory, R. L. (1974) Perception as hypothesis. In S. C. Brown (ed.) *Philosophy of Psychology*. London: Macmillan, pp. 195–210.

Gunderson, K. (1971) *Mentality and Machines*. New York: Anchor Books.

Gurwitsch, A. (1964) *The Field of Consciousness*. Pittsburgh: Duquesne University Press.

Hayes, P. J. (1973) In A. Elithorn and D. Jones (eds) *Artificial and Human Thinking*. Amsterdam: Elsevier, pp. 45–59.

Head, H. (1920) *Studies in Neurology*, Vol. 2. London: Hodder and Stoughton.

Hertz, H. (1956) *The Principles of Mechanics Presented in a New Form*. New York: Dover Publications. (German edn first published 1894.)

James, W. (1912) *Essays in Radical Empiricism*. New York: Longmans, Green and Co.

Kenny, A. (1968) *Descartes: A Study of his Philosophy*. New York: Random House.

Kullman, M. and Taylor, C. (1958) The pre-objective world. *Review of Metaphysics 108*: 108–32.

Lucas, J. R. (1961) Minds, machines and Godel. *Philosophy 36*: 112–27.

Minsky, M. L. (1975) A framework for representing knowledge. In P. H. Winston (ed.) *The Psychology of Computer Vision*. New York: McGraw-Hill. pp. 211–77.

Neisser, U. (1967) *Cognitive Psychology*. New York: Appleton-Century-Crofts.

Neisser, U. (1976) *Cognition and Reality*. San Francisco: Freeman.

Newell, A. and Simon, H. A. (1971) *Human Problem Solving*. Englewood Cliffs, N.J.: Prentice Hall.

Oldfield, R. C. (1954) Memory mechanisms and the theory of schemata. *British Journal of Psychology 45*: 14–23.

Oldfield, R. C. and Zangwill, O. L. (1942) Head's concept of the schema and its application in contemporary British psychology. Part I. Head's concept of the schema. *British Journal of Psychology 32*: 267–86.

Polanyi, M. (1967) *The Tacit Dimension*. London: Routledge and Kegan Paul.

Pylyshyn, Z. W. (1973) What the mind's eye tells the mind's brain: a critique of mental imagery. *Psychological Bulletin 80*: 1–24.

Schiff, W. (1965) Perception of impending collision: a study of visually directed avoidant behaviour. *Psychological Monogragh 79*: Whole No. 604.

Shaw, R. (1971) Cognition, simulation and the problem of complexity. *Journal of Structural Learning 2*: 31–44.

Suppes, P. and Zinnes, J. L. (1963) Basic measurement theory. In R. D. Luce, R. R. Bush and E. Galanter (eds) *Handbook of Mathematical Psychology*, Vol. I. New York: John Wiley, pp. 1–76.

Tolman, E. C. (1948) Cognitive maps in rats and men. *Psychological Review 55*: 189–208.

Wang, M. (1973) *From Mathematics to Philosophy*. London: Routledge and Kegan Paul.

Wittgenstein, L. (1922) *Tractatus Logico-Philosophicus*. London: Routledge and Kegan Paul.

Wittgenstein, L. (1969) *On Certainty*. Oxford: Basil Blackwell.

8 Phenomenology and psychology: Being objective about the mind

Neil Bolton

> The third part of the life of a human being, a part that we cannot ignore, is an intermediate area of experiencing, to which inner reality and external life both contribute. It is an area that is not challenged, because no claim is made on its behalf except that it shall exist as a resting place for the individual engaged in the perpetual human task of keeping inner and outer reality separate yet interrelated.
>
> (D. W. Winnicott)

Introduction

That contemporary academic psychology is content to exist without reference to phenomenology is evident from the manner in which influential psychologists describe the recent history of their subject in such a way as to show how being a psychologist is incompatible with being a philosopher. The story is a straightforward one. The failure of introspection to yield a reliable account of the contents of consciousness signifies that the only possible approach is methodological behaviourism, which does not confine itself to studying non-verbal actions but which does insist upon our defining 'what is meant in terms of observed events: that is, situations, to which a man must respond, and actions or words which he produces' (Broadbent, 1961,

p. 41). We thus overcome the major difficulty of the introspectionists, that of obtaining agreement from different investigators, and we advance to a theoretical language which enables us to investigate the causes and demonstrable antecedents of behaviour (Mandler, 1975). As the science of stimulus and response, of input and output, psychology is concerned only with statements that can be verified empirically and not with value judgements which belong to an entirely different realm of discourse (Broadbent, 1961, p. 47), presumably philosophy, although the accumulation of knowledge can make our moral attitudes more effective. On the other hand, psychology is closely allied to the biological sciences and attempts to view man in his biological setting. Like such sciences, psychology has reached the stage where it can advance by application of the experimental method:

> It is unlikely that we will see any more revolutions that completely redefine what we mean by mental life. Probably we will see increasing specialization as our factual information continues to grow in depth and detail. The dream of a single philosophical principle that explains everything it touches seems to be fading before the realization that man is vastly curious and complicated, and that we need a lot more information about him before we can formulate and test even the simplest psychological laws. (Miller, 1966, p. 369)

From this perspective phenomenology can only be seen as an aberration which has been overcome by psychology, for not only is it, as philosophy, purely speculative, but, worse, it is speculation about consciousness, an exercise which was observed to fail with introspectionism. Psychology, it may be concluded, is an empirical science; phenomenology is philosophy superceded by psychology. Thus psychologists are able to close ranks against philosophers, for any defence of the role of philosophy in psychology could only be an indulgence in philosophy.

It is clear, however, that the indifference or hostility shown by these authors towards phenomenology rests, not upon a systematic analysis of this movement, but upon a simple identification of the aims of phenomenology with those of introspection on the grounds that they are both concerned with the analysis of consciousness without reference to observed behaviour. Now this interpretation is mistaken since the purpose of introspection is to state facts of conscious experience. Phenomenology, however, has the more fundamental purpose of gaining essential insights into the nature of consciousness, that is, of reporting what consciousness has to be in order to be consciousness. This it does by attending to the phenomena of conscious experience as they present themselves to us. Thus the phenomenological method may be characterized as a critical reflection upon experience in order to discover its necessary structure and not as the reporting of facts, such as whether the subject uses imagery in problem-solving or feels depressed. If this ambitious project turned out to be defensible, yielding genuine insights into mental structures, phenomenology would play a major role in determining the course of empirical psychology, for it would define the proper use of psychological concepts. Moreover, it would cause us to reflect upon the assumptions that guide contemporary psychology. We might ask about the possible limitations of the input-output model of the mind; or whether it is in the nature of mental functioning to allow us to make a sharp distinction between moral and scientific realms of discourse and investigate man solely through use of the latter; or, again, whether mental life *is* best viewed within a biological perspective. For the phenomenologist the progress of psychology is not guaranteed by the application of the experimental method since what is required is the more fundamental investigation of how the area of psychology is essentially constituted.

What is ultimately at stake in any authentic comparison of the aims and methods of phenomenology and psychology is the question of the proper way of being objective about the mind. Psychology claims to have solved this problem by methodological behaviourism, which insists upon the verification of statements by reference to observable behaviour that occurs in response to manipulable stimuli: once we are sure of the connections between input and output, inferences can be made about the structures which control the processing of information. From such a perspective introspection is not only unreliable; it is unnecessary. For the subject develops and functions in interaction with his environment and the object of study *is* that interaction, not a private realm to which only each subject has privileged access. And, correspondingly, the method of study is an impersonal one in which the investigator reports the results of experimental manipulations, not his personal experience. If, following Mead (1934), we define the mind as that which can be an object to itself, it may be said that the purpose of scientific psychology is to discover what the mind has to be in order for it to be treated impersonally as a determinate part of the world of objects. Phenomenology, on the other hand, is the attempt to be objective about the mind through attention to mental phenomena themselves in their necessary function of revealing a world of objects. Phenomenology attempts to discover what the mind has to be in order for a world of objects to exist for it. To ask this question is to step back from the natural attitude, in which we take for granted that a world of objects exists for us, in order to understand how such a world can come about. We may say, therefore, that phenomenological analysis is concerned with how the objective is subjectively constituted; and that its method of investigation is necessarily personal, since it requires of the investigator the effort of having to abandon the natural attitude in order to be able to report phenomenological truths. The burden of responsibility lies, as with introspection, on the investigator truly reporting his own experience, but his aim is now to discover its necessary structure rather than the idiosyncratic facts contained within it.

Because of these different aims and methods, scientific psychology and phenomenology must remain separate disciplines. But in certain fundamental respects, the present chapter will argue, the phenomenological perspective is the determining one. This follows of necessity from the definition of mind as that which can be an object to itself, for this definition entails that the mind is not only an object but that which has the power to constitute objectivity. My contention is, then, that since it is consciousness that constitutes objectivity, the discipline which investigates the essential nature of that constitution, namely phenomenology, is the necessary foundation for that which investigates consciousness as part of the objective world, namely psychology.

The phenomenological method

The procedures of phenomenology may be viewed as attempts to found a discipline which can validly claim to investigate the way in which objectivity is constituted. The first step is to set aside that attitude of mind in which we take for granted that the world exists for us. In this, the natural attitude, it is taken for granted that, through perception and thinking, we can reveal more and more about the world around us: the possibility of human knowledge is a self-evident fact. But, since it is impossible to understand the constitution of reality from within a perspective which simply accepts reality as constituted, we must put the natural attitude aside, 'in brackets', in order to focus clearly on those acts of consciousness in which we experience the world of objects. For within the realm of the

natural attitude we remain incapable of solving the problem of the
possibility of knowledge; the commonsense belief in reality is a totally
implicit theme in the way in which we relate ourselves to the world,
not an act of judgement. But phenomenology seeks to investigate this
very theme and it must begin, therefore, by suspending that belief.
This is the meaning of the phenomenological *reduction* or *epoché*. In
Husserl's (1931) words:

> We put out of action the general thesis which belongs to the
> essence of the natural standpoint, we place in brackets whatever it
> includes respecting the nature of Being: this entire natural world
> therefore which is continually 'there for us', 'present to our hand',
> and will ever remain there, is a 'fact-world' of which we continue
> to be conscious, even though it pleases us to put it in brackets. If
> I do this, as I am fully free to do, I do *not* then *deny* this 'world',
> as though I were a sophist, I do not doubt that it is there as though
> I were a sceptic: but I use the phenomenological epoché which
> completely bars me from using any judgement that concerns spatio-
> temporal existence. (pp. 110–11)

The purpose of the reduction is to separate us from what commonsense, culture and science tell us in order to return to a world of
original experience, a world which the investigator himself must enter
before he can understand how objects appear to consciousness.

Once the investigator is able to attend to the phenomena themselves, that is, to the acts of consciousness themselves, he can concern
himself with the question of the essential nature of those acts. Just as
it was necessary to turn from the natural attitude to a philosophical
attitude, the latter enabling us to question and thereby understand
the achievements of the former, so it is now necessary to shift
attention from particular facts to essential qualities. Husserl argued
that every empirical and individual experience can be transformed
into an essential insight through a procedure he termed eidetic
intuition. Intuition is simply that form of experience in which an
object is given to us as present to consciousness and eidetic intuition
is intuition of the essence of something. We can achieve essential
intuitions in the formal sphere (e.g. understanding a syllogism), in
the material world (e.g. the essence of red or triangle), or in the
realm of consciousness (e.g. thinking, memory). Husserl at first
believed that eidetic intuition took place upon the basis of experiences
of particular individuals of a class of objects, but came to attach an
increasingly important role to the imagination, until he saw the

imagination as crucial in revealing the essence of things. Thus, starting with an actual or imagined individual sample, the investigator explores through imaginary variation what changes can be made in the sample without altering its essential nature; thus we discover what the object has to be in order to be the object it is. The roots of eidetic variation develop within the natural attitude; there is nothing mysterious about eidetic intuition since it is through this activity that we understand the nature of the triangle or of the concept of dog, but it reaches its true significance only when the natural attitude is abandoned. For it is only after the facticity of the world and of the self observing that world have been bracketed, that phenomena can be attended to as possibilities to be actualized. The essential structures of consciousness can be seen only when they are viewed in isolation from the objects in the world to which they relate. Husserl (1927) says:

> We may in free fancy, vary our actual world and transmute it to any other which we can imagine, but we are obliged with the world to vary ourselves also, and ourselves we cannot vary except within the limits prescribed to us by the nature of subjectivity. Change worlds as we may, each must ever be a world such as we could experience, prove upon the evidence of our theories and inhabit with our practice ... My psychological experiences, perceptions, imaginations and the like remain in form and content what they were, but I see them as 'structures' now, for I am face to face at last with the ultimate structure of consciousness. (p. 701)

Enough, I hope, has been said to indicate that carrying out the phenomenological reduction cannot be a routine performance undertaken within the natural attitude. To invite someone to do phenomenology is to invite them to abandon this attitude in which, as Husserl put it, one lives in one's acts, to attend to the acts themselves in their essential nature. Phenomenology is, therefore, a profoundly reflexive discipline, since in its attempt to understand the taken-for-granted objectivity of the natural attitude it requires of the investigator himself a shift in the direction of attention from that objectivity to the subjectivity in which the objective world is constituted.

The problem of constitution

How then does phenomenology account for the constitution of objective reality? What, more specifically, are the characteristics of consciousness that permit us to make the distinction between the subjective and the objective and how is the relation between these two to be described? Sokolowski (1970) has shown how Husserl's ideas on these questions developed over his lifetime, but I shall content myself with attempting to outline the solution to which he was eventually drawn.

Phenomenology advances a view of consciousness which is fundamentally opposed to that formulated by the British Empiricist philosophers which regards the mind as 'nothing but a bundle of different perceptions which succeed each other with inconceivable rapidity, and are in perpetual flux and movement' (Hume, 1739, p. 252). But, if this is the case, how can identical and identifiable objects exist? How can there be objectivity for a subject whose consciousness consists of acts which perpetually succeed one another? Husserl's solution to this problem was to point to the *intentionality* of consciousness. When an object is perceived, thought of, remembered, and so forth, there is, on the one hand, the act of perception, thinking or remembering and, on the other hand, that which is perceived, thought of or remembered. That is, within consciousness, we can distinguish what Husserl (1931) called the *noesis* (the act of consciousness) from the *noema* (the object as it appears to consciousness). Now the noema is distinct from the noesis in the sense that it does not constitute a part of the act and does not, therefore, exist within consciousness in the sense that the act does. For example, when looking at a thing, I alternatively shut and open my eyes and experience a number of perceptual acts which are all different from one another. But through every one of these acts I experience the same object. The tree that I perceive presents itself now exactly as it did a moment ago, as it did yesterday, as it is expected to do tomorrow. In the noema, then, we have something identical which cannot for this reason be mistaken for a part of the corresponding acts. We can generalize from this to say that consciousness is always consciousness of something: a conscious act presents the subject with a sense, an identifiable meaning which retains its identity over and above the temporal acts in which it is presented. Objectivity may be defined, then, as the independence of the object of the mode of its apprehension. Objectivity, as Gurwitsch (1940) points out, is not a mysterious something which locates things beyond consciousness: it simply indicates the possibility of keeping the object before our mental eye as persisting.

The doctrine of the intentionality of consciousness is the foundation of phenomenology, determining the way in which the movement could develop. For it points, on the one hand, to noetic analysis, that is, to an exploration of the structure of intentional acts in their function of constituting a world of objects; and, on the other hand, to noematic analysis, that is, to a description of the essential natures of the objects revealed to us. I shall return to this latter objective in our discussion of psychologism. Let us now pursue the former as Husserl elaborated the theme in *The Phenomenology of Internal Time Consciousness* (Husserl, 1964), *Formal and Transcendental Logic* (Husserl, 1929) and *Cartesian Meditations* (Husserl, 1960).

The theory of constitution which initially appealed to Husserl (1900, 1901) was the Kantian thesis by which sense or perception is opposed to understanding: it is the function of the latter to provide the universal and necessary *form* of experienced reality, whilst its *content* can only be given through sensation. As is well known, Kant argued that certain concepts, for example, time, space and causality, are not abstracted from experience: thus the notion of causality signifies a necessary connection and cannot be derived from any number of observations of the fact that A is followed by B. But, the position, shape, size and sequence of things is derived, not from such *a priori* concepts, but from our experience of the things themselves. On this view, therefore, objectivity arises when sensations are interpreted by intentions.[1] This theory of constitution may be referred to as the matter-form schema. It was current in Husserl's time (e.g. Natorp, 1893) and is widely accepted today within cognitive psychology (e.g. Garner, 1974; Neisser, 1976), but it was this schema which Husserl was led to abandon by his analyses of internal time consciousness.

In perceiving an external object we perceive a series of aspects of the object: I perceive the tree before me from a variety of perspectives, in different lights, and so forth. Corresponding to this are a series of sensations animated by intentionality. Sensations and intentions are immanent objects: they are experienced as occurring within consciousness, unlike the external object which is experienced as transcendent to consciousness. Now, Husserl (1931) talks of animated sensations *representing* objective qualities, an immanent red sensation, for example, serving as the appearance of an objective red quality. It is important to note that the notion of representation does not mean that we should treat sensations as signs or symbols of real things, so that the latter remain forever unknown. Rather, we perceive reality directly through appearances and sensations, even though reality remains distinct from and transcendent to consciousness. Husserl (1931) argued that, just as an animated sensation functions to allow an objective quality to appear, so time apprehensions are subjective phenomena which serve to manifest objective time to us. But, and this is a crucial point, although time appearances are similar to other appearances in serving to make manifest the objective world, they are prior to all other appearances and make it possible for us to experience them. Time appearances make it possible to have other appearances within our subjectivity for we can only experience objects in so far as they persist through the dispersion of our acts in time (see p. 164) and thus internal time consciousness is the structure basic to all experience.

An immanent object is not known in the same way in which a transcendent object is: Husserl says, we do not encounter our sensations or intentions, but experience them. However, just as external objects are encountered through a manifold of appearances, so immanent objects are experienced through a manifold of temporal phases. For an immanent object to be an object of experience, it must be located within the flow of time phases. But what is the nature of consciousness which permits this location to be accomplished? Husserl answers that we experience the present, the now-moment, together with its horizons of retention and protention. Thus, hearing a tone sounding involves a present experience together with a retention of that which was originally given (which is experienced as 'having been heard just now') and an anticipation of something 'just about to occur'. The structure of present moments situated within the context of retentions and protentions is the unchanging form of inner consciousness. As Sokolowski (1970) points out:

> ... the essential point to be retained from the discussion of temporal phases is Husserl's claim that elapsed moments of intentionality do not fall out of consciousness. Elapsed now-instants do not disappear as soon as they give way to a succeeding now-instant; rather they are held in retention ... The importance of this point is that it allows us to say that a manifold of temporal phases can be present to our consciousness at one and the same instant, and that consequently an immanent object can be constituted for our experience in such a manifold. The manifold is composed of the actual now-instant together with a series of phases that have elapsed but are still held in retention. (p. 86)

Thus, we have seen that intentions and sensations are immanent objects that are constituted in the manifold of time phases. Here we reach the heart of Husserl's argument for he goes on to identify time phases with intentionality itself. This identification is a necessary one because, if it were denied, I would experience temporal phases as occurring over and against the intentionality which informs my consciousness. Consequently, the intentional act constituted in these temporal phases would be experienced as being opposed to my present stream of consciousness. But this cannot be, for in experiencing our immanent acts we exist in the same stream of consciousness as that in which the acts themselves are formed. As Landgrebe (1973) points out, all experiencing is experiencing in a horizon of possibilities, given to us through retentions and protention, and the experiencing consciousness is at the same time consciousness of such a horizon. This is precisely what *experience* is, as against *perception*, which involves encountering an object which stands outside our stream of consciousness. Now, if partial intentions are identical to constituting temporal phases, they themselves cannot be constituted, but belong to the originating stream of consciousness. Sensations, as immanent objects, are also constituted by temporal phases, that is, by our intentions. What is sensed, says Husserl (1901), is no different from the act of sensing. There is no duality between sensation as an object and sensation as awareness, and to have a sensation is to experience it as an immanent object in my subjectivity. The radical implication of this reasoning is that, since both sensations and intentions arise from internal time consciousness, there is no longer any basis for making a distinction between them: there is at the most primitive level only a unity, the world of 'lived experience', the consciousness in which sensations and intentions are undifferentiated. The schema of intentional acts informing sensory content is shown to be false.

This conclusion about the nature of immanent objects is extended to the constitution of objective time, and of objectivity in general. The matter-form schema does not apply to the constitution of objective time, the time which seems to exist independently of our consciousness, since there is no such thing as a temporal sense datum independent of intentions. If we wish to explain objective time, we must look to the structure of subjectivity; there, we see that our explanation must be couched, not in terms of acts, but of the pre-act structure of intentionality itself. In his later works, Husserl (1948) developed the viewpoint of a genetic analysis which would trace the origin of objective thought from our pre-reflective encounters, showing, for instance, how our concepts of space or causality arise out of that 'lived' experience which takes place before any acts of judgement. Objectivity refers, then, to those judgements, which have arisen out of the flow of intentional life and which, therefore, both owe their existence and meaning to consciousness and 'stand before' it for inspection. Merleau-Ponty (1962) faithfully carries on the Husserlian tradition when he affirms that 'perception is not an act but the background against which all acts stand out' (p. x). It is precisely because phenomenology in its account of constitution grounds its explanation at the level of consciousness in which no distinction is possible between the intentional activity of the subject and the material of the objective world that it can avoid the errors of empiricism and constructivism, the former reducing experience to environmental determinants, the latter reducing it to the activities of the subject, without falling into the false compromise of a *critical realism* which rests upon an opposition between intentions and sensations.

The critique of psychologism

Thus far, we have seen the necessity for adopting a threefold classification in describing the relationship between subjectivity and objectivity – the world of objects encountered in perception, the world of immanent objects experienced as intentions or sensations, and the world of the constituting flow of consciousness. It would be easy to make the mistake of believing that, since it is subjectivity that gives sense to reality, that reality is nothing other than the meanings imposed by subjectivity. But phenomenology is not an idealist philosophy of this kind. Husserl insisted that reality cannot be reduced to consciousness for it is transcendent to it. Consciousness must be, then, a necessary but not a sufficient condition for the emergence of sense: it does not create the meaning of objects but allows that meaning to come about. At the centre of phenomenology is the avoidance of attributing priority to either subjectivity or objectivity: the objective is 'relative' to consciousness but consciousness reveals the objective.

I pointed out earlier that the notion of the intentionality of consciousness implies both a noetic analysis of the structure of intentionality in its function of constituting the objective world and a noematic analysis of the essential natures of the objects revealed to us. We are now in a position to see how the latter necessarily complements the former, for a genetic or constitutional analysis will show how an objective sense originates, whilst an analysis of the object itself will show us the essential nature of that sense. In this latter analysis we focus upon the constituted meaning in order to describe it as it is given to us. There is no question here of reducing the objective to the subjective, of explaining the object in terms of the conditions that give rise to it, for this would be to commit the error of psychologism, the reduction of objectivity to psychological processes such that a distinction can no longer be made between that which is subjective and that which is objective: Husserl's (1900) attack on psychologism included a number of criticisms. He argued that if logical laws were derived from experience, then they could deal only with probable, and not with necessary, relationships, but this is a mistaken account of the exact laws of logic, in which conclusions follow premises in a valid syllogism with absolute necessity. Psychologism also confuses a law with the act of knowing the law, but the law is true irrespective of whether it is known or not. Further, in insisting that objectivity is relative to consciousness, psychologism could only lead to sceptical relativism, which for Husserl was a self-defeating position, claiming absolute necessity for itself whilst denying the possibility of universally necessary statements. Genetic phenomenology, however, can claim to avoid psychologism; it shows how objectivity is relative to consciousness through tracing the development of judgements from pre-predicative experience (p. 167), but affirms that consciousness *reveals* the objective. For, having abandoned the dualism of matter and form at this, the most primitive level of experience, there is no dualism of subjective and objective. We are aware of reaching out to a reality which exists beyond ourselves precisely at those moments when self and world coincide. The fulfilment of our intentions is at once the recognition of the identity of the intention and its fulfilment and of their distinctness.

We have seen that intuition is that form of experience in which an object is given to us and essential intuition is said to reveal the object in its necessary structure. Husserl's analysis of internal time consciousness was an attempt to understand the necessary structure of intentionality by means of a critical reflection which would bring the objective sense to full clarity in intuition. The concern of such a study is not to reduce the phenomenon to antecedent causes but to describe its necessary sense. And since consciousness gives us the world, our own revelation of the aspects of consciousness can only be to show how they give us access to the truth of the world. Thus, for example, Dufrenne (1974) characterizes aesthetic experience as a 'sympathetic reflection' which attempts to understand how a work of art unfolds itself to create its own world, a world of expression. Through feeling we connect ourselves to the inherent expressiveness of the aesthetic object. Aesthetic feeling is, therefore, one way in which we grasp the truth of the world. Psychologism, by contrast, attempts to understand solely from the point of view of the subjective consciousness: the psychological object is explained by reference to the mental operations themselves, as when aesthetic perception is 'accounted for' in terms of moderate levels of arousal, perception as a series of interpretive actions, and creative thinking as a collection of associations. The differences between behaviourism and cognitive psychology fade into insignificance in the face of their common psychologism, the reduction of the objectivity of knowing to purely psychological processes which in themselves allow us no means of distinguishing truth from falsity. Whilst phenomenology entails a 'bracketing' of the natural belief in the reality of the world in order to understand how there can be a real world for human consciousness, psychology's acceptance of the reality of the world, its unawareness of the problem of constitution, leads to a false objectivism that obscures the difference between the subjective and the objective. Whilst phenomenology centres itself around the paradox that reality is relative to consciousness and yet transcends it, psychology sees its task as being the objective study of the subjective, that is, of that which makes no reference to the objective and can, therefore, only fall into the error of making the subjective the measure of the objective. It is not a question of opposing a humanistic perspective, which deals with meaningful actions, to a positivist one which talks of causal mechanisms, for the error that they share outweighs the differences between them.

In summary, the rejection by phenomenology of the ultimate dualism of inner and outer reality leads to a rejection of psychologism, the reduction of objective sense to subjective processes. It thus leads onwards to an account of mind whose central preoccupation is the distinction between authentic experience which reveals, if always partially, the reality to which subjectivity is directed and inauthentic experience which fails to do so. In this sense phenomenology may be characterized as a moral discipline: it perceives the actual as ways in which the possibilities of being human are fulfilled or not. It is, hence, also a reflexive discipline, for how can the investigator himself remain indifferent to the demands of making clear what is authentic in human experience?

On the relation between phenomenology and psychology: a dialogue

Psychologist: You say that we cannot consider psychological processes in isolation from the truth of the objects to which they refer, but surely there are general structures discernible in processes such as thinking, memory and perception. The mind works in ways determined by the structure of the brain, so that we can describe stages in problem-solving, different kinds of memory, the nature of anxiety, and so forth.

Phenomenologist: I do not wish to argue that there are no general structures in the mind, but I do wish to propose that the identification of those structures is bound up with the correct identification of the truth or falsity of the objects that are revealed through the operation of the mind. Let it be quite clear that I am not supporting a naive realism which believes that things in themselves can be analysed and brought to clarity independently of the mind's constitution of them. Just as we should avoid supposing that because subjectivity constitutes reality it therefore creates it, so we should avoid the assumption that it is simply a question of putting subjectivity aside in order to attend to reality itself. It is a commonplace to say that both these views lead ultimately to a denial of truth or rather of the objectivity of truth; the former because it identifies what is true with what is intended or felt; the latter because everything that can be attended to is thereby true: both leave no room for the process by which one overcomes error.

Psychologist: But wait! I think that you are consigning us to a quite unnecessary mystery. Granted that simple idealist and realist views are mistaken, then the solution is obvious – a combination of the two. The mind is an hypothesis-testing device and the reality which exists independently of it provides the information that enables us to confirm or reject hypotheses. Such a view is quite consistent with the present activity of psychologists: they can take for granted that this is how things are and continue to study pure processing.

Phenomenologist: I am quite content to agree that our ideas are tested against a reality which is independent of them, but your conclusion leaves at least two fundamental questions unanswered. First, in order for ideas to be tested against reality there must be some form of relationship between the realms of the mental and the actual. How else could the one be translated into the other? The notion of hypothesis-testing can only make sense within a context which is not a result of such testing but its necessary pre-condition. The model of input and output is not the fundamental one, therefore, since it is necessary to determine that form of being which makes it natural for us to check our ideas against the facts. Second, the model is superficial also in that, whilst accepting the basic drive to seek the truth of one's beliefs, it does not enquire into the question as to how that which is true and real determines our mental life. This is the reason why such a position ultimately degenerates into naive idealism. On the other hand, if one regards subjectivity as aiming at the truth, as it were, then our approach has to be broad enough to include both terms, the mental and the real, in their essential unity. One would then study, not perception, but what is essentially revealed through perception, not emotion but how feeling forms the world for us, and so forth.

Psychologist: But, if I have understood you correctly, this would mean the introduction of value judgements into our inquiries, for we would have to ask ourselves what is true and real and of value before we could do anything else. We would be passing, not from facts to values, which is a bad enough mistake, but from values to facts, which seems utterly absurd. For how on earth are people ever going to agree on what is an 'essential truth'? This is armchair philosophizing at its worst.

Phenomenologist: Every endeavour presupposes certain values; even your own espousal of an empirical science is based upon a choice, a preference for certain norms rather than another set. What I am suggesting is that, rather than accept the role of values unquestioningly as we tend to do if the values happen to be our own, we should systematically investigate them with a view to determining the sorts of truth they reveal. With respect to verifying our insights, I have evidently more faith than you in our capacity to reflect upon our thoughts sensibly and communicate with one another in a critical fashion. It is important to remember that we are not reporting private 'facts' through introspection, but discussing essential ways of interpreting reality: thus insights can be verified by participants checking each other's perspectives in the same way, possibly, that a child learns a language in contact with the speech of adults, except that in these matters we are all children. I find it deeply satisfying that a direction of inquiry is warranted in which there is no discontinuity between the investigator and the investigated in the sense that I shall only truly understand the object of study, the mind, by advancing my own thoughts as to the truth revealed to us as human beings. This total correspondence of subjective and objective parallels that identity which occurs at the most fundamental level of human being, as Husserl has shown. It is the authentic way of being objective about the mind.

Psychologist: Are you saying that it is the only way in which an objective understanding of the mind can arise? There might be a slim chance of this being true for certain areas of investigation, but for many, surely, this sort of involvement is just unnecessary. To find out how a subject learns to solve a problem or why he perceives a certain type of stimulus in the way that he does must entail the investigator detaching himself from the situation in order to view it objectively. In this and countless other situations the psychologist need not concern himself with what is 'true' but just with how things happen, and this is the heart of psychology which your criticisms do not affect.

Phenomenologist: I think that there are three arguments that may be used here. In the first place, in the situations you describe it might be very helpful for the investigator to place himself in the subject's shoes and ask what he might be attempting to achieve or how he might be perceiving things in order to gain some insight into the subject's perspective, which is, after all, an important variable. Second, one supposes that experimental situations have been chosen by the investigator to throw light upon the basic processes of perception, learning, and so forth. I would argue that the investigator must justify his selection of an experimental situation as potentially able to reveal basic processes and the source of that justification must be an analysis of what the essential natures of perception, learning, etc. are. So we are back at our beginning: your empirical investigations must occur within a framework that goes beyond psychology. And this brings me to an attempt to answer your question. A number of authors (e.g. Macmurray, 1961; Polanyi, 1967; Merleau-Ponty, 1962) have pointed out that our impersonal knowledge must be seen in the context of a form of understanding which is both the source of that knowledge and which constantly transcends it. The error of psychology, which it is led to through an acceptance of the ultimate dualism of subject and object, so that as a science it becomes 'merely objective', is a failure to recognize this context. And seeing our empirical generalizations against this background is crucial to the task of giving them sense and coherence. If you refuse to do this, you will condemn our subject-matter to an artificial and unbridgable division, whereby psychology will study man in his inessential aspects and something called philosophy – in our case, phenomenology

– will be concerned with his essential nature – as a being for truth.

Do you remember Miller's (1966) view that psychology has seen the end of conceptual crises and can now look forward to steady growth as a result of the accumulation of empirical findings? Compare that view with Heidegger's:

> The real movement of the sciences takes place when their basic concepts undergo a more or less radical revision which is transparent to itself. The level which a science has reached is determined by how far it is *capable* of a crisis in its basic concepts. In such immanent crises the very relationship between positively investigative inquiry and those things themselves that are under interrogation comes to a point where it begins to totter. (Heidegger, 1927, p. 29)

I maintain that the importance of phenomenology for psychology is its suggestion that psychology is capable of such a radical crisis.

Note

1 In contemporary theory, the term 'sensations' is replaced by 'stimuli' and we talk of plans or schemata instead of interpretations, but the meaning is essentially the same.

References

Broadbent, D. E. (1961) *Behaviour*. London: Methuen.

Dufrenne, M. (1974) *The Phenomenology of Aesthetic Experience*. Evanston: Northwestern Universities Press.

Garner, W. R. (1974) *The Processing of Information and Structure*. Potomac: Erlbaum.

Gurwitsch, A. (1940) On the intentionality of consciousness. In M. Farber (ed.) *Philosophical Essays in Memory of Edmond Husserl*. Cambridge, Mass.: Harvard University Press, pp. 65–83.

Heidegger, M. (1927) *Being and Time*. Oxford: Basil Blackwell (1967).

Hume, D. (1739) *A Treatise on Human Nature*. London: Oxford University Press (1888).

Husserl, E. (1900) *Logical Investigations*, Vol. 1. Halle: Niemeyer.

Husserl, E. (1901) *Logical Investigations*, Vol. 2. Halle: Niemeyer.

Husserl, E. (1927) Phenomenology. In *Encyclopaedia Britannica*, 14th edition.

Husserl, E. (1929) *Formal and Transcendental Logic*. The Hague: M. Nijhoff (1969).

Husserl, E. (1931) *Ideas: General Introduction to Pure Phenomenology*, Vol. 1. New York: Macmillan.

Husserl, E. (1948) *Experience and Judgment*. London: Routledge and Kegan Paul (1973).

Husserl, E. (1960) *Cartesian Meditations*. The Hague: M. Nijhoff.

Husserl, E. (1964) *The Phenomenology of Internal Time Consciousness*. Bloomington: Indiana University Press.

Landgrebe, L. (1973) The phenomenological concept of experience. *Philos. Phenom. Res. 34*: 1–13.

Macmurray, J. (1961) *Reason and Emotion*. London: Faber.

Mandler, G. (1975) *Mind and Emotion*. New York: Wiley.

Mead, G. H. (1934) In C. W. Morris (ed.) *Mind, Self and Society*. Chicago: University of Chicago Press.

Merleau-Ponty, M. (1962) *The Phenomenology of Perception*. London: Routledge and Kegan Paul.

Miller, G. (1966) *Psychology: The Science of Mental Life*: Harmondsworth: Penguin.

Natorp, P. (1893) *Einleitung in die Psychologie nach Kritischer Methode*. Freiburg: E. C. Mohr.

Neisser, U. (1976) *Cognition and Reality*. San Francisco: W. H. Freeman.

Polanyi, M. (1967) *The Tacit Dimension*. London: Routledge and Kegan Paul.

Sokolowski, R. (1970) *The Formation of Husserl's Concept of Constitution*. The Hague: Martinus Nijhoff.

9 Theory in psychotherapy

John M. Heaton

In this chapter I want to do two things. First to show that psychotherapy is best understood as the beginnings of a science of action and its disorders rather than a cure for disorders of the mind; it is therefore, to use an old-fashioned word, an ethical science rather than a psychological one. I will examine some important concepts used in therapy to show the confusions that result from not understanding it in this way. Second, I want to show that if it is to develop as a science of action then the nature of theoretical work in psychotherapy is very different from the way it is envisaged at present.

There is little doubt that psychotherapy is in a state of deplorable confusion. There is a profusion of different therapeutic schools – Freudian, Kleinian, London Jungian, Zurich Jungian, Reichian, Gestalt, Rogerian, construct therapy, behaviour therapy, primal scream and so on. There is confusion as to whether therapy is best given individually, to the family, in groups, within a community or should be directed at society itself. There is even argument as to whether any training is necessary to give therapy, for example the co-counselling movement. These therapies and ideas tend to have little contact with one another, and are more like a heap of recipes for a state of mental health which is left undefined than the products of a healthy systematic and self-critical science.

Psychotherapeutic theory is equally confused. There is great uncertainty as to the nature of psychotherapeutic knowledge. Is psycho-analysis a science or a pseudo-science (Cioffi, 1970)? Is behaviour therapy the only rational scientific therapy? On the whole therapists see theory as purely abstract or as a pragmatic exercise. In the former it passively reflects in words what is observed and done in therapy so that theory is made rather a pointless exercise, a pale copy of practice. In the latter, theory is written like a cookery book, rich with advice and recipes of practices which are alleged to produce therapeutic change. This leaves therapy wide open to every sort of opportunism and quackery, for the desirability of the changes allegedly produced is never examined.

Action

It is first necessary to indicate briefly what is meant by action, a concept in which there has recently been much interest (Arendt, 1958; Louch, 1966; Searle, 1969; Taylor, 1964; Winch, 1958 and many others). The idea of action is linked to that of an agent. For every act there must be an agent whose act it is – a self in the language of therapy. This immediately contrasts it with behaviour in which no agent initiates the complex of movements. Furthermore action cannot be imagined outside a society in which there are customs, rules and language. For action is a performance and there are right and wrong, adequate and inadequate performances which have been learned; all actions are embedded in norms and ways of living which enable them to be performed and judged.

Actions and their failures are explained in terms of the actor's intentions, purposes, and the reasons governing the society in which he lives. The language of action is used and shaped in the course of action by the actors so action can only be identified by concepts and norms familiar to the actor. It would be impossible for an actor to initiate an act of which he has no concept.

Thus a disordered act such as a slip of the pen is done inadvertently, so the agent is not fully behind the act – he did not mean to do it. Its reasons are explained in terms of the norms of the society in which the agent lives – fear of exposing his sexual desires to himself and others, veiled insults, envy and so on. For the explanation to be effective the agent must understand the concepts used; he must know what an insult is, what it is to be envious, etc. and these concepts depend ultimately on the norms of his society.

Men are responsible for their actions because we hold them so. An action simply is the sort of thing that can be commanded, forbidden, praised, blamed, or thought mad, in contrast to behaviour which just happens. So action is not something we can define by simply pointing at it. Thus I might write my signature in a moment of idleness or use it to win a fortune or commit treason. The same movement can in various circumstances constitute any of these actions and many more, so in itself it constitutes none of them. To understand an act we always need to look beyond physical events into language and society.

The patients that go to psychotherapists and are treated by them always exemplify disordered action. Things happen to them like pains, guilt, phobias, obsessions and tics, yet to the agent there seems to be no cause and no convincing reason either. Their lives feel empty, they do not know what they want or ought to do, they cannot get on with people or people cannot get on with them, they are unhappy and are unable to love and work satisfactorily. They are usually in a state of conflict which means that they have no clear sense of agency in their actions.

Observation and discovery

Now the study and treatment of disordered action is very different from that of pathological processes in the mind having a cause which may be found by induction and observation. Enormous confusion has resulted from not clearly differentiating the two.

Freud (1963, p. 83) wrote 'It was discovered one day that the pathological symptoms of certain neurotic patients have a sense. On this discovery the psychoanalytical method of treatment was founded.' He clearly thought he had made a discovery based on observation. He often emphasized that psychoanalysis was not speculative but was a direct expression of observation. 'A tireless elaboration of facts from the world of perception' (Freud, 1961, p. 217). In his popular lectures he describes the findings of psychoanalysis with the aplomb of an astronomer or physiologist talking of his observations and experiments. Most psychotherapists have followed him in this although with less persuasive power.

Take Freud's 'discovery' of the Oedipus Complex – the cornerstone of his theory. He 'discovered' it during his self-analysis which was initiated by his father's death. His self-analysis preoccupied him as did his relationship to his own father and mother, and problems of sexuality and masturbation. He wrote during this time, 'Everything is still obscure, even the problems; but there is a comfortable feeling that one has only to rummage in one's own storeroom to find sooner or later what one needs' (Freud, 1966, p. 267). At about that time (1897) he announced the discovery of the Oedipus Complex and most of his other basic notions. But he did not behave like one who had made a discovery based on and confirmed by careful observations. He was more like a person trying to make sense of his experiences and using myth in the way it has traditionally been used. But myth is not an empirical matter that can be observed as Freud seemed to think; it is a logic of desire, a way of creating meaning.

Freud's shift from seeking the causes of symptoms to concern with their meaning was not a discovery and not based on any new observations. He was misled by the analogy between discovering new things by observations with microscopes and telescopes and the 'discovery' of meaning and new meanings. When we try to discover causes in the material world we search systematically by experimenting with and observing different states of affairs, for we have an idea of what the cause is like in advance.

The search for meaning and its development is very different. This, I suggest, is why Freud intuitively developed his method of free association. For here we do not search with some empirical object in mind as we do not know what we will find until it turns up and we recognize it. The activity of finding meaning does not constitute a deliberate search, even if it results in finding what we want.

Take the case of Freud's insights into slips of the tongue. He turned the inquiry away from causes such as dysfunctional brain activity towards reasons. Thus he turned from considering behaviour to assessing speech acts. He judged them as being inadequate actions; they were not allowed to be excused, so he stopped patients, himself and even members of his family from saying that they just happened. He made them free associate until a justifiable reason for the slip was found. It was a process of evaluation and not of observation and induction.

Telling

A central confusion of Freud and most therapists is that they do not distinguish between reporting and telling. They assume that dreams, fantasies, emotions and thoughts are occurrences in the mind which can be observed and reported to them by their patients. So the therapist's job becomes one of listening to these reports and when they become confused or appear to report confusions, some intervention is necessary. Similarly patients often think they should 'report' what is on their minds or what happened to them in the past, and will try and get clues from the therapist as to what he wants reported.

Now there is a big difference between the logic of telling someone something and reporting it. If a girl said that her lover 'reported' to her the night before that he loved her, we would think it odd and probably interpret her statement as meaning that she thought there was something peculiar about him. But if he *told* her he loved her there would be a sense of personal revelation and intimacy appropriate to the avowal. In telling someone something it is for us to say what we had in mind. This contrasts with reporting which always, in principle, can be verified or corrected by someone else.

Of course when we are told something we may not agree with it. The girl may not believe that her lover's declaration is genuine but, if this is so she will respond in ways that will affect him so that he reveals more of himself. She will not ask him to inspect the contents of his mind and find that they are false in so far as he does not really love her. Telling people things calls for a response or series of actions between the people concerned, whereas a report that is suspect requires inspection of what is reported on (Hunter, 1973).

By confusing reports with telling, therapists grossly distort the nature of their patients' utterances. For they turn them into reports on the supposed goings on in their patients' minds rather than utterances which call for a response which reveals. Taking up the analytical attitude of a dispassionate observer implies that the therapist has privileged access to the patient's mind, that he is the better observer, the patient being too involved. It alters the natural logic of telling and so easily throws the teller into a state of confusion. This, of course makes him insecure, and so more likely to be dependent and more open to the therapist's suggestions, which although implicit are nevertheless powerful. Hence there can start an endless exploration of what is 'in' the patient's mind of which the therapist is assumed to be the more knowledgeable observer.

Thus Freud, Klein and others try to reconstruct the inner world of their patients from what they are told by and observe in their patients. They come up with elaborate accounts of mental mechanisms, phantasies, instincts and so on. When people ask them if a small child can speculate upon its being born through its mother's anus or not, or whether a little girl regards her clitoris as an inferior penis, then they retire to mystification. 'None, however, but physicians who practise psychoanalysis can have any access whatever to this sphere of knowledge or any possibility of forming a judgement that is uninfluenced by their own dislikes and prejudices. If mankind had been able to learn from a direct observation of children, these three essays could have remained unwritten' (Freud, 1953, p. 133). It did not occur to Freud that his theories could be a manifestation of his own inability to respond to what patients told him. Instead he regarded his observations as reliable and concocted theories on the basis of them.

Therapeutic practice however can and should be rather different. The therapist's use of notions like infantile sexuality, the castration complex and so on is best understood as a way of giving form and meaning to various experiences which therapists sense underlie their patients' actions. They are notations or myths and therefore do not stand in any direct relation to observable reality. They carry no information and any attempt at refutation or experimental confirmation is therefore futile. These theoretical notions are meaningful but are not empirically true.

This helps to account for the great variety of therapeutic theories. Jungians elicit material about archetypes and individuation, Kleinians about early experiences around the breast, Rogerians about 'basic instinctual goodness' and so on. None of these theories is refutable in terms of observation on empirical material. They should be seen as notations which enable the therapeutic process to get going; so they are not true (nor are they false) although they may strike one as crude.

However therapists insist that their theories are true. They presumably feel that if they were seen as myths it would somehow deprive them of any persuasive power – this is doubtful for myth has a tremendous hold on mankind. However they are not scientifically respectable. So therapists cling to their myths, which helps explain the dogmatism and exclusiveness of the various therapeutic schools and the grave doubts of some of their critics as to whether their activities are 'scientific'.

If therapists were to realize that no therapy can be understood in the terms of its own notations and myths but that its basic theory lies in the light it throws on action and its disorders, then they would have an answer to critics such as Popper (1957) and Cioffi (1970) who claim psychoanalysis is a pseudo-science as it is designed to escape refutation. Nor would they need to resort to apologists such as Rycroft (1966) who claim that analysts are some sort of humanists who are experts at deciphering a special inner psychic reality. Furthermore they would realize that they had two transferences to analyse – the transference onto the analyst and the transference onto his particular therapeutic school and its myths and language.

Experience

A key notion in therapy is experience. It is held that one's own experience is the highest authority of truth. Thus, 'The touchstone of validity is my own experience. No other person's ideas, and none of my own ideas, are as authoritative as my experience. It is to experience that I must return again and again, to discover a closer approximation to truth as it is in the process of becoming in me. Neither the Bible nor the prophets – neither Freud nor research – neither the revelations of God nor man – can take precedence over my own direct experience' (Rogers, 1961, pp. 23–4). 'When an activity feels as though it is valuable or worth doing it is worth doing ... I have learned that my total organismic sensing of a situation is more trustworthy than my intellect (Rogers, 1961, p. 22). This dogma is almost universal amongst encounter group leaders, Gestalt therapists and radical therapists. Freud held a similar view: he held that only those who have experienced psycho-analysis are able to judge it. The ordinary man has too great a resistance to the shockingness of its findings to keep his head (Freud, 1961). Freud at times seemed to think that the greater the resistance to psychoanalysis the more likely is it to be true. He forgot that early Christianity, Galileo's ideas and many other original ideas and movements have come up against far greater resistance and per-secution. In fact psychoanalysis in the western world rapidly became extremely popular and analysts soon were wealthy and influential members of society.

Freud thought that his notion of the unconscious which showed that the conscious ego is not sole master of man, provoked the greatest resistance. He none too modestly compared himself to Copernicus and Darwin who also, according to him, aimed blows at man's narcissism. He could not acknowledge that many thinkers from time immemorial have pointed out that man is not sole master of himself, but more wisely were not so concerned at aiming blows at narcissism which tends of course just to increase it as well as being rather an arrogant thing to do. He also did not see that the term conscious ego is a technical term and that the ordinary man if asked the rather odd question as to what ruled him would be unlikely ever to have answered that it was his conscious ego, but would probably say that something outside him did – the government, money or his wife.

The dogma that one's own experience is the touchstone of truth is an old one with a long and chequered history. Thus Locke in 1680 wrote:

> Let us suppose the mind to be, as we say, white paper void of all characters, without any ideas. How comes it to be furnished? Whence comes it by that vast store which the busy and boundless fancy of man has painted on it with an almost endless variety? Whence has it all the materials of reason and knowledge? To this answer, in one word, from *experience*; in that all our knowledge is founded, and from it ultimately derives itself. (Locke, 1961, p. 77)

Rogers's argument is contradictory. To say for example that 'my total organismic functioning is more trustworthy than my intellect' is to contradict oneself for presumably it is one's intellect that makes the judgement.

Whatever we experience, see, hear or feel we experience hear or feel as a determinate object; that is, under a certain description. There is no such thing as a pure experience. Thus whereas I see curious marks in the snow a hunter sees the tracks of a rabbit. What the layman hears as a momentary lapse of memory the analyst hears as a repression of a sexual impulse. But the hunter and I see the same thing and the analyst and layman hear the same thing. There is no difficulty for us in telling each other what we see the marks as, or what we hear the sounds as, or in understanding one another. What we can never do is to say what it is we see as marks or tracks or as a memory lapse or an act of repression. There is no basic present experience.

To believe that the touchstone of validity is one's own experience is to tie oneself down to what is immediately given. It is using a notion of experience to define the world or the most valid part of it which leads to the neglect of the role of language and society in the creation of knowledge. It creates the problem of knowing what grounds there are for moving from the actual to the possible – a crucial one in therapy.

In therapy this belief encourages the dogmatism of the various schools, for each remains fixed to its own experience. Any therapy becomes a reflection of the therapist himself. Patients learn to describe and refine their experience in the way their therapist does, for their concept of experience helps determine what they experience. So if they 'do well' they become essentially like their therapist.

As there are no objective criteria as to what experience is worthwhile, value becomes quantified or glamorized. So the more intense or glamorous the experience the more value becomes attached to it. Strong emotion, orgasms, pre-birth and so called transcendental experience become good and desirable in themselves. There is in addition a profound neglect of the political roots of therapeutic activity. All this inevitably leads to the '*belle âme*' described by Hegel (1805) which

> lives in dread of besmirching the splendour of its inner being by action and by existence; and in order to preserve the purity of its heart it flees from contact with the actual world.... In this transparent purity of its moments, an unhappy, so called 'beautiful soul', its light dies away within it, and it vanishes like a shapeless vapour that dissolves into thin air. (Para. 658)

Self-knowledge

Freud and most therapists agree that they have developed techniques for self-knowledge. Freud (1963) for example says his techniques must be learned and applied to oneself and others just as the techniques of histology or surgery must be learned. Perls et al. (1972, p. 3) say 'self-discovery ... involves the adoption of a rather special attitude towards your self and observation of your self in action. To observe your self in action – ultimately, to observe your self as action – calls for techniques strikingly different from those you may have tried already and found wanting, in particular introspection.' They all assume that we get knowledge of our desires, pleasures, emotions, thoughts and feelings by observing ourselves. They believe that there is an internal psychical reality which is on the whole inaccessible to most of us, but that can be observed by part of the ego with training. This view of the mind has been criticized radically by Wittgenstein (1958), Ryle (1949) and many others, so I will not repeat the arguments. I merely wish to spell out some of its consequences for psychotherapy.

It reduces self-knowledge to being a technical matter which is done poorly by ordinary folk but really needs an expert. In thinking technically we make representations of the end we desire and then devise the most efficient means to attain it. We define the end within a system of concepts and then devise the means to reach that end, the whole process remaining by necessity within the system of concepts.

Medical practice is technical in this way. If we become ill we have a picture of what health is, which is usually the state we were in before we became ill. The doctor then devises means to restore us to that state as quickly and comfortably as possible.

Technical activity always implies there is a content or material to work with. So in the case of the mind the assumption is that it is some sort of internal thing or series of processes which has to be observed and worked upon – analysed, synthesized, allowed to grow, explored, altered in its behaviour and so on. In addition it may be seen as a repository of resources which contains energy to be unleashed and used by the owner under the guidance of the technician.

Any technique or method of self-knowledge is always limited to seeing and dealing with that which lies within the conceptual system of the method. So to be restricted to a method of self-knowledge is to give up any possibility of radical self-criticism. For to know what method to adopt one must have arrived at some knowledge of the nature of the subject matter and so about knowledge of the self. If one defends this knowledge by the use of one's chosen method, one is open to the charge of circularity. Alternatively if one seeks justification for the method in its success then one is still no better off. For the method cannot justify the crucial assumptions that are in dispute. The methodologist is unable to show why his successes should be judged as successes and not mere alterations. To call them successes is simply begging the question.

Pure science makes certain phenomena of nature intelligible. The applied scientist uses these concepts to alter nature in a way thought desirable. He is given a picture of nature to which he can apply his techniques. So there must be univocity of concepts and specifications between the conditions, prescriptions and goals of the applied scientist. The products of applied science become standardized ideal objects which means that they keep the same meaning however often repeated – hence the possibility of mass production. In the case of the 'mind' it becomes seen as a standardized material which has been described by psychologists and so can be disposed of with a view to calculable goals. The psychologist decides what healthy functioning is from his examination of the mind and then the applied psychologist uses methods to produce healthy functioning when there is dysfunction (Shapiro, 1975). It should be noted that the same argument applies whether the psychologist regards 'the mind' as an obsolete concept and only studies behaviour or whether he believes in 'the mind'. In both cases he sees 'the mind' or behaviour as something very complex which belongs to people and so it can be disposed of technically.

Psychotherapists fail to differentiate between what Aristotle called the productive sciences and the practical (Heaton, 1976). In the productive sciences the object is to produce a work or result apart from the doing or making. The important thing is the product and the technique necessary to produce it and not the state of mind of the producer; the arts and crafts, medicine and physiotherapy are examples.

The practical sciences have as their object the manner of living. They are sciences concerned with human affairs and try and define the best life and indicate the way to live it. In these sciences it is the state of mind of the actor that is crucial for his end is acting in a satisfying way. Politics and ethics are examples of such sciences. The important point is that in the productive sciences the end is known – the physiotherapist is clear that his aim is to increase mobility and reduce pain. In the practical sciences on the other hand the end is not known. It can only be indicated, according to Aristotle, by a dialectical regress to basic principles from the experiences of ordinary living.

So satisfactory action – happiness – is not something that can be pointed to; there are no foolproof instructions on how to attain it; it is impossible to define the exact conditions which make love possible, for example. By happiness I do not mean pleasure or any particular experience – one can have a happy holiday although one may have experienced pleasure, misery and much else during it. It is not an experience that occurs over a specific length of time as do pleasures and pains. It is perhaps best considered as not an experience at all – which does not mean it is not important. 'But I do have a real *feeling* of joy.' Yes, when you are glad you really are glad. But of course joy is not joyful behaviour, nor yet a feeling round the corners of the mouth and the eyes. 'But "joy" surely designates an inward thing! No "joy" designates nothing at all. Neither any inward nor any outward thing' (Wittgenstein, 1967, para. 487).

Now it is one of the basic illusions of neurotic patients that they can somehow be told how to be happy (Heaton, 1972). And it is a common illusion of psychotherapists that some technique or other will make their patients happy or at least turn neurotic suffering to ordinary human unhappiness. So patients are subjected to a never ending series of techniques in the vain hope that one or a combination will produce some sort of happiness. Or the more cautious therapist sees himself as a technician of the mind who cures neurosis and leaves ultimate questions like the nature of happiness to the clergy or

good luck, thus opting out of responsibility for clarifying the basis
for his therapy.

Rituals

Distinguishing between the productive and practical sciences enables
one to differentiate between techniques and rituals, which is of
considerable importance to psychotherapy. Techniques are connected
with the productive sciences and rituals with the practical ones. A
technique is a means to produce a specific end product whereas a
ritual has no end product, it is an action done for its own sake, a pure
act if you like. In rituals we are attentive to the language and correct
way of performance, we are made very aware of the rule dependence
of the acts. They must be done in the right state of mind to be
efficacious and may have to be repeated many times. They are not
individualistic and arise from the society in which they are meaningfully performed. Rituals enable people to get in touch with the powers
in themselves and in their society and may bring about a union
between separate groups in which there is asymmetry.

Ritual is an important form of symbolic knowledge: one has, for
example, to partake in the mass to know its full meaning. Now this
knowledge is not of things or words but of conceptual representations
(Sperber, 1975). These are not a property of objects, acts or utterances
but interpretations of them; they indicate how they are to be taken. They
are a form of evocation that creates a common meaning. Some
procedures of psychotherapy could be seen as rituals designed to evoke
the recognition of powers latent in the patient which are necessary to
his being able to act in a satisfying way.

Interpretation

An important activity in many forms of psychotherapy is interpretation. Now interpretation is often conceived as a two-way process in
which the patient observes his mind and reports what he sees while
the analyst observes the patient and his productions and interprets the
hidden meaning of the patient's words and behaviour. By this means
the patient's endopsychic perceptual field – to use Freudian jargon –
is widened and the unconscious made conscious (Sandler et al., 1971).

According to the view outlined, making the unconscious conscious
is done by allowing oneself to be observed and thus learning to observe
oneself correctly and so acquiring knowledge about one's self. It is

mysterious how this can lead to any change in one's actions in the ordinary world, for observing something and acquiring knowledge about it does not change it. This is well exemplified by Fenichel's anecdote of the analyst who unsuccessfully interpreted, for weeks on end, a patient's wish to kill him.

Furthermore, Freud undertook to reconstruct the past, especially the sexual past, from the present. He used the analogy of archaeology in which the investigator reconstructs the actual building from its ruins. Here again it is difficult to see how this can help in making the patient act more effectively unless we distinguish vestiges from sources, which Freud failed to do.

Vestiges are fragments of a past object that have survived and assist in the reconstruction of the object of which they are a remnant. Sources on the other hand constitute a power, a tradition which opens up possibilities for the future. Thus Freud's own writings are the source of the psychoanalytic tradition, they are not mere vestiges of the past. Patients need to get in touch with their own sources with the aid of interpretations which enliven them and give them meaning rather than mechanically trying to reconstruct the past with vestiges from the present.

Freud thought of interpretation as a method of getting to the truth of what really happened in the past or to the processes occurring in the patient's mind. He forgot that any historical episode resolves itself into a multitude of intentional acts. History is always history, for it involves selection which is guided by interests. Similarily with what is 'in' the patient's mind. There can be no independent criterion as to whether what the patient observes in his mind is correct or not. In fact we do not learn to know ourselves by observing our minds.

A seasoned soldier who has fought in many a battle knows himself better than a raw recruit who comes to the battle full of enthusiasm. The former knows what it is like to face great danger, he is familiar with his own resources and responses in the face of death and so is likely to remain calmer than the recruit. He has not found this out by observing himself but by interacting with danger.

It is the same with therapy. Patients get to know themselves better by interacting with the therapist in relevant ways. Interpretation is an event in their history in which past and present become a moment of their effective history: a moment that is productive but one that, like all others, will be overcome. The past thus becomes an inexhaustable source of possibilities of meaning; a resource rather than a still life which can be passively investigated.

The language of therapy

A basic illusion shared by most psychotherapists is that there is a method, or collection of methods, of therapy. They all believe that self-knowledge or healthy living can be taught or brought about by means of techniques that they know. As a consequence they assume that they have discovered facts about the mind and so are in a position to tell us how we ought to live. Thus Freud (1961) tells us that we should be less strict towards our instincts and more truthful, Bowlby (1953) said that we should love our children more, Reich (1948) that health and morality depend on orgiastic potency, and so on and on to the pronouncements of the latest psychotherapeutic guru. All of them claim authority with false modesty – it is 'the facts' that speak. None tells us how we are to go about doing the things he says we should do, except implying that we should go to a member of his school to learn. They reduce ethics to the crudities of advertising.

It is important to distinguish ethics from morality. In morality we are concerned with rules that regulate behaviour: do not commit adultery, do not steal and so on. In ethics we are concerned with constitutive rules (Searle, 1969), that is rules that constitute the society in which the regulative rules apply and which make them meaningful. Thus the rules of the road would be meaningless unless we had rules which constituted such distinctions as the reality of life and death and the importance of saving time and money. If a society decided that life was crucial but that the more car smashes we had on a journey the better, then the constitutive rules of the society would differ from ours and the rules of the road would change. Any member of the latter society would see little point in our highway code.

Constitutive rules are basic to our actions and of course action includes speech. But because they are basic they cannot be directly represented in words. If we tried to formulate in words such basic propositions we would inevitably find that we had not got what we were looking for because there would be nothing in the proposition to tell us how it is to be taken. No proposition can be formulated to tell us how it is to be understood. Any sign for example can be variously interpreted. I could take a finger pointing at the moon as meaning I should break into song, or jump into the water in which it is reflected, and so on. Moreover, if what I call interpreting the sign consists in producing a further sign, exactly the same difficulty arises for the interpretation of this sign.

It is no longer reasonable, therefore, to search for an ultimate nugget of sense in ethics. Instead we have to make 'gestures' in the right direction or speak symbolically so that the symbol gives an indirect presentation of the concept – a symbol for reflection in Kant's phrase (1951). He gives as an example the beautiful as the symbol of the morally good. This mode of symbolic speaking is widely used in therapy (Cheshire, 1975; Heaton, 1976).

There is no ultimate insurance, no guarantee, that notions like 'love', 'truth', or 'curbing one's instincts' will be taken by other people and projected into different contexts in the way we would do. When this does happen it is because the people concerned share interests and feelings, humour and significance, and, in general, have a life in common. Unless a therapist can guarantee that we share his interests and dreams then his generalizations about methods of self-knowledge are likely to be fallacious; since the very nature of self-knowledge itself is an extremely difficult and ambiguous question.

A lot of the confusion arises because scientific talk has not been clearly differentiated from ethical talk. The language of science has been devised over centuries to have a univocal meaning which is precisely understood within the scientific community. This is done by definitions which construct ideal objects by means of strict rules. Thus the straight line in geometry, chemical formulae, etc. are, as objects of science, only given through their definitions. Definitions are built on conventions which are explicit such as technical rules, common measures and units of measurement. Scientific institutions define what is recognizable by science, for example the motions of the planets are, while movements produced by poltergeists are not. Knowledge of some scientific theory is also necessary to understand its terms; to know the meaning of a light wave we must have a smattering of theoretical physics. But of course at root scientific language is founded on one's mother tongue and this cannot be rooted in definitions because one has first to learn how to recognize a definition.

All the depth therapies depend on recognition rather than definition. They contrast with behaviour therapy which, being constructed from definitions arising from learning theory, appears more scientific. Its disadvantage is that it can only remain on the level of morality and simply helps patients to keep to the rules or to learn them. It has no concept of constitutive rules and so cannot question the patients' form of life in the way depth therapies do.

Therapeutic activity in the depth therapies is very like learning one's mother tongue. The child learns to recognize words and use them, although it could neither define the words nor state the conditions in which they are correctly used. In the therapies the various forms of resistance, transference, judging when it is appropriate to make an interpretation and so on, can be recognized by an experienced therapist and patient but cannot be defined because they depend on timing and context.

This matches the problems which the patient brings to the therapist. It is impossible to define the exact conditions in which it is appropriate to make love but the impotent man or frigid woman needs to find them. It is much the same with the other problems that confront therapists. It is impossible to make completely explicit all the conditions for happiness, for making friends, for a happy marriage and so on, but they can be recognized by experienced people.

The basic language of any particular therapy must show what it says for it must aid understanding and recognition. Its basic propositions are like the basic propositions of mathematics – they have no empirical content. Thus they have no proper subject matter, convey no information, do not admit of meaningful alternatives and they presuppose their own correctness (Shwayder, 1969). Their function in therapy is solely to aid understanding and insight and so enable the person to act rightly.

When therapists take their basic propositions as containing empirical content then endless contradictions result. They usually take them as conveying information about the mind and behaviour. A good example is Freud in his introductory lectures on psychoanalysis. But who is he talking to and what is he doing? He tells people that they are sexually repressed but how are they to take it? What usually happens is that they take it as information about their minds told to them by an expert which is precisely the way Freud talks. So this talk becomes a series of empty definitions which are given a private meaning by each hearer, e.g. I should go out and have sex. It leads to therapists and patients accumulating a lot of information about envy but showing envy in the way they talk, talking about the psychological defence of splitting and yet manifesting it, talking about enlightenment but not living wisely. So Freud, by writing of his early insights as if they contained reports about the mind, manages to block understanding and prevent inner change.

Similarily Jung by failing to develop a synoptic view of psychotherapy projects his lack of understanding into the idea of a medium – the psyche – in which most astounding things are possible.

Psychotherapists fail to realize that theorizing should not drown the voice of thought which can be 'so soft that the noise of spoken words is enough to drown it and prevent if from being heard, if one is questioned and has to speak' (Wittgenstein, 1967, para. 453).

The dimensions in which each therapist tries to locate the phenomena he describes are never exhaustive of the dimensions in which the phenomena exist. For descriptions are always for a particular use, they are not word pictures of facts for there is no one-to-one correspondence between words and things. The case histories of different therapists are a good example of this for they all differ. Some are on the look out for parapraxes and sexual involvement with parent figures, others for birth traumata and their consequences, others for games people play and so on. Every therapy has an attraction for some people but none is ever, or can ever be, complete. What is important is to make clear the point of view from which the things they say look compelling; to find out the nature of their attraction.

Representation

The crux of theoretical work in psychotherapy is to confront the representative powers of language, to recognize its limits and what can and cannot be said. For the object of therapy is right action; there is no method of instruction as to how to act rightly yet speech and action are called for. It is only such work that might eventually stem the empty theorizing of most therapists. This is aptly described by Medawar (1972) in discussing the twenty-third International Psycho-analytical Congress:

> The contributors to this Congress were concerned with homo-sexuality, anti-semitism, depression, and manic and schizoid tendencies, with *difficult* problems then – far less easy to grapple with or make sense of than anything that confronts us in the laboratory. But where shall we find the evidence of hesitancy or bewilderment, the avowals of sheer ignorance, the sense of groping and incomplete-ness which informs an international congress of, say, physiologists or biochemists? A lava-flow of ad hoc explanation pours over and around all difficulties, leaving only a few smoothly rounded prominences to mark where they might have lain.

Therapists, especially when they theorize, perpetually confuse meaning with truth and so become dogmatic as to the nature of reality. Therapeutic notions about the structure of the inner world, families and groups usually make sense, that is they are logically coherent and the words in which they are stated are connected with ordinary language. But to what do these theories refer? How is their truth to be assessed?

Now the notions which therapists use to construct their theories are taken from the society lived in by the creator of the theory. But the theories are usually expressed and applied as if they arose spontaneously out of the heads of their inventors like Athene springing fully armed with a mighty shout out of Zeus' head. They often seem to be intuitions from their solitary mental life.

In solitary inward speech we communicate nothing to ourselves, we can at most imagine doing so. We tell ourselves nothing because there is no need of it. We simply conceive of ourselves as speaking. The self-communication of the self could not take place because there would be no finality to it, there would be no finite existence to call it to a halt. The existence of this inward speech does not have to be expressed because it is immediately present to the subject. It is imaginary and the spoken words float before our minds although they have no grip on existence.

This non-existence of the words in inward speech leaves the words' sense unaffected. But the words can perform no function of indicating anything beyond themselves, they have no objective reference. They do not indicate the existence of mental acts for example. Such indication would be pointless as the acts in question are themselves experienced by us at that very moment (Husserl, 1970).

Now therapists nearly always assume that their theories are true. They believe they refer to some observable reality – to real processes in the inner world, or to real processes that occur in families and in groups. They do not realize that theorizing is not merely a matter of reflecting inward speech, of having intuitions, but that it involves thought. For if language is used to communicate an understanding of other people then 'There must be agreement not only in definitions but also (queer as this may sound) in judgements' (Wittgenstein, 1958, para. 242). Therapists assume that they are describing real processes because they assume that their imaginary presence to their own inward speech constitutes understanding themselves and others. But this assumption hides from them the otherness of people; that other people have different experiences and interests and so may judge differently.

Therapists often appear to assume they are in touch with psychic or social reality which they can know. They fail to realize that no process by itself can constitute understanding and knowledge of reality. Reality is not what gives sense or meaning to language but it shows itself in the sense language has.

Conclusion

I hope to have shown that psychotherapy must be based on theoretical work on the nature of action and its disorders. Such work will throw light on the actor and his situation. It is not technical work and so will not produce a series of instructions as to what the actor is to do; if it is any good it is enlightening rather than instructive.

Psychotherapy should not be based on psychology. It is not concerned with observing the mind or behaviour and reporting on what is going on but with attending to the movement of a situation and recognizing how to judge and respond appropriately to it; that is respond with desire rather than react to demands and compulsions. Neurotics lack judgement not knowledge.

If psychotherapy bases itself on psychology it can only become an applied psychology, as is behaviour therapy. It then develops techniques which enable a person to conform to some abstract norm – the average or some goal thought up by therapist and patient. It contains no critique of these norms or goals.

If it bases itself on the analytical therapies it can only wander in the darkness of the therapeutic schools with their feuds and rivalries, techniques, gurus and catch-phrases.

Theoretical work in psychotherapy must foster the recognition of the limits of language and the contexts in which words come to represent. It should combat the craving for generalizations about human nature which besets therapists when they theorize and should help them to see the part that different therapeutic practices play in the life of people and societies.

References

Arendt, H. (1958) *The Human Condition*. New York: Doubleday Anchor Books.
Aristotle. *The Nicomachean Ethics*. 1095 ^{a}30–^{b}4.
Bowlby, J. (1953) *Child Care and the Growth of Love*. London: Pelican Books.
Cheshire, N. M. (1975) *The Nature of Psychodynamic Interpretation*. London: John Wiley and Sons.
Cioffi, F. (1970) Freud and the idea of a pseudo-science: In Robert Borger and Frank Cioffi (eds) *Explanation in the Behavioural Sciences*. Cambridge: Cambridge University Press.

Freud, S. (1953) Three essays on the theory of sexuality. Preface to the 4th Edition, *Standard Edition*, Vol. VII. London: Hogarth Press.

Freud, S. (1957) Five lectures on psycho-analysis. 3rd Lecture, *Standard Edition*, Vol. XI. London: Hogarth Press.

Freud, S. (1961) Resistances to psycho-analysis. *Standard Edition*, Vol. XIX. London: Hogarth Press.

Freud, S. (1963) Introductory lectures on psycho-analysis. Lectures III and V, *Standard Edition*, Vol. XV. London: Hogarth Press.

Freud, S. (1966) Extracts from the Fliess Papers; Letter 73 *Standard Edition*, Vol. I. London: Hogarth Press.

Heaton, J. M. (1972) Symposium on saying and showing in Heidegger and Wittgenstein. *The Journal of the British Society forPhenomenology 3*: 42–5.

Heaton, J. M. (1976) Theoretical practice: the place of theory in psycho-therapy. *The Journal of the British Society for Phenomenology 7*: 73–85.

Hegel, G. W. F. (1805) *Phenomenology of Spirit* (Trans. A. V. Miller). Oxford: Clarendon Press (1977).

Hunter, J. E. M. (1973) *Essays after Wittgenstein*. London: George Allen and Unwin.

Husserl, E. (1970) *Logical Investigations*, Investigation 1. London: Routledge and Kegan Paul.

Kant, I. (1951) *Critique of Judgement*. 59 (Trans. J. H. Bernard). New York: Hafner Publishing Co.

Locke, J. (1961) *An Essay Concerning Human Understanding*, Book II. London: J. M. Dent and Sons. Chapters 1 and 2.

Louch, A. R. (1966) *Explanation and Human Action*. Oxford: Basil Blackwell.

Medawar, P. B. (1972) *The Hope of Progress*. London: Methuen.

Perls, F., Hefferline, R. F. and Goodman, P. (1972) *Gestalt Therapy*. London: Souvenir Press.

Popper, K. R. (1957) Philosophy of science: a personal report. In C. A. Mace (ed.) *British Philosophy in the Mid-Century*. London: George Allen and Unwin.

Reich, W. (1948) *The Function of the Orgasm*. New York: Orgone Institute Press.

Rogers, C. R. (1961) *On Becoming a Person*. London: Constable.

Rycroft, C. (1966) *Psychoanalysis Observed*. London: Constable.

Ryle, G. (1949) *The Concept of Mind*. Harmondsworth: Penguin Books.

Sandler, J., Dare, C. and Holder, A. (1971) Basic psychoanalytic concepts: Interpretation and other interventions. *The British Journal of Psychiatry 118*: 53–9.

Searle, J. R. (1969) *Speech Acts*. Cambridge: Cambridge University Press.

Shapiro, M. B. (1975) The requirements and implications of a systematic science of psychopathology. *Bulletin of the British Psychological Society 28*: 149–55.

Shwayder, D. S. (1969) Wittgenstein on mathematics. In P. Winch (ed.) *Studies in the Philosophy of Wittgenstein*. London: Routledge and Kegan Paul.

Sperber, D. (1975) *Rethinking symbolism* (Trans. A. L. Morton). Cambridge: Cambridge University Press.

Taylor, C. (1964) *The Explanation of Behaviour*. London: Routledge and Kegan Paul.

Winch, P. (1958) *The Idea of a Social Science and its Relation to Philosophy.* London: Routledge and Kegan Paul.

Wittgenstein, L. (1958) *Philosophical Investigations* (Trans. G. E. M. Anscombe). Oxford: Basil Blackwell.

Wittgenstein, L. (1967) *Zettel* (Trans. G. E. M. Anscombe). Oxford: Basil Blackwell.

Name index

Figures in italics refer to bibliographical references.

Subject index